SOMETHING IN LINOLEUM

Something in Linoleum

A Thirties Education

PAUL VAUGHAN

faber and faber

This edition first published in 2011
by Faber and Faber Ltd
Bloomsbury House, 74–77 Great Russell Street
London WC1B 3DA

Printed and bound by CPI Group (UK) Ltd, Croydon, CR0 4YY

A CIP record for this book is available from the British Library

ISBN 978-0-571-28161-9

For all these people –

Kate
Tim
Matthew
Lucy
Ben
Tom

and, of course,

Pippa

ACKNOWLEDGEMENTS

'Juvenilia' by C. Day Lewis from *The Complete Poems of C. Day Lewis* ed. Jill Balcon, Sinclair-Stevenson; 'Trowbridge' by A. L. Rowse from *The Road to Oxford*, the Estate of A. L. Rowse and Jonathan Cape; 'As I walked out one evening' by W. H. Auden from *Collected Poems* by W. H. Auden ed. Edward Mendelson, Faber and Faber Ltd; *The Ascent of F6* by W. H. Auden and Christopher Isherwood, Faber and Faber Ltd; 'Autumn Journal' by Louis MacNeice from *The Collected Poems of Louis MacNeice* ed. E. R. Dodds, Faber and Faber Ltd; 'Ode' from *Poems* and *Why Was I Killed?* by Rex Warner, the Estate of Rex Warner and The Bodley Head; 'The Condemned Playground' by Cyril Connolly, Routledge.

I am as one eavesdropping upon a captive past
Of which nothing remains but echoes and chains.
Yet, could I lay bare that primitive mural
Whereon I am superimposed,
What boldness of line and colour, what pure quaint moral
Emblems might be disclosed!

– C. Day Lewis: lines from *Juvenilia*

One

WRITING ONE'S AUTOBIOGRAPHY is at the best of times a somewhat vainglorious act. 'Any account of adolescence is necessarily a study of the fatuous', Henry Green warned us as he embarked on an autobiography of his own. And the usual thing is to attempt a justification.

I want to show what it was like to live in a certain district of England in the 1930s, and to have been part of the mass migration to the outer edge of London which was one of the outstanding social changes of the inter-war years.

I want to write about my own family, not untypical of the middle-class families who joined the rush to an illusory Arcadia, and also about the founding headmaster of my school in south-west London, one of the forgotten men of the period – a fringe member of the Auden circle, who had collaborated with Auden and briefly enjoyed his friendship. His name was John Garrett, and the school he started was built to accommodate the children of the local suburban estates. Hence my life was shaped by two quite different phenomena of the 1930s: the rapid redistribution of the population that went with the creation of the London suburbs; and the literary and artistic movement of the times. In Raynes Park, SW20, the Man on the Clapham Omnibus came face to face with the Auden Generation.

With his new school community, started in 1935, John Garrett set out to show the people living in an unremarkable district that there were other worlds beyond the frontiers marked by the railway route to London and the high road to the country and the coast. Garrett took it upon himself to apply the force of his personality to his small area of the English school system as it was then, and he represented an exciting standard of intellectual adventurousness in an environment not noted for that virtue. With the manners and bearing of an Oxford aesthete, he brought an exotic distinction to an ordinary, outwardly colourless corner of suburban England.

But when it comes to dedication, well, this book should be offered to the shades of two people: both John Garrett and my father, George Vaughan, respectable secretary of a trade association, third of five children and one of the tens of thousands of suburban immigrants. Like Garrett, he too 'got on' in life and, as middle-class fathers hope to do, made it possible for his own two sons to 'better themselves'. In fact it wasn't obvious to me at the time that, for all his upper-class camp flamboyance, Garrett came from roughly the same social stratum of turn-of-the-century England as George Vaughan. Their own fathers were, respectively, a gents' hairdresser and a prison warder.

Both Garrett and my father are dead now. My father, three times married, retired to the South Coast to eke out his state pension on whisky at the local Conservative Club; he died of a stroke when he was eighty-six. Garrett, who had become headmaster of a grammar school higher up in the educational pecking order, 'came out' as homosexual when it was difficult and dangerous to do so, then also fell victim to a stroke, though still in his fifties; he retired before his time and died of a second stroke a few years later. He was only sixty-four.

When Raynes Park County School opened in 1935, Garrett was in his prime, aged thirty-three, and the kind of man people noticed. His voice was loud, with a posh accent. He had a large nose, fair hair brushed close to his head, and he would grin with his chin thrust forward, lips pursed a little. He took care about the way he dressed, favouring the kind of clothes that suggested the fashionable thirties intellectual – woollen ties done up in a fat knot, shirts with soft collars, tweedy jackets and suits. When he walked, it was with a swift, tripping stride, shoulders wagging a little from side to side.

The boys thought he walked like a cissy, but didn't have much of an idea what that might mean. We knew he had a persuasive, bullying charm and a knack for getting people to do what he wanted. In due course we learned he had a gift for friendship – particularly if it could prove useful and profitable. High among his claims to posthumous repute is the product of one of those friendships – his collaboration with W H Auden over the anthology *The Poet's Tongue*. He also persuaded Auden to write a school song. And when it came to choosing staff, he had the nose for talent of a *Vogue* columnist. The teachers at Raynes Park tended to be high-fliers – future headmasters, university professors or administrators in their profession. Among them were the novelist Rex Warner and the painter Claude Rogers, co-founder of the Euston Road school. Patrons of the school included Cecil Day Lewis and the film director Basil Wright, and the red-brick school on the bypass became a recognised stopping place on the intellectual lecture circuit: it was the *New Statesman* school, where the boys were treated to a succession of visits from the men and women whose bylines were familiar to *Statesman* readers, a procession of celebrities from literature, the older universities, journalism and the stage. Garrett knew the Lehmanns and the Messels and the Redgraves; he talked T S Eliot and Lord David Cecil into giving away the prizes on successive Speech Days. All these connections were used to advance the reputation of the school, and so the reputation of John Garrett.

When Garrett started his school, there were only some 200 pupils aged between ten and fifteen, children of the dormitory suburbs, rest and recreation areas from which armies of commuters trooped into action in the morning and to which they returned wearily at night. Some hadn't far to go. In our area of this scene of headlong change, there was a mixture of housing estates and light industry, with small factories built along the ten-mile stretch of the Kingston bypass, a road opened in 1927 and extended during the thirties out to Esher and Guildford, a highway that was recognised in the estate business as a magnet for the land speculators and builders of bijou properties.

Huge new estates were spreading fast across the rural acres, street after street of Tudor-type semi-detacheds with their brand-new railway stations, pubs and gleaming art-deco Odeons. My family's house was on one of these estates. It was a thriving, comfortably-off region of Britain. Thirty years earlier, the area around Raynes Park itself had been the centre of the greatest increase in population of all the London suburbs: between the two census returns of 1901 and 1911 the populations of Merton and Morden had shot up by 156 per cent. In the thirties, another boom was happening: between 1931 and 1939 the population of the area rose by another 75 per cent, with more and faster trains and buses going into the centre of town from the new communities that were nevertheless within striking distance of the countryside and the sea.

It wasn't only the improved transport that made these new settlements so popular. The air was purer, too, with prevailing winds blowing from the open rural counties. Jobs were easier to find in the small factories on the edge of south-west London: it was one of the areas that had escaped the worst of the depression. Life was cleaner and more comfortable: electricity was on tap, whereas in the Victorian and Edwardian terraces of the inner city many households still relied on gas. There were new gadgets to keep the house clean and the family fed: electric cookers (their sales trebled between 1930 and 1935), electric kettles, electric fires and vacuum cleaners. And the customers for these commodities, as for the houses themselves, were the better-paid factory employees and white-collar workers in banks and offices and shops.

New communities, built mainly by private developers with no special concern for any principles of town planning, had settled into haphazard networks of new residential roads, generally handy for not much else than the local railway station. Shopping 'parades' had established themselves on some of the estates, with brief rows of 'nice' shops whose proprietors generally lived above in a flat, meeting some but not all the basic needs of the local households, usually at extra cost.

This was the territory to which the parents of the boys at Raynes Park had come, a small fraction of the one and a half million people who moved into Outer London between 1921 and 1937. Whenever John Garrett interviewed a prospective parent, he made notes of the conversation in a series of school exercise books. If he hadn't met the family before, he generally wrote down what kind of job the boy's father had. Mostly they were clerks, small shopkeepers and tradesmen, with a sprinkling of men from the professions or more out-of-the-way occupations. He noted a merchant seaman, a civil servant (clerical grade), a Diplomatic Correspondent and a Lobby Correspondent, a trumpet-player, a Central School Headmaster, a butcher, a cook-housekeeper (and single mother), three or four policemen, a naval pensioner, a sergeant-major, an accountant, a bank official, an army bandsman, an insurance salesman and a widow who kept a sweet-shop.

Starting a new school gives a community a chance to express whatever ideals it may entertain about its children's future. It also prompts some sort of choice about the values to be preserved from the system under which those same children's parents were brought up. In a new community like the catchment area for Raynes Park County School, the prospect of a clean slate, a fresh start, must have been exhilarating. Yet in many ways the new school clung to traditional ideas about boys' education: Garrett was out to show that the best features of a public school could be reproduced in a suburban day school, and he was also bent on letting light and air into what he saw as the convention-fixated society all around him. 'Suburban' had been a term of disparagement, but the existence of the new suburbs had darkened the word still more: Garrett was one of those who would frown disapprovingly over the cultural values supposedly nursed by the families in those sprawling great estates, spreading malignantly into the green countryside.

When John Garrett interviewed my father in November 1935, with my brother and me in attendance, he failed, for some reason, to write down what my father's occupation was. It wasn't something you could describe in a word: he might have put down, 'Something in linoleum'. My father evidently told him he wanted us to go to a university and Garrett decided we were the right type.

Certainly, we were exactly right for this suburban environment. My family were part of the new middle classes, moving out from Brixton in 1934 when the exodus was still in full stride, to New Maiden, a small township that wasn't yet a borough, on the outside edge of south-west London.

This was where the postal district numbers came to an end. We weren't in London, we were in Surrey, and it mattered. My mother was captivated by the newness of it all, the 'villagey' High Street, with a neat little railway station, trees growing out of the pavement and hardly a Cockney accent to be heard. There was a tea shop with tables outside, fixed into the pavement in the form of concrete mushrooms. There wasn't much traffic, and, instead of noisy double-decker omnibuses labouring along the city roads, there was a single-decker 'country' bus that chugged through New Maiden on its way to the county town (county town!) of Kingston-upon-Thames.

We failed to realise that history was yet again repeating itself, even if, this time, the new version was on an altogether larger scale.

Brixton, SW2. A clattering, grimy district, but in its time it too had been a semi-rural refuge for the better off, seeking escape from the crowds and the dirt of the city. True, Brixton in the twenties and thirties still retained a few signs of Edwardian desirability. Certain roads were favoured by members of the respectable middle class, and for some reason – it was said they found the rents lower – quite a few theatrical families who helped to elevate the tone of the place: the Lotingas, the Lupinos and the Liveseys, Naughton and Gold (later of the Crazy Gang), and the O'Gorman Brothers, Dave and Joe, who performed a cross-talk act on the variety circuits. The overdressed daughters of one of the O'Gormans, called oddly Maureen and Noreen, went to my first school, arriving each day in frilly dresses and patent leather pumps, dressed alike as though they were twins.

My mother knew all about these families: all her life she was mildly stage-struck. As a girl, she had been friendly with Edward Chapman and Elsie Randolph, both of whom achieved minor celebrity in the theatre and in films, he as a character actor, she in musical comedy, partnering Jack Buchanan. My mother's early life was full of stories about such people and it was punctuated by alleged sightings of the near-famous: she had glimpsed Esmé Percy, so she said, in Streatham High Street, George Arliss on the front at Budleigh Salterton, Leslie Henson emerging from a doorway in Margate. She had known a family of four blonde sisters, with a Norwegian mother, whose names were Ingë, Tingë, Sylvia and Louise; they had formed themselves into an accordion quartet, touring the variety theatres under the name *The Fair Four*. On another occasion my mother was invited to a birthday party of Ernie Lotinga's, and Hetty King was there taking charge of the games, dressed in man's clothes, with short hair and a long cigarette-holder, an image of daring *chic* my mother never forgot.

I can remember some of my grandmother's furniture in the flat at 89 Upper Tulse Hill: a Turkey rug on the polished parquet, a wicker armchair that seemed to creak even when no one was sitting on it, a sewing box on legs, an oak bureau and a gramophone that played 'The Blue Danube', The Merry Widow Waltz', the 'Radetsky March', a movement from *L'Arlésienne*. 'Gaga's' husband, my grandfather, was known to be 'musical'. When he died in 1918, he left a banjo and a small violin which had an inscription inside: 'Antonius Stradivarius Cremonensis Faciebat Anno 1732'. In fact it had been made in Czechoslovakia around 1900.

Gaga's flat was on the first floor of a sizeable house in one of the 'better' roads, up on Brixton Hill, where many of the large mansions were still occupied by single families, like the Lotingas, who kept servants and lived in Edwardian affluence. Now, vast blocks of flats occupy these spaces, containing dozens of families. Gaga's house, 89 Upper Tulse Hill, disappeared long ago. It had a garden with a summer house you had to climb steps to get into; there was a double swing and a tennis court, and room left over for a spacious, elm-shaded lawn. When we sat out there on a warm afternoon, you could hear the maid next door ringing a little hand-bell at four o'clock to summon the family to tea, a sound that will for ever remind me of warm June afternoons, the fragrant smell of the hot kettle, of freshly-made Mazawattee, the gasps of laughter and effort from my uncles playing tennis, my grandmother with her aura of lavender-water and her poised, dignified, affectionate ways with my brother and me.

Photographs were taken on some of those occasions. My mother, in her short-skirted, one-piece flapper's frock, her hair fashionably shingled, adopts an athletic pose in the long grass behind the summer house, the liberated twenties girl. In another she is on the swing, waving at the camera, a favourite I-am-being-photographed pose. In yet another picture my brother and I are collapsing on the grass, under either arm of our youngest and jolliest uncle, who in those days travelled for Batger's, makers of fine confectionery, and would sometimes open up his sample case and give us our choice of the box: one sweet each.

Both my father and my mother were second-generation London-ers. A movement of the population earlier than the great migration out to the suburbs in the twenties and thirties had brought their parents to London, in my mother's case from the West Country, in my father's from the Midlands. His father

8

spent thirty years of his life in the prison service, with a four-year gap when he went to fight in the Great War. He was a prison officer in an obsolete rank known as the Clerk and Schoolmaster grade, at Brixton Prison. He died before I was old enough to remember how he would bounce me on his knee and call me Paulinus Suetonius, and then say, 'And the Romans would add, as a mark of derision, *et Brittanicus.*' This rigmarole may have had something to do with the Ancient Order of Druids, of which he was a member. People liked my grandfather. He was a burly, ruddy-faced, kindly man with a stupendous Imperial moustache, and he was known as 'Father' Vaughan in the prison, perhaps an ironical allusion to Father Bernard Vaughan, a noted controversialist of the day. Grandpa too had some musical talent, dabbling at the cornet and said to have been capable of getting a tune out of several instruments, an attribute probably more useful than it sounds because he was a member of a minstrel troupe formed entirely of prison warders (blacked-up? moustache and all? a peculiar idea). He supported the Labour Party and even spoke at street corners during General Elections. My father claimed to remember being introduced as a small boy to Keir Hardie. Others in the family told of the steely look that came into my grandfather's blue eyes when provoked, a reminder that he was in a hard and unpleasant profession.

In 1915 he enlisted in the Royal Artillery, served four years in France and was awarded the Belgian *Croix de Guerre,* but used to disclaim any credit, saying 'it came up with the rations'. I think he may have had a dangerous and uncomfortable time during those four years. I have a letter he wrote to my father in August 1918. My father had been called up but the war was in its final stages and my grandfather wrote optimistically, in a flowing copperplate hand, about the state of affairs on the Western Front. 'All is gas and gaiters, we seem to have Fritz by the short hairs and am [*sic*] giving him no end of a bustling . . . I should not be surprised if the enemy called "pax" any minute . . .' He left the army as a Battery Sergeant-Major in 1919; back he went to Brixton, stayed there until 1926, then retired and, pursuing his own dream of rural tranquillity, bought a pub in Hoddesdon called The Green Man. He lived to draw his pension for only eight more months, and in 1926 he died from the delayed effects of a gas attack in Flanders. On the death certificate it said 'Cardiac asthma'. He was fifty-six.

His wife, my grandmother, was a country girl, humorous and gossipy, with a broad Brummagem accent. We called her Nanny. In my mother's opinion she was feckless, unpractical, and not very hard-working, none of which registered with me. Nanny and my grandfather had seven children, but only five survived into adulthood. One was accidentally suffocated in his parents' bed while they slept – a not uncommon mishap then. Of the survivors, two were girls and three were boys, and in a patriotic era, all were given kingly names: Alfred, then my father, Albert George, then Arthur. Between the first two boys came Millicent, and between George and Arthur came May, so there was a pattern to the children's initials, perhaps for some whimsical reason of my grandfather's. My father, born in 1899 and so just qualifying as a Victorian, occupied the middle position in the family and was also assumed to be the cleverest: for that reason he was a bit of a favourite, the one who had the treats and the special privileges. He used to talk of being taken to the Empress Theatre to see Fred Karno's troupe, The Mumming Birds, with Charlie Chaplin as the boy in one of the boxes, doing interruption gags. Fred Karno's headquarters were not far away in Coldharbour Lane, in a building later converted to an ice-rink and later still to the offices of a pharmaceutical firm, the same firm that, in due course, gave me my first job. The office was nearly opposite a turning called Vaughan Road.

The summer of 1938.

My father is Secretary of the Linoleum and Floorcloth Manu-facturers' Association. He is proud of the job and the privileges it brings him – travelling to foreign capitals, eating expensive meals he doesn't have to pay for, hobnobbing with rich, successful and even one or two titled men in the lino trade. He knows John Garrett is in the habit of inviting a succession of people down to the school to lecture and he proposes to Garrett that he should be one of them, inviting himself to come to the school and give a lecture on – oh God – the manufacture of linoleum. Garrett, all charm, agrees.

For me, it is an occasion of matchless discomfiture. I imagine Garrett grimacing at the idea of having to agree to put the lecture on; but instead of arranging for my father to speak in the Hall or the Library, Garrett has him come to the Geography Room. And it isn't Garrett who takes the chair and introduces him, it is Gibb, the Second Master, who teaches Geography. He also acts as host.

The audience is confined to one form only – my own. And the lecture itself is terrible – boring, ill-organised and trite. The boys listen in listless silence, laughing once at some joking reference to me. Even ordinary Geography would have been preferable. My father, in his business suit, stands in front of a line of little bottles containing things like linseed oil and dyes used for colouring lino, which he thought necessary for illustrating his description of a not very exciting process, miles away from the concerns of anyone else in the room. I understand with awful clarity how parents, pitifully well-meaning, can plunge their children into terrible embarrassment. I am racked with vicarious guilt and love for my father as he stands up there, I am convinced, making a fool of himself – and by association, of me too.

An early encounter between Suburban Man and the Auden Generation – with the next generation caught between the two.

Two

SELF-BETTERMENT IS a middle-class preoccupation, and the idea of 'getting on' was to hang around those suburban estates like the smell of cooking on Sunday mornings.

A sign of my father's reaction against his parents: at some time around 1910 he dropped the 'Albert'. For the rest of his life he was always known as George. Perhaps he merely followed the example of the reigning monarch, who had been Prince Albert but became King Edward. But it is more likely he thought the Cockney nickname 'Bert' would have been like a ball and chain round the ankle for a youth with a talent for languages and maths, determined to move up in the world.

At the age of eleven, he had won a scholarship to Alleyn's in Dulwich, a better school than his father, who earned three pounds a week in the prison service, had any reason to expect. Six years later, in 1916, George Vaughan took the Matriculation exam, and with vague ambitions towards foreign travel – which must have been very vague indeed, considering what was happening across the Channel at the time – went to work in the Banking and Exchange Department of Thomas Cook & Son. As he must have expected, the job was short-lived. In May 1917 he was called up and posted to the Middlesex Regiment, and quite early identified as someone who possessed what were known in the next war as 'OLQ' (Officer-Like Qualities); he was sent off on a succession of courses to be trained as an instructor in

various military skills which now have a distinctly archaic ring
– drill, musketry, map-reading, Lewis gunnery. Then he was
posted to an Officer Cadet Training Battalion, but it was an out-
of-the-ordinary posting, in a choice location – Balliol College,
Oxford.

His arrival there, a gawky, rather tense but pushy young man
from a relatively humble family, brought about a peculiarly
English class confrontation. He and his fellow cadets were a
group that included only a sprinkling of what would have been
regarded as natural Oxford men. When they arrived, they were
invited to assemble in Hall for a speech of welcome from a
senior officer, who lectured them on what was expected of
officer-cadets. Dinner, with college ale, was served by mess
waiters and a few ageing college scouts. This was the life! The
Master of Balliol was the historian A L Smith, a strong supporter
of the Workers' Educational Association, a University oarsman,
propagandist of the bicycle and the ice-skate and renowned for
his kindness to successive intakes of Balliol cadets, to whom,
because of his unexpected socialist leanings, he was ironically
known as 'the Working Man'. My father remembered Smith
speaking to the young cadets after dinner, impressively attired
in evening clothes and academic gown, and explaining to them
that, because there were virtually no undergraduates, they must
consider themselves *locum tenentes*, guardians of the traditions
of the University and of Balliol College. Their officers would of
course be dining at High Table with the Master and such of the
Fellows as were left. He invited them to undertake their sporting
activities in the name of the College rather than the Battalion: to
his surprise my father found himself rowing and playing cricket
for Balliol. It was the first time the Oxford Experience figured in
my family and my father was profoundly impressed.

In those days changes occurred slowly at Oxford and it isn't
difficult to imagine the place, even in the summer of 1918, still
drowsing in a late-Victorian torpor. The Examination Schools
may have been converted to a military hospital, but, after all,
Oxford was still a small university town. The Cowley phenom-

enon, with all it represented, belonged to the future. William Morris's bicycle shop was even then doing business in Longwall Street, but many great Victorian figures were about in the quads: Walter Raleigh, G O D Allen, Quiller-Couch. Warden Spooner was at New College, the college barges flew their jaunty rows of bunting on the Isis and bicycles swarmed in the narrow streets. My father and his friends hired bikes and rode them around Oxford and the nearby countryside. Once, a party of them went by bicycle for a weekend in London, a heroic endeavour which A L Smith would doubtless have applauded. Such expeditions, the punting trips on the Cherwell with complaisant local girls, and the fact that on Wednesdays they were allowed to hang up their uniforms and don grey flannel trousers and white cricket shirts, reinforced the cadets' view ('the fiction' my father called it) that they were privileged young gentlemen. You could forget the war. In Oxford, you couldn't even hear, as you could in London on still afternoons or at night, the low rumble of the guns from across the Channel.

One of my father's comrades was called Thompson. He had been an undergraduate at Merton. Now, he was posted over to Balliol and the OCTB, and was one of the three cadets with whom my father shared rooms in college. The others were called Vigil and Wainwright: it seems the billeting arrangements had been made on the Army's usual arbitrary alphabetical lines, but Thompson became a friend. He was the one who knew his way about Oxford, knew about college customs and could give advice on the peculiar traditions and nomenclature of the University.

Another friend was to play a larger part in my father's life: a jolly and flamboyant man, with a bad stammer, called Cecil Hicks. He too would become a suburban immigrant, but he gave the impression of being somehow left over from the Edwardian period – debonair, roguish and a little vain. At Oxford in 1917 he was a cadet in the Warwickshire Yeomanry, and he and my father had something in common: Hicks also came from Brixton, where he worked as assistant in a draper's shop. Asked on arrival at Balliol to state his civilian occupation, Hicks said he was an actor. He told my father it sounded better and carried more prestige, but his habitual stutter must have made it hard to believe.

When my father's three-month training course was nearly over, in the summer of 1918, another equally deadly enemy intervened: Spanish 'flu.

The cadets had taken their final exams and also gone through 'Field Service' training, practising the kind of formal manoeuvres military commanders like to devise – symbolic, almost choreographic representations of the real thing. My father used to describe with pride, almost as if it had genuinely taken place 'in the field', a favourite procedure called Fire and Movement, in which a platoon attacked in sections. While one section lay still and gave covering fire, the other made a four-second dash forward, that being the estimated time it would take a German gunner to get a running infantryman in the V of his rifle sights. Then the first section would run forward while the second section gave them cover.

Luckily, my father never had cause to put this risky-sounding manoeuvre, or any other war-game, to any practical test. While he and the others were waiting for their results, cadets began to go mysteriously sick. Wainwright died. So did many of the others, but my father, though he too was on the sick-list, was lucky. Dosed with the standard medicines, namely aspirin and quinine, he got better, and although still groggy, was sent home to recuperate. He was also advised that he could anticipate the results of the final test, remove his white hat-band, badge of the officer-cadet, and have a single pip sewn on either sleeve of his jacket.

Cecil Hicks had also escaped death by 'flu, and scraped through the final exams by sitting next to my father and copying his answers. I doubt if the examining officer would have worried overmuch. Field officers were badly needed but, in any case, it was by now the first week of November 1918. The 'fearful bustling' my grandfather had written home about had produced the expected result. There was nothing much for my father to do but wait about at home. Thompson, his fellow-cadet, sought him out: a moment of embarrassment as he appeared at the door of the family's flat – in the Prison Officers' Quarters. My father managed to carry it off, and took Thompson on a tour of the local pubs. Cecil Hicks also called, with his wife. And on Armistice Day, my father went to see him in the Brixton draper's shop, owned by his aunt, where he had rooms with his wife and baby. They were being kept frantically busy selling penny Union Jacks. The two young men, wearing officers' uniform, took a bus to the West End and were treated as heroes by people in the streets. Both of them enjoyed the irony of it: neither had seen the front line.

The Oxford experience had given George Vaughan enough *savoir-faire* to take command of a battalion on parade, give orders and speak up for himself to superior officers. He had inherited a lot of my grandfather's bluff charm, he had a winsome, slightly crooked smile and a look of boyish, if rather gaunt attractiveness.

Somewhere there is a photograph of him taken at about this time, in uniform and wearing, at a debonair angle, his tin hat – unnecessarily no doubt, but it looked gallant, a favourite word of the period. He stands with legs apart, in riding boots with Sam Browne belt, holding a swagger cane. His hands are on his hips and he is smiling jauntily, a little loftily, at whoever was taking the picture, probably some brother officer. To be honest, it is the picture of a swank. It was taken outside the Officers' Mess near Cologne, where by this time, 1919, he had been posted with the 52nd Battalion of the Middlesex Regiment as part of the British Army of Occupation. Here his way with languages got him noticed. He was made Battalion Interpreter because he was the only one capable of asking the local people anything, and what was more, he spoke German and French with no trace of the self-consciousness for which the Englishman abroad remains a byword. The appointment earned him an extra eight shillings a day.

His stay in Germany was not particularly eventful. The only hint of excitement was the scare that followed the Germans' reluctance to sign the first draft of the Versailles Peace Treaty. Was the fighting going to start all over again? The Army of Occupation mobilised itself to march on Berlin. Flotillas of London buses, lorries and armoured cars – an updated re-run of Mons – were collected for the advance to the capital, and 2nd-Lt Vaughan, who knew how to ask the way, was seconded to the regiment which was going to form the vanguard of the force. They were told they would have to move along a road enfiladed by the field artillery German gunners had kept back after the Armistice.

But the German negotiators changed their minds. The scare subsided and my father's bit of the Great War fizzled out before it had started. He was demobilised in 1919 and came back to London, where his father had preceded him by a few weeks; nervous about the large number of idle ex-servicemen hanging about London, he placed an advertisement – without asking his son – in the *Evening News*: 'Ex-officer, skill at languages, seeks employment. Anything considered.' My father was not too pleased: this move was at variance with his plans to spend his gratuity in prolonged celebration. But the advertisement did get a reply – from a Birmingham metallurgist, who had been appointed by the Belgian Government to supervise the renewal and repair of the country's devastated coal mines. He gave my father a job as Company Secretary, with a salary of £200 a year.

My father and mother had known each other since they were both in their teens, and they had developed the kind of holding-hands, sentimental friendship that in those days represented the normal limits of youthful romance. But they had seen very little of each other until they met again after my father's return from Germany, a dashing, glamorous figure in his subaltern's uniform.

My mother's family occupied a position a step or two up the social ladder from the Vaughans. Her father was Ernest Stocks, son of a man with a small drapery business in Plymouth, and he had moved to London in his twenties, bringing with him his pretty wife, born Ada Ernestine Stuttaford. In London he became a commercial traveller for the firm of Pawson and Leaf, wholesale cloth merchants.

Ernest Stocks was a chunky, gregarious man, not very tall, a clever mimic, a frequenter of saloon bars who took care to look well turned-out. He liked his clothes made to measure – suits, shirts, even underwear. A single item of his clothing has survived into the present – a smoking cap. It was a small pill-box hat made of blue velvet and embroidered with gold thread. From a button on top depended a gold tassel. We have seen such things in drawings by Tenniel or the Cruikshanks. I am not sure what my grandfather smoked when he put his hat on – Havana cigars, I should think – but had his headgear also had a function as a drinking-cap, it would all too often have adorned his skull. His favourite tipple was whisky, and his profession probably encouraged its consumption.

His territory as a travelling man was the South Coast, which he would cover on sometimes lengthy trips away from London. It was a respectable occupation. The term 'commercial traveller' had by no means the servile, faintly comic character it acquired later, and Jimmy Stocks' excursions, as the representative of a large and well thought-of City firm, were journeys of no small consequence. He would arrive at Margate or Eastbourne in topper and morning suit bringing cases packed with samples, and take a carriage to the hotel of his choice, where he would be received with respect. He would already have advised the leading local dealers of his impending arrival with a note that let it be known he would be at the Grand or the Promenade or the Adelphi at such-and-such an hour. The buyers would call. Bargains would be struck, and sealed with a glass of something.

As for what other entertainments he favoured when not conducting his business, that is a mystery. He was a popular man, well-dressed and not short of a shilling or two, and I picture him as, at the least, relishing the cheery society of business acquaintances in the seafront hotels of Bournemouth, Brighton, Worthing and Dover. At home with the family in Brixton, he was brisk, not particularly patient, and, although kind enough, quite stern with the children.

There were five surviving, four boys and one girl. The oldest was Ernest, then my mother, Ada Rose, then Graham (always called Joe), and the two youngest boys, Billy and Philip. In the first decade of the century they all lived in a large house in Trent Road, in the better part of Brixton, off Brixton Hill, with a living-in maid. It was a comfortable middle-class life, the family on the whole keeping to themselves, making their own amusements and not often entertaining company. When he was not on the road, my grandfather's social life found its fulcrum in the saloon bar of the George Canning, the pub on Brixton Hill. But it was a family divided quite sharply across the generations. My mother's stories of life in that house were fixed upon its juvenile population, stories of high jinks in Brockwell Park, larks in the bedrooms or somewhere else out of adult earshot, with Ernie the ringleader. Joe was more serious, but tagged along, with Rosie and the two smallest boys as the rank and file. Ernie was the one with the ideas. 'I must have adventure,' he would declare, and one day in 1918, although he was under age, he enlisted in the Royal Artillery. Meanwhile the grown-ups continued their self-contained Edwardian life, with my grandfather the unchallenged head of the household and neither parent showing much affection towards their offspring.

One prank perpetrated by Ernie caused particularly grave displeasure. He and Billy were instructed to prepare more paper for the lavatory. At that time bought toilet paper was rare. In the Stocks' household, small squares of newspaper were carefully torn out and hung on string from a hook in the wall. Ernie and Bill produced pieces of various dimensions, from very large to postage-stamp size, strung them on the cord and placed a notice alongside: 'All Sizes Kept in Stock'. Father was not amused. 'Which one of you boys is responsible for this?' Ernie owned up and received a severe telling-off.

It was the kind of household where there were few outward signs of love, and it was surely male-dominated in a period when womankind was the weaker vessel. The females were outnumbered. My grandfather was not given to demonstrating his affection and grew irritable if the children intruded too noticeably. My grandmother, a quiet, docile woman, left most things to her husband. He met the household bills and made all the major decisions, such as which school the children would be sent to. In the circumstances, the double blow that fell upon the family in 1918 was catastrophic. Ernie, now eighteen years old and in hot pursuit of the *Boys' Own Paper*-style adventure he longed for, was in the Artillery and stationed at Folkestone. Within a few weeks of enlistment, he caught pneumonia and died. Shortly afterwards, my grandfather too was taken ill. Six weeks after the death of his oldest son, he died also. The cause of death was cirrhosis of the liver. He was only forty-six.

Why does history repeat itself in families? It is a strange coincidence that my great-grandmother, too, had been left a widow while still in her thirties: not only that, but she had married a man whose first wife had died, leaving him with four girls – a step-family to which they added a fifth, my grandmother. Now, although she was not yet forty, my grandmother too was a widow, with four children, all of them still at school. She had very little to live on, only a small insurance policy, but she owned the house. Joe, the steadiest of her sons, was to be the breadwinner. An incident that Christmas sums up much of the bereaved family's plight. All the Stocks children had been used to a generous spillage of presents from their father and from some of his clubby, bibulous friends. In 1918, foreseeing empty stockings in Trent Road, Joe made it his business to buy something for everybody, and scraped together enough for a small parcel each – sweets, a cheap toy, a book. He had already had to leave school and had taken a job in an old-fashioned City bank, assuming straightaway the dapper, bowler-hatted persona that he maintained for the rest of his working life – a banking career interrupted only by the Second World War. Billy, meanwhile, spurred on by motives not unlike Ernie's, took a bolder path: he sailed to Australia, as the family said, to seek his fortune.

The family had well and truly broken up. Like Joe, Ada Rose went to work in the City, in her father's old firm, Pawson and Leaf's, first as a clerk, then briefly as assistant to one of the travellers. She accompanied him in his brougham on his rounds in the London suburbs, until he began making advances to her, whereupon she took fright, and left to go to work at the Prudential Assurance Company, joining the hordes of young office girls who daily trooped into the huge Victorian Gothic building hard by St Paul's, and who were employed on humdrum clerical work under the supervision of severe and unbending office managers.

It was from this tedious situation and the financially straitened home life in Trent Road that she escaped into matrimony.

Three

MY FATHER AND mother were married in 1922. Although they had known each other since 1916, something had happened to make their juvenile romance turn sour; my mother later used to hint that my father's conduct thereafter and his adventures in Germany during their estrangement were something to be ashamed of. It's true his tales of his few months with the Rhine Army had now and then a boastful, disreputable side – brief trips to Paris 'with a few amenable girl friends . . . *Vous souviendrez que je parle français*', he once wrote to me by way of – inadequate – explanation; and he dropped hints now and then about escapades with local girls in the public park in Cologne.

I doubt if he behaved worse than any other young officer in that victorious but idle army, but, at all events, when he was back in London he and my mother began to see each other again. The question was eventually popped, the affirmative answer given, and the ceremony performed. For some mysterious reason, there were no photographs of the event – or none survived. On her honeymoon in Margate, my mother took her favourite dolls along, evidently needing their moral support during the coming ordeal. Afterwards, the two future colonists of the suburban wasteland settled down for the time being in a small flat in Brixton, the town they knew.

My mother had her first baby in 1923. It was a girl, and she lived only a few minutes. Another mystery: all we were ever told, as children, was that the baby's name 'would have been' Barbara, but later they told me she had some birth defect so serious that the family doctor, Dr Gilchrist in Coldharbour Lane, somehow made sure she didn't survive.

Soon afterwards, perhaps out of sympathy for them, my father's benefactor, the metallurgist Dr Gifford, offered the unfortunate couple a large flat, this time in Acre Lane, Brixton; they moved there in time for my brother to be born in the house in May 1924, and I was born there too, seventeen months later.

Apart from a few months in their first flat, they only ever lived together in two houses, and those two addresses were nothing like each other. No 88 Acre Lane was a tall three-storied late Georgian house with a basement. When it was built, in the 1820s, the surroundings must have been very different. It had been part of a terrace which had been demolished, leaving only No 88 and its semi-detached neighbour, No 86. At the back, the house had a large window opening onto a curved balcony: a hundred years earlier, a person standing on it must have had a view of meadows sloping down to a valley where lay the village of Stockwell. In the distance, you would have seen the spires of the city churches and the great dome of St Paul's.

Now, in the 1920s, buildings came right up to the back of the house. There was no back garden, only a small concreted yard, without a plant in sight, not even a weed. No view, no vista, only a high brick wall, shutting off a view of the small terraced Edwardian houses that had swarmed up the sloping terrain between Acre Lane and the railway line, the former London, Chatham and Dover Railway running to Victoria.

To reach the front door of No 88, with its handsome fanlight, you ascended a wide flight of seven stone steps. In front of this was the garden, a generous space with a wide gravelled path set around a circular flower bed. A brick wall, about waist high but with a privet hedge, gave us some seclusion from the passers-by and the traffic going up and down to Lambeth Town Hall or westward to Clapham Common. Open-topped buses honked along the road, and a few cars, and trade vehicles delivering milk, bread, or coal.

Immediately next to a cobbled passage at the side of our house, the Acre Lane shops began, each with its characteristic smell. The first shop was an off licence: I recall its dank, beery odour and the clink of bottles. A Mrs Clay kept the premises, a small, cheery woman with pink cheeks and absurdly prominent front teeth. Her husband was seldom visible and was understood to suffer from some mysterious and possibly shameful ailment connected to his trade. Next to Clay's was the shop kept by Mr Godden the chemist, a courteous, white-haired, well-scrubbed man in gold-rimmed spectacles whose orderly displays of coloured liquids and long-forgotten household remedies (Zam-Buk, Zubes and Zoids) also had a unique smell – sharp, clinical, and good for you. A little way along was David Greig's the grocer's, where men in black serge coats with white sleeve protectors up to the elbow sold ham, Gorgonzola cheese, fresh coffee, and biscuits dispensed from square glass-fronted boxes ranged before the counter, and where the bacon slicer gave out a sinister hiss as it peeled off slice after slice of home-cured streaky. Further along still was the ironmonger's, smelling of tarred rope, paraffin and bundles of sticks for lighting the fire; then a baker, Bamford's, whose manageress was said to have been glimpsed doing bit parts in the films we saw at the Brixton Pavilion. 'Look,' my mother would excitedly exclaim, 'There's Mrs Bamford!' I cannot believe she wasn't making this up.

Both 86 and 88 are still there but the walled front gardens have gone and the flower beds have been concreted over to make a car park. The tall hedge that divided the two front gardens has been torn out. When driving past I have noticed, inside our house, neon strip lighting where our gas pendants used to hang: we had no electric light until 1930, when one night a glowing gas-mantle fell down after the family had gone to bed, and set fire to the sitting room carpet. At some time in its history, the house became the offices of a direct mail advertising firm. Once, I happened to find an advertisement they had placed in a trade paper. Under a picture of the two houses, with the background blanked out, was a caption: 'New People Have Moved In.'

When we were the new people, No 88 was already old and shabby, and, like its next-door neighbour, converted to flats. What was more, the ground floor and basement of 86 formed part of a garage and repair business managed by a man called George Mesurier, who used to drink with my father and whose name we were schooled to pronounce in the correct French manner.

Our flat consisted of the top two floors of No 88 and another family occupied the rest. Soon they moved out, whereupon my father's family moved in: his widowed mother, his two unmarried sisters and his younger brother.

My mother was appalled, and began making plans to escape, determined to protect her memories of a more genteel style of life, the golden age on Brixton Hill before the double disaster of 1918. And for the first time in their married life their ambitions began to pull in different directions: on one side, his loyalty to his family, and on the other, her dreams of a 'nicer' life. Eventually it tore their marriage apart. But for the time being, it produced only short-lived, easily forgotten irritations. Newly-weds are usually sure they can do something about differences of temperament, major or minor. Love conquers all – even the proximity of the in-laws.

As a small boy I was aware of the change of atmosphere once I descended the elegantly curved staircase of No 88. Down there, on the ground floor, Nanny had made the back room into a bedroom, shared at one time by all four. It was all a bit rumpled and frowsty, with a hint of unmade beds and unemptied po's. In the basement below, the smells were of Nanny's huge copper, where she did the weekly wash with her little bag of 'Dolly' blue dye to bring out the whiteness, and of big frying pans of dripping from which she offered us 'dip' – a thick gobbet of bread dunked in the smoking fat. There was a dog called Pat and a cat called

Poosh, both of whom probably added their own smells to the other homely odours. Quite a lot of what I remember from that below-stairs household, and of many other times and places in my childhood, comes back to me in the form of smells – like the sweet scent of the Icilma face cream Nanny kept on the mantelpiece and which she would rub into her hands after she'd done the wash, working it into the slack skin '(Me fingers are all washing-tub', she would complain); or the sharp, piny, resinous smell from inside the new, French-polished gramophone cabinet she had bought on HP from Drage's and which they kept in their front room on the ground floor. On it they played *Indian Love Lyrics,* 'Pack Up Your Troubles', the Two Leslies singing 'Ain't it Grand to be Blooming Well Dead', and Carl Brisson singing 'I'm Going to Maxim's' from *The Merry Widow.* Perhaps because the words reminded me of some marital tiff, I chose to interpret this as the song of a man who had decided to leave his wife but changed his mind at the last minute with the words, 'And you, why, *you can come too!*'

Meanwhile our flat upstairs was as neat and orderly as the old house would allow, and smelled, if at all, of Min Cream, Mansion Polish and other cleaning agents. Another dominant smell was from the steaming gas geyser in the bathroom, mixed with the Coal Tar soap my mother favoured for the bath and the Izal disinfectant she poured prodigally into the ancient lavatory with its broad, scrubbed mahogany bench – a bench with two holes, one for grown-ups, the other of smaller diameter to accomodate childish behinds. Such things now fetch extravagant prices.

In the front room on the first floor, the furniture was regularly dusted and the floor gone over with Ewbank and O'Cedar mop. On a tall, narrow oak stand reposed the telephone. The number – very low – was Brixton 1001. It had a separate ear-piece that you unhooked from the main apparatus with its daffodil microphone, and that too was dusted every day, along with the Boehringer and Strohme upright piano. When I was ill, I would lie in bed upstairs and listen to the sound of my mother dusting the keys, blip-blip-blip, unrelated chords from altissimo to deep bass and back again, and sometimes she would take a sudden fancy to play, sit down on the piano stool, and sketch a few bars of 'Roses of Picardy', or 'The Wedding of the Painted Doll'.

Home music-making had not yet been extinguished by the gramophone, still less the wireless. The tradition persisted at No 88, both upstairs and downstairs – less so in Nanny's household, in spite of my grandfather's reputed prowess on cornet. For a while, my youngest uncle, Arthur, had a drum kit on which he would thud and crash randomly now and then, perhaps accompanying a dance record, and there were times when there would be hymns round the piano. My Auntie Mill played: she was very pious, or what her sister May called 'churchy', and was always taking us to church bazaars and jumble sales, even, once, a church pageant on Clapham Common in honour of William Wilberforce.

My father was the most musical of his brothers and sisters. He had a light tenor voice and had sung solos in the church choir. As a boy chorister, he had sung a solo in Southwark Cathedral, and never forgot the event: he was still referring to it in his eighties. He continued to sing for a while as a young man, the mainstay of his repertoire being a duet he used to sing with one or other of the Stocks brothers-in-law, called 'Watchman, What of the Night?' ('Do the Dews of the Morning Fall?'). I hated this song, with its gloomy and portentous words, which may have been the work of the composer, one J Sarjeant. The song required one of the singers, a tenor, to question the other, a bass, about the approaching dark. The bass represented a symbolic night watchman, and his replies were meant to be encouraging, but the effect was lugubrious in the extreme, with references to funeral palls, the cheerless tomb and the arrow of death speeding towards its next victim. Probably the lyricist had in mind some sort of picturesque medieval official but to me the word 'watchman' suggested the sort of obscure figure you could sometimes see in Acre Lane, sitting in a canvas bivouac, crouched over a brazier. I sometimes wondered about greeting such a man with the words of the song, but knew the reply would be unlikely to refer to the orient skies or the morning of joy.

That song's metaphorical burden was above my head, but understanding wasn't improved by my father's and uncles' articulation of the opening words, which became 'Do the Jews of the morning fall?' There was the same difficulty with another of their repertoire, 'You Are My Heart's Delight', popular in the family a little later on. 'Shine, then, my whole life through, Your light divine bids me hoe upon you', my Uncle Billy would quaver, struggling at the top of his range. I could not understand this figure of speech.

Music-making was not very expert, but it was casual and spontaneous and gave the family circle of aunts and uncles a sort of half-hearted, frustrated pleasure. The songs and piano solos were not the business of whole musical evenings but interludes of an hour or so, perhaps when the conversation had petered out and someone would suggest a song. The music would be taken out of the hinged rack in the piano stool, up would come the lid of the Boehringer and by way of prelude my mother would execute a few arpeggios, with much use of the sustaining pedal. Standing at her side, one hand in pocket, or with both hands clasped before their waistcoats, the men would give forth with 'Because', 'Bless This House', 'Rose of my Heart', (a special favourite, for obvious reasons) or another song I loathed for its soppy sentiments, 'Trees'. 'Poems are made', pleaded my uncle, straining at a top B-flat, 'by foals like me . . . But only *God* can make a tree!'

There was also a volume of music bound in red, obtained from the newspaper my father took all his life, the *Daily Express*. It was called *Songs that Won the War*. These were considered suitable for me to sing, and sometimes at idle moments during the day I would stand at the piano by my mother's side and warble 'Tipperary', 'Goodbye-ee', 'Who Were You With Last Night, and 'Sister Susie's Sewing Shirts for Soldiers'. They soon became part of the fabric of myths and folk-memories about the great convulsion that seemed to have happened to them all. Early in my life, *The War* took on a special, exciting aura. Those four years were close in time: it was still The Great War. Sometimes my father used to speak of it, with a serious thinker's frown, as The War to End War. My mother, full of awe, would tell stories of Zeppelins over Streatham Hill, bombs falling, the night when one of the airships crashed in flames and the cheers could be heard all over London. I became an avid listener to tales of 'those poor boys out there', the never-ending Casualty Lists, of still summer nights when you could hear the guns in France. Somewhere in the house there was a book of drawings by Bruce Bairnsfather, and gradually I formed a picture of some unimaginably dangerous yet romantic place . . . No Man's Land, a grim terrain lit by star-shells, a sound-track provided by the mutter of machine-guns, the crump of artillery fire, the sad music of a harmonica.

I have an early memory of Armistice Day in 1929 or 1930. My mother and I are shopping in Brixton. Outside Lambeth Town Hall, everything suddenly stops. The trams come to a halt where they are, in the middle of the road, so do cars and lorries and the odd horse and cart. It is as if a magic spell has been cast over London. Pedestrians stand still, with their hats off, their eyes downcast, and a clock strikes eleven. In the distance, there comes the rumble of artillery fire. Dogs bark. 'Did you hear the guns?' whispers my mother. 'The guns in Hyde Park.' The guns! You could almost believe yourself back in The War again. I stand holding my mother's hand, thrilled by the idea of two minutes' silence observed by everybody and all of them, together, thinking about the same thing – that huge, mysterious and frightening event that all grown-ups knew about.

There were other reminders when we travelled about the city: the Cenotaph in Whitehall, where my father, like all the other men in the bus, would doff his hat. (He did the same, standing to attention, if a funeral procession passed by.) There were certain statues: Jagger's Artillery Memorial near Hyde Park Gate, with a gunner standing in steel helmet and gas cape with his arms outstretched on the parapet behind him, gravely regarding the passers-by; or the Royal Fusiliers' Memorial in Holborn, on which a fusilier in what my father taught me to call Field Service Marching Order, with rifle at the trail, stood silhouetted against the city skyline, one hand held out behind him as though to steady himself, perhaps to call his comrades to join him – or caution them against doing so. On our bus journeys round London I hoped we might pass one of these dramatic memorials so that I could register once more the fortitude, endurance and reproach of those stern figures.

Nevertheless, my father's tales of Army life, experienced mostly after the fighting was over and the last shot had been fired, were of a cheerful, optimistic kind, in which he featured as a debonair young infantry subaltern being cheeky to the Colonel or Adjutant. To my slight disappointment, nobody was ever killed in his stories. The discomfort, the boredom of service life, not to mention the hardship and mortal danger, had been forgotten. The comradeship, the jokes and freedom from domestic care all took precedence, as they did in the memory of many ex-soldiers, especially if they had managed to avoid the Front Line.

Another member of my father's circle who helped him to indulge in this cheerier view of recent history was a man called Pinchard. I never knew his other name because even in the late 1920s, he liked to be called by his Army rank: Captain Pinchard. He didn't appear to have a job, but he ran an amateur dramatic troupe which my father and mother joined, appearing in one-act plays written by Pinchard himself and usually based on life in the Army – once again, the sort of life in which no one was in danger of anything but mild ridicule. One play was called *The Disorderly Room* and was a comedy of mistaken identity involving some harmless duping of an Infantry Colonel, and another was called *The Adjutant,* written in rhymed couplets. Pinchard, perhaps fulfilling an ambition not realised during the war itself, cast himself as the CO, and when he appeared in his uniform, undoubtedly preserved from his Army days and kept in meticulous order, I was seriously impressed. This trim, neat, bouncy little man in cavalry breeches and Sam Browne, with his waxed moustache and stock of Army lore, helped to piece out my view of the military life, just as my father did with his anecdotes of life in the regiment, the Middlesex – nicknamed, he would tell me meaningfully, 'The Diehards', and he would recount yet again the tale of a Peninsular War colonel falling in battle and calling out with his last breath, 'Die hard, men, die hard!'

Whatever the Great War had done to dent the tradition, King and Country and the Empire still meant a lot to my father and his friends: the very words quickened the pulse. When I went to my first school, Empire Day, 24 May, was an occasion to be looked forward to. The school was hung with flags and we were given a special tea. At the climax of the celebrations, all the children marched round and round the school hall in file singing *Land of Hope and Glory* and waving small Union Jacks, purchased and brought to school for this purpose.

So, like other children of those days, I was infatuated with military matters and my infatuation lasted a long time. Throughout childhood I indulged it in games with toy soldiers. I always asked for soldiers at Christmas and birthdays, and no seasonal pillow-case was complete without at least one slim, exciting oblong box of W Britain & Co's Bluejackets, or Horse Artillery, or Infantry of the Line, one box of which, I am ashamed to recall, came with the soldiers, their rifles at the trail, wearing gas masks. It became a tradition for all the uncles to play with my soldiers after Christmas dinner when the table had been cleared and the washing-up was proceeding in the kitchen. The men and women in the family, in other words, were assigned roles according to stereotype: a menial domestic chore for my mother and the aunts, while the men went, figuratively, to war. Not that I cared: it was fine by me. Their jokes and cries of simulated woe as a field gun misfired or a rampart collapsed caused me more merriment than anything I can remember except Blow Football, a game played preferably on a table-top with small cardboard pipes and a miniature celluloid ball, and guaranteed to make me nearly incontinent with mirth.

Not only did my uncles enjoy the war games, they even took to buying me Christmas presents they had specially selected for their own use during the annual Yuletide pitched battle – a miniature howitzer, or naval guns with long, thin barrels that you could fire with unpleasant accuracy, especially with an amorce cap slipped into the breech. War or no war, nobody saw anything wrong with such simulated carnage, nor did they see anything wrong with giving me toy guns and other weapons to play with. Nor was the weaponry only toys. My father allowed me to play with a small Colt revolver which had come to him from his father, and the story was that it had been discovered inside a loaf of bread sent in to one of the prisoners in Brixton gaol – presumably with some ammunition as well, which must have made the loaf improbably weighty and hence easily detected. Instead of being used in a prison break-out, the gun's new function was to make my games of war and gangsters fleetingly more realistic, though unlike the usual kind of toy six-gun and rifle, my real revolver didn't go Bang, it only gave out an uninteresting click and didn't even have the right smell of cordite.

We kept the Colt until 1940. My father found a way of exchanging it for a Webley service pistol and six rounds. He kept them in the glove compartment of his Wolseley saloon car – in case he met any German parachutists.

The people in my family liked getting up in front of an audience and performing. My parents' acquaintance with a few pro-fessional actors might have been the reason why they joined one of Brixton's groups of amateur Thespians called the Punchinello Players. They were what was known as a Concert Party. For their opening and closing numbers they wore special Pierrot costumes designed and made by my mother, who was handy with her Singer sewing-machine: clowns' one-piece suits with baggy trousers and white ruffs at the collar. At wrist and ankle there were black lace fringes, and on their feet, neat black dancing-pumps. The costumes were light brown with a black spider's web motif all over, and the ensemble was completed by a black skull-cap. There were eight or nine in the troupe. In addition to their chorus numbers, which involved a few simple dance routines, there were comedy sketches in which my father usually played the Funny Man, for with his breezy manner and toothbrush moustache, the kind later known as a George Orwell, he had a talent for perky stage humour and was considered a bit of a wag.

My brother David and I were sometimes taken to the Punchinello Players' shows. Usually they took place in church halls and similar places. One of them featured a ten-minute playlet in which my mother and father were the only actors, called *The Burglar and the Girl*. As the curtain rose, a burglar with a black mask was seen climbing through a window at the back, only to be surprised in mid-robbery by a cool and aristocratic girl. In his gorblimey accent, he talks her out of calling the police. When he's gone, she turns out to be not, as we had thought, the daughter of the house, but another burglar, who makes off with the jewels he'd come for. *The Burglar and the Girl* began with the stage in darkness as the villain made his entrance through the open window. The creepy atmosphere was too much for my brother, who hid under the seat and had to be taken out. Though not entirely at my ease, I stuck it out, aware of my mother and father talking incomprehensibly and of my mother, at one point, drawing a gun on my father – *my* gun, doing duty as a stage prop, and so I must have known nobody would get hurt.

Back at home, we set to and produced for the benefit of luckless visitors our own versions of some of the items in the Punchinello repertoire, complete with programmes, tickets, and an admission charge of one ha'penny. My brother took things further. Captain Pinchard had a daughter, Biddy, who started her own dancing class, which David attended once a week, and took part in her end-of-term displays, so gaining an introduction to a métier he has followed ever since. Biddy Pinchard also figured in a Punchinello Players sketch, devised by the Captain, in which my father played a floor-walker who falls in love with a wax mannequin, played by Biddy. She dances before her admirer, but all of a sudden there is a fire in the store, and she 'melts', leaving the hapless shop assistant inconsolable: curtain. Biddy was still running her dancing school in her eighties: her obituary in the *Dancing Times* in 1987 noted that among her pupils had been the dance writer David Vaughan.

Eric Gill in his autobiography speaks of memories of early childhood as 'Holes in Oblivion', isolated pictures or single images that stand out clearly from a surrounding fog in which a thousand others remained, for him, for ever obscured. From this life that precipitated us into suburbia, a very early memory comes to my mind: sitting on a chair with one leg held stiffly out while my mother fastens knee-length gaiters. She takes pride in dressing us smartly, and uses a button hook very fast, with deft fingers, popping the little brown buttons, like beads, into their loops. On my feet I see little patent leather shoes with a strap across the instep. We wear elegant matching overcoats, David and I, with velvet facings, and blue berets. The picture is faded, but real.

From being ill in childhood, sharper memories remain. Lying in bed during the day, listless, hot, aching, with sounds drifting in from Acre Lane: the slow, heavy clip-clop of a dray-horse hauling a coalman's cart, with the coalman crying 'Co-aal! Co-aal!' And on a winter's night, when being ill had brought the ultimate in luxury, a fire in the bedroom grate; and after dark you could lie awake with the reflection of the flames dancing on the ceiling. Some of the memories are fearful: those disordered dreams when the scale of things, their number, depth, density, all became horribly distorted, and my own body seemed at once preposterously small and frighteningly huge, stretching like rubber – dreams that always began manageably enough but soon became imbued with such horrors that I had to cry out for my mother to come and coax them all away.

Perhaps once every six months, as I ran around the flat in Acre Lane, I would suddenly feel the floor tipping, my head starting to spin, the walls, the furniture reeling across my vision from right to left over and over again, and I hear my childish, frightened voice calling out, 'Mummy, the room's going round!'

Our doctor was a kindly, comfortable Scotsman called Dr Gilchrist, famed for his prescription for a healthy lunch: a glass of milk and an apple. He decided these peculiar turns of mine were minor epilepsy. But by the time I was seven or eight they had gone away. The episodes were the extremes of that sinister experience called illness, the worst because of their unpredictability and the suddenness and violence of the attack, as if some power outside yourself had taken hold of you and made inexplicable things happen to your body. The same power gave you spots and scabs and fevers, causing your skin to become dry and papery and your limbs to be heavy, languorous and dull. It gave me measles, jaundice, and impetigo, the latter with a foul sore that spread across my lip and up my nose and had to be painfully soaked off with cotton wool dipped in Mr Godden's best olive oil. To a boy we knew it gave a fatal illness – the name was spoken in hushed voices, *meningitis* . . . and a friend, it was reported to us, awoke from a feverish sleep to utter words that reinforced this notion of the mystery and nightmarishness of disease, as he told his mother, 'I dreamt I'd fallen a million.' With those words, he died.

When I was five I witnessed my mother and father fighting. It was the first adult row I remember. They were at the foot of the stairs on our landing. He was gripping her arm behind her back and she was sobbing and gasping. He said to her, 'That'll teach you to be a naughty girl.' It was said in a tone of contempt, almost of banter.

He saw me staring at them and told me to go back into the dining room where I had been playing. A few minutes later I heard him go downstairs, and crept timorously into the front room where my mother was sitting by the window, alone. I went to her and clung to her, but she pushed me away. What was it about? How did it end? I have no idea. But I think it was important, a short, unhappy trailer to the misfortune that overtook and destroyed their marriage twenty-five years later.

Another memory of that Saturday afternoon. It remains like a single snapshot, as though in slightly blurred sepia. I stand looking out of the same sitting room window and see my mother walking on her own, down Acre Lane, with her cloche hat pulled down over her hair, a small, forlorn figure.

Four

ABANDONMENT AND LONELINESS moved me more than anything. One day, by way of a weekend treat, I was given a book from Rupert Bear's sixpenny library. Rupert's adventures appeared in daily instalments in the *Express*, drawn by an artist called Mary Tourtel and written by her husband Herbert. In due course they would be published in book form, one or sometimes two complete stories. The one I had this time was *Rupert Bear's Christmas*.

The title would have led you to expect on the cover a picture, say, of Rupert surrounded by his friends, such as Bill Badger and Edward Trunk, perhaps handing out festive gifts from an outsize Christmas tree, with Mother and Father Bear, the latter smoking his pipe, contentedly looking on. This would have been the style of the later, blander Rupert adventures devised and drawn by Alfred Bestall, who succeeded Mary Tourtel when she retired in 1935. Not this time. As usual, the Tourtels' vision was much darker. The drawing on the cover of the book showed a truly appalling sight: Rupert, wandering in the snow blindfolded, with his arms tied behind his back, cold, wretched and cast out. I looked at the picture, and burst into tears.

Several hours went by before I could bring myself to read the story and face up to the events that had landed Rupert in this dire predicament. They were as follows: sent off, as usual, on some well-meant errand, such as delivering a basket of firewood or some home-made cakes to a neighbouring widow, Rupert had been waylaid by two long-standing enemies, Freddy and Ferdy Fox. Rupert's sheer virtuousness made the Fox twins hate him, and out of nothing but spite they had tied him up and left him to wander helplessly through the snowbound countryside around his home village of Nutwood. Worst of all, it was Christmas Eve.

But help did come, and from an unexpected quarter. A jingle of bells and harness, a cry of concern – and it was Santa Claus himself out on his rounds, who untied Rupert and carried him back by sleigh to his workshop. There Santa offered Rupert the rewards of virtue: his pick of the toys, and a trip, as his guest, on his seasonal journey, distributing presents to all the children, or rather, the animals dressed as children, in Nutwood . . . all, that is, save the malicious Fox Bros, whose exclusion that Christmas was richly deserved.

I loved Rupert, with a deep and unquestioning love, and I don't believe Mary Tourtel, his inventor, has received her due as a creator of these stories for children. They were quintessentially of the 1930s, and must have occupied a commanding place in the reading life, and quite possibly shaped the moral universe of an entire generation of middle-class English children, juvenile readers of the *Express*. Indeed the newspaper's proprietor, the first Lord Beaverbrook, once said that the Rupert stories sold more copies of the paper than anything he had ever published about the Empire.

Mary was a book illustrator who had already published one or two mildly successful stories for children. Herbert, her husband, was an *Express* sub-editor. Considering how newspaper offices work one can easily imagine how the job came Mary's way. At the *Express,* they decided they needed a 'reply' to Teddy Tail, mouse star of the *Daily Mail* children's page. And so from 1923, they had the Rupert stories, in which a teddy bear in a small boy's clothes, though often daunted and far from home, triumphed against such adversaries as a family of Robber Wolves, a sisterhood of ugly witches or, one of Mrs Tourtel's most sinister creations, a Black Dwarf, scuttling down secret passageways like some evil rodent. There was a Magic Toyman who plotted to turn Rupert into a mechanical toy bear, a forest full of moronic giants with slack jaws and matted hair who came after him with clubs, and a character called the Old Man of the Sea who emerged from the waves dripping salt water and attired in a suit of seaweed, attended by a bodyguard of seals.

The settings for these adventures were semi-medieval. They would begin in Nutwood, a place straight out of middle England, looking like a Cotswold village but with a population of humanoid animals: dogs in 1920s uniform 'manned' the police station and the post office, with their tails poking out of the seats of their specially-cut trousers, and a benign sheep in spectacles and mob-cap served behind the counter in the village shop. Within a few frames Rupert would somehow be transported to a romantic fairyland world where turreted castles would be inhabited by stupid but violent ogres, or by a prince who had been turned into a boar but was still dressed in velvet doublet and silk hose. After perilous adventures, help might come to the Little Bear from a talking black cat, a woodbird or a regular member of the cast called the Wise Old Goat, a Merlin-like figure in a cloak, whose superior learning allowed him to function as a kind of *deus ex machina*. As a rule he remained in Nutwood but was in possession of certain more or less supernatural gadgets which would help him locate Rupert when the Bear family became seriously worried by his prolonged absence. There was a crystal ball in his cottage, and once, a kind of primitive TV – his 'wondrous magic glass' – on which the Goat, shrouded in his usual necromancer's cloak and peering through donnish pince-nez, could see the faraway scullery in which Rupert was imprisoned. At once, a neighbourhood elf was despatched to organise the escape.

These astounding, riveting tales were told by means of a daily pair of drawings in Mary Tourtel's precise, graceful, Kate Greenawayish style. She was particularly good with animals, her cats and horses always drawn in wonderfully expressive poses.

Beneath the drawings would be four lines of verse supplied by husband Herbert; and accompanying the verse, a prose version, possibly to satisfy readers who found his poetic gift inadequate. That would have been understandable. Even at an early age I realised the work was feeble doggerel, though still to be preferred to the prose alternative, feeling, I think, it suited the pictures better. But Herbert's prosaic words were all part of the charm of these stories and did nothing to diminish my enthusiasm, nor my brother's, for the continuing Rupert Bear canon, or corpus.

Fans like us could affirm their loyalty to Rupert by joining the Rupert League, an 'official' association of Rupert followers. My brother was already a member of the Teddy Tail Club and the League of Youth, an organisation not affiliated to any news-paper: it didn't seem to require you to do anything, although its rather off-putting motto was *Res non verba,* translated as 'Deeds not words'. The Rupert League was another thing entirely, and when David joined up I naturally followed suit, even though the benefits were not especially numerous. It was the thought that mattered. League members had a small enamel badge and a membership card on which there were spaces for Good Conduct stamps, awarded for various achievements. If you thought you deserved a stamp, you sent in your card with an account of what you claimed to have done, vouched for by a parent. Back would come a congratulatory letter and a gummed stamp, to be stuck into your membership card like a savings certificate. You could also win a stamp by recruiting a new member of the League. Priggishly, I sent in my card once or twice when I was top of the form but never collected the ten endorsements which would have filled the page and entitled me to the Rupert Good Conduct Medal, which, the aged Alfred Bestall told me, when I called on him once in his tiny flat in Surbiton, bore a curious resemblance to the Victoria Cross.

In the end the *Express* was forced to disband the Rupert League because it had grown too big. More than a million children had enrolled and servicing the organization was costing the paper £3,000 a week. And Mrs Tourtel's imaginative world was eventually too much for the *Express* management: the paper was committed to a policy of comfortable, thumbs-up optimism, which applied to absolutely everything – and the Rupert saga was casting a dark shadow across the heart of the paper. When Mary Tourtel was forced to retire through failing eyesight, Beaverbrook gave orders that her successor, Alfred Bestall, should cut out the witches, dwarves, ogres and wolves: henceforth the stories would be brighter, cheerier, cosier – and incomparably more dull.

My senior by seventeen months, David was well-placed for intellectual leadership, and set an example of studious, neat and cultivated behaviour even at an early age. Now and then he exploited the advantage. Once he told me there were spiders at the bottom of the bed – anyone's bed, just as there were cobwebs in ceiling corners or bogies between your toes. I half-believed him. Just to be on the safe side, I took to sleeping with my knees drawn up and my grandfather's revolver pointing downwards in case any spiders decided to try anything. It wasn't loaded, of course, but I reasoned the spiders wouldn't know that.

On the whole, my brother and I were on good terms, and shared many games and fantasies. Like all older brothers, he was the instigator, the one with the ideas – looking out for toys you could make, using the instructions on the *Express* children's page or in the comics we used to buy . . . a miniature tram from an empty box of Christmas dates, or a peepshow inside an empty shoe-box, with a piece of coloured toffee-paper pasted over an eye-hole at one end through which you shone a torch to illuminate the scene you had painted. We both had teddy bears for whom we invented extravagant biographies. Between us, however, there were differences of temperament and of appearance. David was thin, I was fat. I liked soldiers, he liked dolls. I liked riding a bicycle, he never bothered to learn: when I went out exploring, he preferred to stay at home.

However, we had a good friend in common, a girl of about our age called Barbara, who lived around the corner. One day I showed her what I had between my legs: we called it a nilly. Then I talked her into pulling aside the gusset of her bathing costume to show us what she had. Never having seen a girl undressed, I was astonished at how little there was to see, and demanded aggressively if that was all there was. I suspected she was cheating me. I asked her what she called this disappointing little handful of flesh she had rather timidly fished out: her answer sent me into paroxysms of laughter almost of Blow Football scale. The name she had invented was *wud*. The blunt absurdity of that monosyllable caused me to roll on the ground giggling.

Probably juvenile embarrassment. On the other hand, when it came to inventing words, we were past masters, making up names for things for which no convenient name existed. In the Brixton department store Quinn and Axten's, the lifts were operated by girls in maroon uniforms with many buttons on the tunics, long trousers and pillbox hats. Such a girl was known to us as a *demmity-fess*. The little figures in Eskimo suits who gambolled across the snowy icing of a Christmas cake were given the name *sallagy-savies*. The pattern made by a knife and fork crossed on your plate to indicate you would like another helping was called a *crossmate,* and a piece of paper rolled in a tight cylinder, with which you could light the fire or the gas mantle, was a *sib*. There were other words I have forgotten, and I suppose we could claim to have made a small, ephemeral contribution to the language since there are, after all, no others words in existence to describe the lift girls or the Christmas cake children or the other things we had singled out. Nor is there a word, apart from the one we invented, for a type of long English face my brother and I had identified among the crowds shopping in Water Lane or Brixton Road. A face with prominent cheek-bones, mouth habitually a little ajar, the impression somewhat simian – this was known as a *goggox* face.

We were a self-sufficient pair, sharing imaginary adventures and inventing games of our own. And when the time came for my brother to go to school, our dependence on each other's company was plainly demonstrated. David was five and a half when my mother took him for his first day at school in September 1929. Sudbourne Road Infants School was ten minutes walk from 88 Acre Lane. I was almost four, and viewed this new adventure my brother was about to enjoy as yet another example of the favouritism based on age to which I had become resentfully accustomed. Accustomed or not, I burst into tears. Harassed but sympathetic, the teacher was ready with a solution: I should be allowed to stay as well. My mother went home alone.

My school career was now, in today's phrase, up and running. From that first day at Sudbourne Road I retain a few mental snapshots: a tray of sand to play with, some small coloured beads to thread on a string. There is a clear memory of the smell of biscuits in a paper bag unwrapped by my neighbour at my first school desk, a small girl called Audrey, pale and nervous, whose daily panic at being separated from her mother probably accounted for the small puddles that appeared regularly under her chair. For this she always gave the same excuse: 'Someone pushed me over in the lavatories.' I could never understand why this clearly irrelevant explanation was accepted by the teacher with no more than a sigh and a shake of the head. But this was school. And the rules were different.

Like reflections in a window, other children's faces float across my mind's eye. A huge, tall, ginger boy called Ivor, boasting about the size of his testicles in the smelly lavatories, and Gordon, the form comedian, with a repertoire of funny faces involving crossed eyes and sucked-in cheeks, who explained to me and another friend, one Cecil Hunt, the meaning of the words bum, shit, piss, and cock. So much for nillies! My education had begun.

This was the school where Empire Day was marked by a

special rally in the hall and where at Christmas the children were allowed to come in fancy dress. I put on a recent birthday present, a cowboy suit, with imitation leather chaps, prairie hat and toy six-shooter. David wore the white silk suit in which he had lately appeared at an aunt's wedding, so that I heard a fellow-pupil telling another, incredulously, that one boy had turned up in his pyjamas. I thanked my stars I wasn't the one wearing the suit.

School was the place where I became aware of the threat of physical abuse from older children, and from adults. A gang of older boys called Geary's Gang were known to rule the playground and were best kept away from. Ivor with the testicles was recognised as dangerous – to be avoided, or placated with sweets. And in the next form up, to which I was removed after a few months, the form mistress, with the ominous name of Miss Sharnock, was known to be bad-tempered, impatient and *strict*, ready to give you a smack for nothing very much. She had a goggox face. She also had thick glasses and seemed immensely tall. She was feared for her personal style of punishment: with boys she would wrench up one leg of your short trousers and give you a stinging slap on the upper thigh where it wouldn't show. It happened to me once. She heard me talk when she had harshly commanded silence. I felt her arm grab me roughly – my trouser leg was yanked up: the slap made me gasp. I gave Audrey a brave smile and Sharnock pounced again. I hear her voice now, angrily denouncing me as her right hand connected on the other leg this time: 'That's for grinning!'

How unfair it could all be! But Sudbourne Road also began a condition of school life I became used to – always being younger than nearly everyone else in the form. We two brothers had started our school careers in a state of innocent precociousness and also one notable advantage. We were known as 'the babies that can read'. We had taught ourselves with the aid of *Tiger Tim's Weekly* and *Bo-Peep,* in which the captions to the pictures were printed with hyphens between syllables. When reading was on the timetable, we were marched off to a higher form: a privileged élite.

And it was at Sudbourne Road that I was first affected personally by adult ideas of class. Ostensibly at least it was a question of accent. 'Don't they speak nicely?' More than once, my mother claimed, acquaintances would make this comment when they heard us talking. Sudbourne Road was changing all that. Little by little, the nasal sounds of SW2 were beginning to sour the Fauntleroy tones of upstairs at No 88. Also I had followed my friend Cecil's example – he had mentioned it casually – and passed on to my mother some of the basic information we had received from Gordon in the playground. Gordon had also been brought home, with Cecil, to tea. Perhaps he had made a bad impression.

Worse still, David had become mortally afraid of being bullied by some of the bigger boys. The solution was clear. We would have to be taken away from that school and sent to a 'nicer' type of place. They chose a school my Uncle Ernie, whom I'd never known, had been sent to on Brixton Hill, with the grandiose name of Surrey College.

That school doesn't exist any longer, but until a few years ago there remained on the hill a low balustrade, formerly topped with iron railings, around a block of post-war flats, and on that low wall you could just make out the name Surrey College in faded black letters. Of the building itself, there was nothing.

It must have dated from the early 19th century, and been built as a house for some comfortably-off family, in a semi-rural place and in a commanding position at the top of the hill, before being converted to a school, perhaps around the 1890s. It looked huge to me. I was awed by the place. As soon as you went in you could tell it was more serious than Sudbourne Road. The school smell, that compound of books, glue, polish, Lysol disinfectant and chalk-dust, was richer and stronger. The form rooms were steeply raked, with tiers of old-fashioned desks made of heavy pitch-pine bound with iron, the tops scoured with lines and initials knifed in by pupils long since gone.

Surrey College took boys up to fourteen, girls up to eighteen. We small children worked, and played during breaks, in areas segregated from the older, lofty senior population of the school, known as The Big Girls. One day I was challenged by one of them for trespassing on their territory, and with unusual boldness told her I was taking a short cut, so she could put that in her pipe and pull it through her ears. I had misjudged the audience for this witticism (I had heard it at home) and next day I was singled out by the headmistress, Mrs Hall, straight-backed, severe, dressed in black, the widow of the man who had started the school. But – no smacks à la Sharnock. Instead, the power of words. After a three-minute lecture I was dismissed, shaken and ashamed. No Sudbourne Road repartee would be tolerated on the heights of Brixton Hill.

My form teacher was a plump, owlish woman called Miss Plumridge, in gold-rimmed pince-nez and a bun, who presided affectionately over the children in the lowest form. She was kind and popular, and she taught everything: arithmetic, English, geography, spelling, grammar, and writing – for the latter there were old-fashioned copy-books in which we had to copy out page after page of letters in copper-plate style. I loved this, especially the capital letters with their ornate, curly serifs, the Q like a 2. When we came to letter F I was carried away with enthusiasm and wrote many pages of them, so many that I had to go to Miss Plumridge's desk and try to explain my sudden orthographic fever. She didn't mind. Even-tempered and placid, she coaxed from me a spirit of academic competitiveness, and I strove to be top of the form. 'Paul is brilliant,' she wrote on a school report, 'but he will *dream*.' At home, they were more amused than impressed. My mother sang ironically at me a song that was currently popular: 'I'm a dreamer, aren't we all?' I think they assumed Miss Plumridge had uncovered a romantic side to my character, but I knew she meant I didn't keep my mind on the lessons.

Being a Surrey College boy carried prestige and responsibility. We had school caps with the initials SC, which we were instructed to raise deferentially on meeting a grown-up, especially a parent or one of the teachers. At the end of the day I would saunter home, six years old and as full of swank as a drum major, certain that passers-by would recognise me as someone out of the ordinary, privileged, enviable. My parents were pleased with the results of the move. Sometimes we were allowed to bring school friends home to tea, friends called Leander, Tony and Basil. Now and then there were parties, where the fare (unlike now) was entirely sweet: we should have rejected the sausages, crisps, Twiglets and nuts expected by children of the 1990s. We wanted iced cakes, jam tarts, biscuits in animal shapes, jellies that wobbled suggestively, and something we knew as blummonge. And fixtures on the agenda were games that would now be considered boring and naive: Poor Jenny Sits a-Weeping, Oranges and Lemons, The Farmer's in his Den, Musical Chairs, Hunt the Thimble, Squeak Piggy Squeak and, in utter innocence, Postman's Knock.

There were signs that our family of four was moving up the ladder. My father was now Chief Clerk in the Counting House at the Greenwich Linoleum Company. He was also a Freemason, a posher version of his father's society, the Druids. Sometimes I would hear him in the bathroom in the mornings, talking to himself: I feared he was exhibiting what I had been told was the first sign of madness – later I realised he was learning something he needed to know for advancement in his lodge. 'Masonics' were beginning to figure in my parents' social calendar, edging out the Punchinello Players and the doings at church, where my father had been a sidesman, going round with a plate collecting money after the service. Now, once a year, there would be something hugely important and keenly looked forward to called a Ladies' Night. Preparations would begin early in the afternoon, with the rooms and landing smelling of exotic perfume, my mother sitting for what seemed hours before the dressing-table mirror, turning her head this way and that, careful to protect her perm, and my father arriving home early from the office and changing into what he called 'full fig' – tail suit with dazzlingly white waistcoat and white bow tie. Smelling of bay rum, he would escort my mother to a waiting car, holding a top hat, having first for our benefit gone through his repertoire of tricks, tipping the hat off his head and rolling it down his outstretched arm into his fist . . . or taking it off like a music hall drunk, twisting his wrist corkscrew fashion and presenting the topper with the back of his hand, with a hiccup. Then, off they would go, to an unimaginably brilliant place known as the West End.

Next morning we would hear stories of glamorous and dizzy entertainment, with a band and dancing, a singer or a comic performing for the dinner guests and my father, perhaps, making a speech. My mother would remove the tissue paper from some lavish present and show it to us – a scent-spray or a powder compact which had been gift-wrapped, one for every lady guest, left by her place at table.

More in our line were set-piece family treats: the Lord Mayor's Show, viewed from the first floor window of my father's office, and once, a procession for Amy Johnson, lone woman aviator, as she rode in triumph to the Guildhall to receive the freedom of the city. On the wireless there was a song about her: *'Amy, beautiful Amy, How can you blame me, For loving you?'* Christmas was the occasion for a major expedition: lunch at Pimm's, inventors of the cocktails, in the Old Bailey, preceded by a visit to a City friend of my father's, also in the lino business. The lobby of his office was dominated by an enormous reproduction of a landscape by Monet. It wasn't until years later that I discovered the name of the artist, but the remarkable thing about this Old Bailey version was that it had all been executed in inlaid linoleum.

Privileged at Christmas, we were taken to two 'pantos' – the one at the Lyceum, spoken in rhymed couplets and with a transformation scene to finish the performance; and the local show, at the Brixton Theatre, with Naughton and Gold (local celebrities) in rôles like the Broker's Men in 'Cinderella'.

We saw our first moving pictures. The first I remember was a talkie, Al Jolson in *The Singing Fool*: my mother bought the sheet music of the tremendously popular song which the dreadful Jolson had sung to his small son. It was *Sonny Boy*, and it made me cry because the child died, lending an awful poignancy to the words: 'Friends may forsake me, troubles overtake me, I'll still have you, Sonny Boy!' On the music there was a picture of the child-star of the film, wearing an Indian suit and gazing up adoringly at his father. I am afraid it is possible that in a vain and lachrymose way I saw myself as that child, vaguely pretending to share his tragic fate. *Then* they would understand, then they'd be sorry . . . I even identified one of my toys, a small lead figure of a boy intended as a juvenile passenger for my Hornby train set, as 'my' Sonny Boy, and I took this peculiar little mannikin, this miniature representative of myself, in my pocket everywhere, taking him out to stand next to my plate in cafés or to look out of the window on the tram to observe the goggox faces.

But tram rides were becoming rarer events, because we had become one of the few families to own a car. First, a small red open sports car, which you could pretend was a fire engine, with a dickey seat – two seats side by side in what would now have looked like the boot. Soon my father changed it for a Morris saloon and my mother, daringly, learned to drive too. My father's luck held: he had been picked out for a new job, Secretary of a new Association of Linoleum and Floorcloth Manufacturers. It brought a big jump in salary. The lino industry, much of it situated in Scottish towns like Kirkcaldy or Dundee, was thriving. Linoleum was the thing, a cheap, durable covering for the floors of the new houses going up all round the outskirts of London and other big cities – lino that looked like marble, like parquet, like tiles or possibly like a carpet, inlaid with a pattern of flowers or scenery or something 'abstract'. Perhaps some family, somewhere, walked on a linoleum version of one of Monet's landscapes.

Meanwhile in our sporty little 'roadster' we would bowl out

of London to the seaside, and every August, to the best event of the year, our seaside holiday: two weeks in Margate, or more accurately its better end, Cliftonville. The routine never varied. We always stayed in the same boarding house, run by Mrs Newlands, with the name Zion House in the glass over the front door, and every day walked in our 'doughboy' hats to the beach, where there were still bathing-machines lined up, derelict and by now irrelevant. Sometimes we would go, not to the beach, but to the bathing pool on the front, which featured a hot plunge bath, with sea water, for cold days.

There are photographs of these holidays. My mother in a smart one-piece bathing costume plus bathing hat – the costume is rather long in the leg, with a stripe. The men are in black bathing suits made of heavy, baggy cotton that, when wet, moulded itself closely to their genitals. Keenly looked forward to was a visit to Dreamland, Margate's famous funfair, for a ride on the underground waterway and a plate of cockles. And there were times when my father's army friend Cecil Hicks and his family would come too, and then we were kings of the beach, with Uncle Cecil organising cricket on the firm sand and posturing absurdly as a Strong Man in his voluminous bathing-suit, with all of us, our parents, his son John and my brother and me, there to provide a ready audience.

Pleasures, it is well known, are curiously intense in childhood. Nothing ever compares with those first holidays: the sea and sky are never again so blue, the sun never as warm nor the beach so balmy and inviting. Our Margate holidays left me with a store of memories, faint now as old picture postcards, which seem part of a childhood Arcadia when everything contributed to my utter contentment: the thrill of arrival and the first glimpse of the sea, the smell of the seaweed, the beach games and competitions, the waves splashing their soothing rhythm as we dug our sand-castles and built our dams, the long, hot sunsets and the walk back to the boarding-house to be in time for the booming crescendo of the dinner gong, and the inviting aroma of Zion House, compounded of English breakfast, gravy, roast meats,

English puddings and pots of tea. Then the clean white sheets that covered your hot, sunburnt limbs, and the sand that got everywhere – between your toes, in your ears, in your hair, on the bedroom carpet and in the bed itself. The standard images of the English seaside of that time, stock-in-trade of a thousand Southern Railway travel posters and the covers of children's annuals: starfish and buckets and spades, crabs and crazily leaning breakwaters, shrimping nets and raggedy mops of sea-weed, distant steamers and scudding yachts, beaming jerseyed fishermen and docile, saddled donkeys . . . year after year at Margate, they all came true.

But it was when my childhood was coming to an end that the family made its decisive move. In 1934, my mother finally persuaded my father to break away from his family and leave the house in Acre Lane. It was a momentous step for them, and we were also about to become part of one of the most revolutionary, though protracted events in the social history of London – the mass exodus to the outer suburbs.

Five

NEW MALDEN WAS a small township in the middle of an area where the rush to the suburbs was at its most hectic. Acre upon acre of fertile farmland had been bought up for the creation of new estates but the district had been a tempting target for developers since the beginning of the century: successive census returns demonstrated that the population of the urban district of Malden and Coombe had doubled every ten years since 1901, and by 1931, three years before we moved out from Brixton, more than 23,000 people were living there. In neighbouring Merton and Morden the rate of growth was faster still. Between 1920 and 1937 the population there increased by 223 per cent, in the course of which the area acquired no fewer than seven new railway stations.

One of the biggest new estates in New Malden lay to the west of the town centre and it was being developed by Wates, the builders. My father's choice was undoubtedly influenced by the fact that his younger sister, my Auntie May, had married a scion of the Wates family, who had not followed his father into the building trade but worked in a succession of jobs, which included, for a while, and to my father's considerable satisfaction, managership of an off licence.

A central tenet in my father's view of life was a belief in the useful connection, the friend or, preferably, relative in the know, who could be relied on to do you a good turn, pass on a bit of discount, help you jump the queue. I suspect this way of thinking figured in his decision to become a Freemason. So I dare say he hoped for some kind of preferential consideration through his sideways connection with the Wates clan – perhaps a few quid off the price of the house. No such advantage materalised, and my father had to find the full sum of £1,000 for the house they chose. It was on a corner, semi-detached, in the 'Swiss chalet' style, and so supposedly had a faint resemblance to some mountain retreat, the phrase suggesting a peaceful, sheep-dotted landscape bathed in continuous sunshine. It had a steeply pitched, red-tiled roof, which side by side with the house next door made the shape of an inverted W. The façade was rendered in pebble dash, protecting the brick and so thriftily obviating the need for re-pointing. The house was a 'semi', but the detachment was almost complete, the only link between our house and its neighbour being a thread-like arch of brick above a thin sliver of ground, about two feet wide, separating the two flank walls. This area of dead and uncultivable land was more or less permanently littered with builders' rubble.

Our house was the last in a row of about twenty in the same style, but it was a little bigger than the others and £250 dearer. This conferred on us a small but lasting social advantage, as did the fact that we were on the corner, and had a garage at the end of the garden. Inside, the bedrooms were larger. There was an extra room downstairs, too, for which as it happened my parents found it difficult to hit upon any specific use. It was variously designated the Breakfast Room, the Morning Room, and the Study, even though none of the functions indicated by those names was important enough to deserve a special room in our household. This extra living space was next to the front door, and it would finally come into its own in 1940, when my father had the floor-boards removed, the ceiling and walls strengthened and the windows sandbagged. With bunk beds installed for all the family, it would look like nothing so much as a dug-out in a quiet sector of the line round about 1917, and it was known as the Shelter.

The single most important thing about the situation of our new house was that it stood on the Kingston Bypass. This was one of the motor roads that had been spanking new in the mid-twenties, and as is the way with such highways it had swiftly become out-of-date. It was one of a series of trunk roads out of London and it had been built at the unheard-of cost of over four million pounds. Some bigwig had opened it in 1927, but by the time the Vaughan family arrived on its border the bypass's usefulness as a fast road in and out of the capital had been irredeemably compromised by thousands of people like us. For what were ostensibly good economic reasons, the builders of the new estates had put up their scaffolding within yards of the new roadways, and so had the builders of new factories. Rows of these structures lined the bypass along much of its ten-mile length, from Richmond Park to Esher. Bus routes had followed. Then traffic lights and traffic jams, pedestrian crossings, pubs and petrol stations and 'parades' of shops with service roads.

By the late spring of 1934 when we migrated from Brixton, the conversion of acre upon acre of rural Surrey to a totally new kind of urban landscape was in full swing. Our house was at a spot where the Kingston Bypass was crossed by an old road called South Lane, winding its way from New Malden to Worcester Park; and at the latter end it was little more than a farm track, barely negotiable in wet weather for the mud. Not for long.

But for the time being, we only had to walk a few hundred yards from our house to find countryside – the real thing. There were green fields, great stately oaks and elms, and a little brook, the Hogsmill, which meandered interestingly along from some-where the other side of Old Malden to New Malden and beyond, watering on the way a farm close to the new railway line being put down from Motspur Park and Worcester Park to Stoneleigh. These place-names, suggesting something faintly Ye Olde, car-ried suggestions of a picturesque Merrie England romanticism soon to be picked up in the décor my parents worked out for the new house, No 14 Malden Way. It was considered essential for the house to have a name as well as a number. My father settled on one he thought appropriate to its situation next to the bypass: 'Wayside'. Through a crony in the City, he had some writing paper printed with the address set diagonally across one corner in old-fashioned Gothic script, giving, of course, both the name of the house and its number.

'Wayside' . . . the name implied a soft-edged, sentimental view of the house's location, and of the murderous traffic that roared past, rising to its peak on hot summer weekends. Acre Lane this was not. Here the needs of the people and the needs of the motor car collided head-on. Most weeks in the *Wimbledon Borough News* or *Surrey Comet* you could read a headline reporting fresh casualties in the war that smouldered on our doorstep. DEATH-TRAP ON BYPASS – People Afraid to Send Children to School . . . TWO KILLED ON BYPASS – Motor Cyclists in Triple Crash . . . BYPASS TRAGEDY – Poor Lighting Criticized. From the landing window or the 'lounge' of 'Wayside' there was a clear view of the South Lane junction where some of the most spectacular accidents would regularly occur – the screaming of brakes, a sharp bang, a reverberating skitter of metal fragments, followed by even more sinister noises: the moans of the victims, the screams of women bystanders.

And yet, despite the carnage, there was a certain excitement and even prestige about our proximity to this tumultuous new highway. You felt *au courant,* up to date, as along its modern dual carriageway bowled the compact little motors, mostly black or navy blue, Morris Tens and Ford Eights or V-Eights, with running boards and starting handles, sometimes dickey seats and windscreens you could open, adventuring to the coast for the day; or, for those richer than we were, making a swift escape to 'glamorous' places like the Ace of Spades, one of the smart new 'road houses' where you could swim, dance, and dine; or to the Bear Hotel in Esher, where (a brief excitement, almost putting us on the map) Max Baer, the heavyweight boxer punningly stayed while in training for his fight against (was it?) Tommy Farr. These were the haunts of dashing young men with toothbrush moustaches and 'sports' jackets with pleated pockets, driving the SS Swallows or Javelins we would see cruising past the lounge windows of 'Wayside' at a shocking sixty mph.

For some reason our move to this up-to-the-minute environment was done in a rush. So much so that my parents didn't wait for a resolution of something that might have been a serious matter but turned out to be only a minor crisis – my brother's removal to hospital with a suspected tubercular hip. He stayed in the children's hospital at Carshalton for twelve weeks until they decided their diagnosis had been wrong: not TB but a mild form of juvenile rheumatism of which we never heard another word. It meant I was unable to share the excitement of leaving Acre Lane with anyone of my own age and it was up to me to make friends outside the family. No trouble at all. The new estates were swarming with children. Uprooted from Inner London or from distant rural communities, they were all eagerly exploring the estates around them. Groups and gangs were formed. My mother indicated that there were some children it would be better not to play with, her disapproval being based on accent, general scruffiness, and probably on the size, position, and hence the cost of the house their parents had acquired – perhaps for a deposit of 11/6d (59p), which was the astounding bargain on offer from some estate agents. A sort of rough pecking-order was establishing itself. Semi-detached was better than terraced, which was rare anyway; better than semi-detached was a house with the kind of token archway we shared with our neighbours at number 12 Malden Way, a professional chef by the name of Gazelli who lived with his wife and a noisy, hysterical spaniel. Best of all was the kind of house that had been built in some of the roads between us and New Malden itself. They had been put up ten or more years earlier, and they weren't particularly large – but they had class, because every house was different.

These roads were among the places my mother and I explored during the first few weeks of our life at No 14, which rather soon, and to my father's annoyance, became No 248. The Post

Office, which had as much trouble as everyone else keeping up with the rush to the suburban countryside, had decided Malden Way ought to begin a few miles further east towards Wimbledon. We were given a new number and my father's fancy headed paper became obsolete at a stroke.

We felt the new number spoiled the modest, villagey scale of our new address, but it was a small sacrifice. There was much to amaze us within walking distance of No 248 or within a short car journey, much of it with just the sort of rustic charm the posters were promising. Our first excursions to New Malden provoked wonderment: the newness of it all, the wide pavements, the leafy roads that led to the main shopping street. It almost seemed like the country retreats you saw in sepia photographs in railway carriages, promising teas with Hovis or a tankard of ale in the open air. My mother at once began to refer to this small township as 'the village', and revelled in every detail of it, in the release the move had brought her and the certainty that we had gone up in the world.

When we began to explore further we found even more surprising sights. In Cheam, only ten minutes away, there were genuine half-timbered houses – models for the new semis which had Z-shaped beams pinned cosmetically across their facades. Nearer, in Worcester Park, which had a quaint teashop called The Kettle Sings (large copper kettle in window), there was a pub called The Plough where, so it was said, there was a secret room in which Dick Turpin had concealed himself while on the run. Best of all, a couple of miles up the bypass and down a series of suburban side roads, there was a vast open-air swimming pool, with bright green water, a cafeteria, a large concrete fountain and grassy slopes for sunbathing and picnicking. It was the Surbiton Lagoon.

Friends to whom I later described this watering-place thought it absurd, its name a laughable fusion of the bowler hat and the grass skirt, a juxtaposition of the humdrum and the exotic. But if the very name Surbiton suggested the archetypal suburb, and the last place on earth where you would expect to find a lagoon, nevertheless in the hot summer of 1934 it was as near as I could ever hope to get to Paradise. All day long my mother basked on the grass and I played in the pool, arriving at nine in the morning as the gates opened, and staying until it was time to go home for tea. A very Cliftonville, and on our own doorstep.

My father's affable view of the move was improved by the realisation that he had taken the recognisable upward step of becoming a property-owner or, at any rate, a mortgagee. To have your own new three-bedroom house on a corner, with a forty-foot garden and a garage with a 12 hp Wolseley saloon inside – by gum, as he would have said, these were things to be reckoned with in the great cost-analysis of middle-class life. With an enthusiasm not quite equal to my mother's, but still real enough, my father joined in the pleasures of establishing the new household, though frowning somewhat over how much it was all costing. By smoking Ardath he collected a complete set of cigarette cards which when pieced together made up the complete *Laughing Cavalier*. If you sent the set in, a small reproduction of the painting came back, ready framed. My father was especially fond of this picture and would point out how the cavalier's eyes, with their smile full of meaning, would follow you round the room, clearly demonstrating Franz Hals' genius. Then by the same means he acquired a second picture, a reproduction of a famous Royal Academy show-stopper, *When Did You Last See Your Father?* – Roundhead officer sternly interrogating flaxen-haired child in pale-blue silk and silver-buckled shoes, evidently the son of wanted Cavalier hero . . . of course, I identified with the noble little boy.

Both pictures were hung on long cord suspended from the picture rail in the dining room, where they went well with the reproduction 'refectory' table and oak sideboard, the deep leatherette-covered twin armchairs brought from Acre Lane, complete with copper ashtrays mounted on strips of leather and draped over an arm, and the floor-length tapestry-style curtains that hung in the bay where the French windows opened on to the small lawn. The walls were painted in cream distemper with a leafy dado below the picture rail which, like the skirting board and window frames, was dark oak. The whole effect was completed by a centre light in the form of a wooden candelabrum, with its four bulbs set in stubby, simulated candles with imitation wax dribbling down. In this room we had the wireless, and it was there that we sat in the evenings, usually, in the winter, round an electric fire ('borrowed' from the office), although sometimes we burnt coal in the grate.

Broadly speaking the back room, with its Olde England bias, represented my father's taste in home decoration. In the front room my mother took the initiative. Through diligent saving – a habit my father never acquired – she was able to buy a new three-piece suite in pale colours with a woolly fringe outlining the arms. There was a pale carpet – 'oatmeal' was the designated shade – in contrast to the dark Jacobean design in the dining room. The walls were done in a pale green 'pastel' tint and the woodwork was cream. A little later, my mother bought some more up-to-date pictures: a modern English landscape in the style of J Rowland Hilder and – audacious choice – two Van Gogh prints. One was of sunflowers in a vase, and the other the *Portrait of a Young Man*, who also kept his eyes on you as you moved round the room, though my father maintained the smile was not so enigmatic as that of the genial cavalier with the big hat next door.

In this front room, 'the lounge', we entertained guests. It was here that we would sit on Sunday afternoons, reading or 'listening in', while my father, deep in one of the armchairs, would read his *Sunday Express*, then sleep off his lunch and the three or four pints he had had in the Malden Manor, the newly built local pub.

Of course there was lino throughout the house. Some of it was jaspé, with a kind of imitation marble finish, but most of it was reproduction parquet. My father had it laid for him, as a 'demonstration' job, and hence not paid for, by one of the professional lino-layers from Barrie, Ostlere and Shepherd or Nairn's, with whom he would have been on Christian name terms, and he would have 'seen him all right' with the price of a drink or two. Some of it, with much cursing and ill temper, my father laid himself. Then, it was up to my mother to keep it polished, which she did with her O'Cedar mop, once a week.

Outside, the exterior woodwork was apple green, a fashionable colour, contrasting with the pale ochre of the pebble-dash rendering and the terracotta roof-tiles. A privet hedge was planted behind the chain fence. One thing that conferred distinction on No 248 was that there was not only a pillar-box outside but a public telephone, although of course we had one of our own, again with a low number: Malden 0471.

We were a smart, up-to-date family, but we didn't go in for the whole-hearted 'Tudorbethan' fashion that some of our neighbours had taken up: some of the halls and drawing-rooms on the estates had oak panelling half-way up the wall with a ledge on top where you could position, say, pewter plates or golfing cups, with perhaps hunting paraphernalia arranged above or maybe a brass warming-pan, some horse-brasses or a post-horn. The pictures might have shown jolly, Farmer Giles-like men in hunting pink, smoking churchwarden pipes in a country inn, or a group of merry cardinals toasting each other around a long, convivial table. Fretwork was also popular: pipe stands, spill-holders or *Home Sweet Home* plaques could easily be contructed with a fretsaw and a suitable piece of three-ply, using patterns in magazines like *Hobbies*. Or a photograph of a member of the family could be mounted on plywood and carefully sawn round, then fixed on to a grooved piece of wood to make a fleetingly life-like image. We had some of these, though in our household the photographs so mounted were more likely to be film stars than members of the family: we had Laurel and Hardy, Fred Astaire, and at one time (my choice) the Western actor Hoot Gibson. These sat oddly next to a small model of the *Golden Hind* (galleons were popular) constructed also from a *Hobbies* kit.

However, these adornments came later. In the first few months of life at No 248, we were for the most part looking outwards, exploring the roads and shops in New Malden, Worcester Park and Tolworth, Cheam, Motspur Park and – more ambitiously – Kingston-on-Thames, where Bentall's the department store seemed intent on creating a more or less instant tradition to chime with the dignity and tradition of the town itself.

Kingston was an historic town – it was where the Saxon Kings were crowned – and its proximity was an extra bonus. Bentall's had a new façade which copied the front of Hampton Court (another stop on our sight-seeing itinerary), an atmosphere that exuded prosperity, with its company motto from Tennyson ('To strive, to seek, to find and not to yield') engraved in stone on the main stair-well and visible as you went up and down on the escalators (so modern), and a Silver Café where as you sucked your orangeade through a straw (another new invention) you could watch a local artist in his beret, in the act of painting a mural depicting the history of the town. And if my mother were feeling generous there was the Tudor Café upstairs, with waitress service and a string trio led by Alfredo, with his Gypsy Violin, later in his career to become Alfredo Campoli, then just Campoli. The Tudor Café was large – two high-ceilinged rooms, one of which could be closed off if customers were few. But that never seemed to be the case. Long queues formed in the corridor outside, and Alfredo had to compete with the rattle of cutlery and crockery, the hubbub of conversation, the din from the kitchen when one of the doors opened on either side of the rostrum, and the intermittent announcements on Bentall's public address system that left us astonished and smiling at the newness of it, messages preceded always by a bing-bong signal, a descending third, and the ladylike voice that cooed, 'Bentall's calling: a small boy has been lost in the store . . .' And if the queue were too long, or funds were short, it would be Lyons in Eden Street, where my favourite dish, taken from a little glass-doored pigeon hole in the modern automat-style cafeteria, was a Mixed Vegetable Hot-Pot (1/3d). All very different from Lyons Tea Shop in Brixton, in which uniformed waitresses called 'Nippies' had served the customers and brought sets of chess or draughts on demand to the men who lingered over pots of tea.

Encouraged by his experience with Ardath cigarettes, my father acquired a ciné-camera of the now obsolete 9.5 mm gauge, by switching brands to Craven-A (slogan: 'For your throat's sake, smoke Craven-A'). There is film in existence of an *hors-série* holiday at Woolacombe in Devon, where we had outings with my Auntie Mill and her husband who were staying nearby in Ilfracombe. She had married a pious, bespectacled teetotaller called Edward Beckett, an un-Vaughanish man whose lifelong aim, frustrated because he had never learned Latin, was to become a clergyman. The closest he came to it was reading the lesson in Kingston Parish Church. He was several years younger than my aunt but she outlived him by some twenty years. He collapsed and died one evening at Wimbledon Station while on his way home, after a lifetime of sober, industrious employment in the accounts department of a firm that made electrical appliances. I had been a page-boy at their wedding, for which event I was decked out in what had become the family white satin suit: having grown noticeably, I had to squeeze myself into it with a struggle and after some clever work from my mother's sewing needle. I remember only one moment of the day, and that was the cry of 'aah' from a group of women spectators as, bright red with embarrassment, I climbed from the limousine to enter the church, hoping none of my friends would pass by.

That family milestone was not recorded on 9.5 mm, but fragments of cracked and unprojectable film have survived of my brother's stay in hospital, walking tentatively in the hospital grounds wearing a white sun hat, with my maternal grandmother, who shortly after this was herself taken ill and died of breast cancer, in the Royal Masonic Hospital.

I wasn't allowed in to the hospital on those weekly visits to see David. But by the time he had been declared well, or his ailment, as it were, conceptually disposed of, my extra long summer holiday was over. I was sent to a new school.

Six

THIS TIME MY parents chose a school called Malden College. In many respects it seemed to match the living style they were keen on, but it was selected after a no more than cursory inspection by my father, who wanted somewhere near, cheap, and private. The so-called 'College' had been set up in a mansion of small-scale baronial appearance with castellated walls, a tower and a large garden, and it was in a side-road close to the main street of New Malden, only a few minutes' walk from the bypass.

Malden College catered for boys only, boarders and day boys, but the boarders were in a special category known as 'Post Office boys'. Some special but unexplained arrangement had been entered into to provide a free or at least cut-price education to the orphan sons of postmen. The Post Office boys made up about one-third of the pupils and, needless to say, were slightly looked down on by the fee-paying sons of the middle class, who for four guineas a term, came in the morning and went home for tea. Lunch, a vile meal, was provided at the school, cooked by the Headmaster's wife. On the whole, the boarders were a rougher lot than the day boys. Their clothes were shabbier and their manners not as polished, and they enjoyed a kinship, a system of jokes and lore, that we could never share.

As for the masters, they were of a familiar English kind: bored, lazy, hard-up and casual, and if they had any enthusiasm or even liking left for their work, it was barely detectable. There were five of them including the Headmaster, whose name was Russell Davies, a small, balding man in his late fifties with gold-rimmed spectacles and a Strube 'Little Man' moustache. His subject was Scripture; nothing else. His teaching was uninspiring and as a disciplinarian he was ineffectual – a little less so, however, than most of his staff, whose hold on the boys' attention was precarious at best. For only one of the masters, a Mr Hayward, who taught English, did we have a vestige of respect, and that was because he smiled at us, made jokes, and had a young, clean-limbed look. The others looked hard-pressed, trapped. Two of them wore gowns. One was Hayward, and the other was the Maths master, called Gurney. The two other teachers were Hugh Russell Davies, the Headmaster's son (History), and a sallow, rumpled man called Marsh (French and Music) who, I told my mother, smelled as if he had just got out of bed. Once, I encountered Marsh walking with a woman along one of the suburban streets not far from our house. It was a warm, quiet evening. Nobody else was about. I raised my school cap to him as I passed. I heard him say darkly to his companion, 'Yes, that's one of them.'

The building these five worked in, along with Mrs Russell Davies as combination Secretary-Matron-Cook, was far from suitable as a school for sixty or so pre-adolescent boys, with its random arrangements of rooms, Gothic tower and heavy, iron-studded front door. At least the garden was spacious, with a few trees around the edge. Most of the rest was grass, trodden flat, or trodden out. The classrooms, of which there were only three, were poorly equipped, with old-fashioned desks and benches bound with iron rivets. There were two boys to a desk, the lids of which were heavily disfigured with initials, and with channels gouged out with pen-knives, suggesting not only long histories of boredom and frustration, but that the equipment had been bought second-hand. Everything was badly in need of redecoration. There were fireplaces where small, mean coal fires smouldered wanly in winter, during which season the whole place was unbelievably cold, so cold that my father, prompted by David and me, complained to Russell Davies Senior, who promised to attend to the matter. He never did.

Malden College had no obvious individual identity nor noticeable school spirit, but there was a school song. It was *Forty Years On*, borrowed without acknowledgement from Harrow. We sang it on special occasions, such as the last day of term, accompanied by the gypsyish Mr Marsh at the piano. There is only one thing I can remember learning there, and that was what used to be called the Facts of Life. I was about ten years old when the news about men and women was broken to me one morning before school by a raffish, sophisticated day-boy called Dawson, bigger and more confident than the rest of us, whose father was said to be in the theatre. Dawson was standing in the centre of a group of boys under a tree, telling them jokes that were evidently uproarious but which I failed to understand. Anxious to be part of the conversation, I asked Dawson to explain, and he did. You know boys have got dicks? And girls have got these holes between their legs? Yes, I lied. Well, babies come when a boy sticks his dick into a girl's hole and it's called fucking. What's more, said Dawson with a leer, it feels very nice. So nice that some men go mad at the thought of it.

On reflection, that doesn't seem to me such a bad description of the activity that holds the human race in thrall. Many of the essential facts were there, though the one that reverberated through my ten-year-old mind was the idea of it driving men mad. Such men were called sex manias, Dawson advised me. Next morning, after ruminating on this information, I discovered Dawson once again in the same spot in the school garden, surrounded as before by an interested audience of Post Office boys. Like a junior officer at a briefing, I had a question or two, prompted by confused memories of Barbara Martin's wud. Look here, you know how your dick gets stiff sometimes? Yes. Does a girl's thing, you know, kind of open out? Yes, it opens out, otherwise you couldn't get your dick in. The small audience of three or four boarders nodded in wise agreement. At this point,

I can hear my ten-year old short-trousered self asking incredulously, 'You don't mean to say *all these chaps know as well?*' Dawson, with casual ease, assured me it was so.

Voilà: I had been admitted into the Freemasonry of *boys who knew* – knew, that is, how babies came (the word sex hadn't been invented, still less school lessons on the subject), and the conspiratorial nature of the conversations before school certainly seemed to fit in with the shiftiness my parents had exhibited when I asked them to explain matters. I had raised the subject two or three times and got nowhere. My father told me I would have to ask my mother. She told me I would have to wait a while before being told, then changed the subject.

Dawson had now pre-empted further discussion with them on the topic. Furthermore his information began to colour the way I thought about people and the things they did, about uncles and aunts and parents, even though the idea of this activity, fucking, seemed too ridiculous, too much of a joke, for them to bother doing. Nor was the word itself the kind you could take seriously – blunt, short, and comical. Why had I never heard it before? On the other hand, fucking was supposed to be very nice and I began to suppose that one day, unless I were one of those who had gone mad at the thought, I would be doing it with a girl if I could find one prepared to try. In the meantime it was a subject for jokes. 'Here,' said Dawson, 'who do you stick up for, you father or your mother?' 'Don't know,' I said. 'I stick up for my father,' said Dawson with a dirty grin, 'he stuck up for me.' I was shocked, then guiltily amused.

For the time being there were more important things to think about. Walking to school, for instance, on those June mornings. My father would walk with me on his way to Malden station, along the bypass, up on the raised pavement that reminded me pleasantly of a seaside promenade, along to Malden roundabout and past the new church of St Mark's, built only a few years earlier and, daringly, not with pews but tip-up seats, like a cinema. We even attended Sunday morning service there once or twice, a last desultory flicker of piety on my parents' part.

The walk to school took about ten minutes, and that was the time when I pestered my father yet again to tell me stories about the war, by now nearly twenty years past – how the Colonel appointed him Brigade interpreter, how it was assumed he could ride a horse like any other officer, and he blinking well got on one and rode it, and how he and a brother officer just managed to get back from leave in Paris in time for something or other that was important. My feelings about military life were further stirred on these morning walks by a house we passed each day. The low front wall, made of brick, was laid to resemble battlements. There was a flag-pole in the front garden and next to it a miniature cannon of the type used to start yachting races. Hanging over the front door was a wooden plaque bearing the name of the house, in Gothic letters. It was *The Fort*. I wished our house looked like that.

Soon my brother joined these walks to school and my father, doubtless to his relief, decided it was no longer necessary to accompany us. Instead, he would go off 'to business' at a time that suited him better. Sometimes, on the way to the College, David and I would meet Mr Hayward, and my brother would chatter on about West End shows, in which he had a precocious interest. Hayward would be amused. We had seen *1066 And All That* at Streatham Theatre and David already had a list, culled from God knows where, of others he wanted to see. 'Well, Vaughan,' Hayward would say teasingly, 'have you seen *Streamline* yet?' I trudged dutifully along at their side, out of my depth, or perhaps hung back to walk with a friend. Lewis was his name: his parents had come back from India and bought a house on the way to Worcester Park, in which they had replaced some inner doors with bamboo curtains, and had Oriental brass on the mantelpiece with files of ivory elephants of diminishing size. Or perhaps I walked with Wilkinson, a tiny, neat, agile boy with a passion for toy motor cars. Or with my special friend Peter Greaves, who lived round the corner from us in a cul-de-sac, mention of which to my father always brought forth one of his standard jokes: Coalman – Here you are, guv, how do you want your coal? A la carte? Or cul-de-sac?

Greaves was one of a family of three children. Their house was called *The Two Poplars*, with the name this time carved in fretwork by his father, hanging on a wrought-iron bracket outside the front door in such a way that you could read it backwards from the front step. I could never think of the name except in the way I would read it, owT ehT sralpoP, as I waited for Greaves to answer the bell.

He was an enthusiastic, merry, deferential boy. Together we organised Guy Fawkes Nights, games of soldiers, fretwork, conkers, stamp collecting. We could see the backs of each other's houses from our respective bedroom windows. When he wanted to attract my attention he would give a sort of Tarzan yell across the intervening 150 yards, shouting 'AH' and batting the palm of his hand against his mouth. My family disliked this signal and I became embarrassed by it: it roused all the dogs in the neighbourhood. The two of us, with Peter's sister Pauline, made up the entire personnel of the Wayside Stamp Club and a looser organisation called the Black Hand Gang, which had no special function except to exist in a state of notional warfare with a gang of boys based a few streets away.

With Greaves and Lewis and Wilkinson, I hung about the great tracts of meadowland that lay a few streets away from us, along the bypass, where soon there would be yet another Close, Rise, Drive or Crescent of freshly painted villas with their rubble-strewn gardens yearning for cultivation. Naming these streets taxed the building firms' not exactly limitless powers of invention. Most of the names seemed plucked from nowhere: the Greaves's lived in Canford Close, named perhaps after somebody's memorable summer holiday. Most of the other roads (never called streets, a designation that would have sounded far too urban) had unspecific, countryfied names: Knightwood Crescent, Fir Grove, Meadow Hill, Amberwood Rise or (*tout court*) Barnfield. A local variation was the so-called Painters'

Estate, where you wandered along Gainsborough Road, Romney Road, and Millais, Landseer, Turner and Kneller Roads. Building work here was complete, and the houses all occupied. Just beyond them, the builders' men were everywhere. In the daytime, the frontiers of the new estates were buzzing with activity. Lorries delivered supplies, bricklayers toted their hods. But after five o'clock it was another story: then, the children took over. There were great dumps of building materials to explore – pyramids of sewage pipes to crawl into and huge stacks of bricks, red and white, which you could rearrange into steps up to a flat platform. Once there, you could remove more bricks from the middle and build a crenellated wall, and so make a camp or fortress, where you could easily conceal yourself from the watchmen who, in theory, were supposed to be on patrol.

This was the extraordinary new territory spread before the children whose parents had joined the rush to the estates. Its pleasures and surprises were legion. Past the Painters' Estate was the Hogsmill, with a rustic bridge and a spot where a tall oak tree had spread its lower branches over the swiftly running water. From one branch someone had tied a length of rope, and, if you had the nerve, you could swing from one bank to the other. Once when I was there, a fat boy swung across, but his courage failed, and instead of letting go at the far side, he clung on and swung back again. By now he had lost momentum, and while juvenile spectators jeered on either side, the fat boy had no choice but to drop into the water. Waist-deep in the muddy tide, he waded to the bank, face red with shame.

Secretly I shared his disgrace. I wasn't even as plucky as he was. Fearful of the same humiliation, I didn't attempt the crossing. Perhaps it was on that same occasion that I decided to try catching a butterfly. The procedure for doing so, if you had no net, had been described in one of the boys' weeklies, like *Hotspur* or *The Wizard*. And so I managed to cup my hands around a cabbage white that fluttered innocently over a clump of nettles and tried to work up the courage to make the prescribed next move, which was to pinch its neck, if that was what it was, between your thumb and forefinger, after which you were supposed to take it home and mount it somewhere with a pin stuck through the equivalent of its chest.

It was another test I failed. Revolted by the butterfly's agitated movements inside my two clammy fists, and overcome with remorse at what I was doing, I let it fly off.

Killing and mounting a butterfly was the kind of thing boys were supposed to take to – something my uncles and my father, so I presumed, would have taken in their stride. Fighting was another. At that, I was hopeless – timorous and jelly-legged in the event of serious opposition and secretly ashamed of the fact. The problem was, my father liked to encourage the idea of boys being 'two-fisted', settling their differences in manly ways, 'squaring up' to each other like characters in fiction. Was it only in fiction? He used to boast to me about what now seems a barely credible incident in Brixton, when he and his two brothers, Alf and Arthur, were insulted in the bar of the George Canning up on the hill. The three of them, he claimed, had lined up shoulder to shoulder, ready to defend the honour of the family: 'the three Vaughans', he would say, glowing with retrospective pride. And what happened? Oh, the others backed down. Alf had been welter-weight champion of his Division in France. Between them they'd have made short work of those fellers!

I suppose this anecdote was a romanticized account of an incipient pub brawl, with my father, at least in his imagination, conforming to some social pattern one part of him would have rejected. In fact he was a man of relatively slight physique, with shapely hands and slender fingers, and he was certainly not cut out for a punch-up, unlike his elder brother and his father, both of whom were heavily built, bull-necked men with Kitchener moustaches. However, they were the ones who supplied him with behaviour-models and ideas of family solidarity; hence my father thought it right to pass on to me a notion I already suspected to be false, that physical force, not argument, was decisive. *Nemo me impune lacessit*, he would say, adding (and

74

expecting a laugh for) a whimsical translation he had read somewhere: Nobody does me dirt and gets away with it.

It is scarcely surprising that on one awful occasion I did do my best to put these views into practice. I conceived the idea, for which there was no basis whatever, that one of the Post Office boys at Malden College with whom I happened to be on good terms and indeed shared a desk with, had spoken insultingly of my brother. Therefore it was my duty to 'avenge' the supposed slight and challenge the boy, who was known as Taylor II, pronounced Taylor-Two, indicating that he had an older brother in the school called Taylor-One. In the same way, I was known as Vaughan-Two. Cornering Taylor-Two in the classroom one day after school dinner, I accused him of whatever insult it was that I had invented, and demanded an apology. Taylor-Two, a pleasant, unaggressive boy, rightly saw no reason for apologising, and refused. I had no clear idea what was supposed to happen next, but decided to adopt the classic pugilistic stance frequently demonstrated by my father, and heart thumping almost audibly, again demanded that Taylor-Two climb down.

Confused, surprised, and possibly as scared as I was, Taylor-Two said No. By now, a group of boys had collected ('Vaughan and Taylor-Two are having a fight' . . . there were disquieting cries from other Post Office boys of 'Bash him, Taylor') but matters were resolved in the nick of time by the arrival on the scene of my brother, I dare say ironically amused by the sight that met his eyes. He assured me there had been no insult offered him, no cause for retaliation. Taylor-Two and Vaughan-Two, no blows having been exchanged beyond a few token thumps on each other's shoulders, shook hands. We took our places at our common desk. I was left with feelings of relief, self-reproach, and utter futility.

I presume the ideas about masculine behaviour my father tried to encourage derived from his own pre-1914 boyhood. A boy should be able to 'look after' himself, he declared, and so he not only tried to instruct me how to lead with my left and bounce on my toes, he actually bought me some child-size boxing gloves and initiated a few perfunctory boxing lessons, urging me to hit him as hard as I could, assuring me that however hard the blow he would be able to take the necessary defensive action. It was an uninteresting thing to do. Moreover I saw no reason for acting so aggressively towards someone I loved. He had no better luck with various outings he organised to sporting events. Reluctantly, but unwilling to show it, I went with him at various times in my childhood to a First Division football match, an evening of boxing matches at the Royal Albert Hall, the Oxford-Cambridge Rugby match and even a dog race, in the course of which the greyhounds actually caught up with the electrically driven 'hare' and tore it to pieces – evidently an extremely rare occurrence. At all these events, I plumbed new profundities of boredom. Yet I think my father was in some way able to convince himself I was having a wonderful time.

With literature he had more success. My father possessed few books, but he belonged to a circulating library and read thrillers and westerns, generally in bed at night. In the glass-fronted book-case in the dining room were one or two volumes by Edgar Wallace and Sidney Horler, an anthology of sea stories by 'Bartimeus', Stephen Leacock's *Literary Lapses* and a boy's adventure story of the 1890s with engraved illustrations called *The Brig 'Audacious'*. We also had a Bible, a Household Encyclopaedia in four volumes, acquired during the newspaper war of the 1930s, and Nuttall's *Standard Dictionary of the English Language* in which I looked up all the dirty words I could think of: none were included. We also had my mother's copy of the New Testament and her *Pilgrim's Progress*, a handsomely bound prize from her Sunday School in 1910. Then there was a book from which my father would now and then read to me, a worn grey cloth-bound text-book which had belonged to his father and probably been used in the course of his work in Brixton Prison. It was called *Composition Through Reading*. Among other improving texts, on which the student was supposed to answer questions, it contained 'Once more unto the breach' and the St Crispin's Day speech from *Henry V*, and Tennyson's *The 'Revenge': A Ballad of the Fleet,* which my father would grimly declaim: 'Sink me the ship, master gunner, sink her, split her in twain! Fall into the hands of God, not into the hands of Spain!'

Truth to tell, his voice was not ideally suited to this work, being high in pitch with a tendency to crack under stress. Moreover he could not pronounce the letter R. Nevertheless, memories of Tennyson's *The 'Revenge'* have proved ineradicable through the years, and so have those of another piece of writing he enjoyed and took to reading aloud to the family annually after Christmas dinner, a humorous sketch called 'Hoodoo MacFiggins' Christmas', from Leacock's *Literary Lapses.*

In general our leisure pursuits conformed to the suburban pattern. There were three cinemas within easy reach of our house and we became regular customers at both local Odeons, one at Tolworth, one at Worcester Park, or the shabbier Plaza at New Malden. If my father was in the mood, and if we had gone to the Odeon at Tolworth, we would cross the road and dine out at the Toby Jug, where the Grill Room, smelling enticingly of steak dinners, had a small dance orchestra and a space for couples to perform the fox-trot or the waltz. There was a Master of Ceremonies, in black tie, with lapel badge bearing the letters 'MC', who would announce the sets with a repertoire of jokey remarks. The food was straightforward: steak or fish. My mother would have a gin and It or a sweet sherry, my father a pint of bitter.

Toby Jug dinners were rare events, but rarer were visits to the theatre. My mother favoured Streatham Hill, but if my father were the instigator, it would be the Kingston Empire for a variety bill. This was much like old-style music hall, with the number of the act flashing up in electric lights at the side of the stage and a bar at the back of the stalls from which you watch the performance. Comic acts were best – Max Miller, Will Mahoney, Billie and Renée Houston or the incomparable Wilson, Keppel and Betty – but there were also Apache dancers, who specialized in hurling their girl partners across the stage with expressions of lascivious disdain, and a mountainous Canadian xylophonist called Teddy Brown, moving daintily behind his gleaming chromium instrument.

We had given up going to the Christmas pantomimes. But on special occasions we went to the West End: once, to the Crazy Gang, when I experienced for the first time in my life the wonderful agony of helpless mirth in a theatre, not at the Crazy Gang themselves but at a tall, thin man in old-fashioned running clothes who did a wordless mime as a football goalie before a backdrop of a yelling crowd. Years later I discovered the identity of this performer: he was Jacques Tati.

By the mid-1930s my father was a Conservative supporter. His own father's Socialist principles he dismissed as out of date and muddle-headed. He liked to quote the cliché that if a man weren't a socialist before the age of twenty-one there was something wrong with his heart. If he were still a socialist after that there was something wrong with his head. How did he reconcile this judgement with my grandfather's beliefs? Had they ever argued the matter out? I didn't know. My grandfather was long dead, and my father, having been an officer in the war and now with a house of his own, plus a responsible job and a family, was drawn ineluctably to the party of possession, privilege, and rank. He took the *Daily Express* and the *Sunday Express*, laughed at Strube's cartoons and Nathaniel Gubbins' humorous column and nodded his head judiciously at the articles on the feature page. He might have been the very model for the Man on the Clapham Omnibus.

In his attitudes to society and politics, he was at one with the rest of the men in the family. My uncles all supported Stanley ('Trust Me') Baldwin and in due course the National Government. The occasions for airing their observations on such matters were family visits, usually for tea on Sundays. My mother would make a fruit cake, or a Victoria sponge with apricot or strawberry jam filling ('This is delicious, Rose!')

which would be brought in on the oak trolley with a large pot of tea and sandwiches of fish paste, Heinz Sandwich Spread or Marmite. Then cigarettes, conversation, sometimes music-making, until at about six, drinks would be offered before the guests departed and my father slipped away to the Malden Manor.

At these meetings there was a general air of accord about the important questions of the day, a consensus of sober and serious-minded opinion among steady men of the middle-class in their Sunday suits, jingling the change in their pockets, talking about their cars ('How's the Ford going?'), driving ('Which way did you come?'), foreign wars (occasionally), household repairs, job prospects and how the garden was looking. My mother's brothers were all doing respectable jobs. Joe was another émigré to the suburbs, with a new semi in Carshalton and still employed by Japhet's, the merchant bank he'd joined when he left school; Philip, living in Doncaster and an infrequent visitor, was in insurance. Billy, back from Australia where the expected fortune hadn't materialised, was at Ford's in Dagenham. He had a girl friend he would bring over to us, a tall, retiring person who had the distinction of having posed for an ad for 'Cutex' nail varnish – but they'd only photographed her hands, which were long, fine, and narrow.

My father's brothers and sisters, who visited less often, were also more or less comfortably employed. Alf, the oldest, had re-enlisted in the army and was a warrant officer in the Service Corps, stationed in Egypt. Arthur, a debonair, independent man, was working for Shell. However, my father's sister May had been the cause of increasing marital dissension in our house. At first she and her husband had set up house in Norbury, close to the rest of the Wates family. To my mother's chagrin she now persuaded her husband to buy a house about two hundred yards from ours. Possibly she was in flight from her own in-laws, but at any rate move they did, with their small daughter, to (naturally) another Wates house, and one of a slightly unusual kind known as 'Sun-Trap' houses. They had steel-framed windows which curved round the corners of the main rooms; some of the houses had flat roofs on which it was theoretically possible to sunbathe, and the small front gates featured a rising sun motif with broad wooden rays. There were about a dozen of these post-Bauhaus dwellings in a small 'parade' of houses just along the bypass.

My mother made no secret of her annoyance that her in-laws had pursued her into Surrey and that the sister-in-law she got on least well with was now within 'popping-in' distance. But popping-in was discouraged: instead, it was the cold shoulder, and it was at the cost of family harmony. At night, after I had gone to bed, I would hear the most frightening sounds in the world: doors banging, shouting, my mother in tears, the stomach-tightening noises of parents quarrelling, the commotion that foreshadowed the final rift that came no more than a dozen years later.

Seven

OF THE FRIENDSHIPS my father made on the officer training course at Balliol, the one that survived the war was with his Brixton friend Cecil Hicks. Around this time, the mid-thirties, we were seeing a lot of Hicks and his family, on joint outings and Sunday afternoon visits – eagerly looked forward to – and the younger of their two sons, John, was my best friend.

Cecil Hicks amused my father. His claim to be an actor when he arrived at Balliol was strictly speaking a lie, and it must have been easily recognised as such in view of his stutter, but it had a sort of truth. Hicks was a natural 'card', roguish, flirtatious, a bottom-pincher, projecting the sexy self-confidence that marks the ladies' man. He liked practical jokes: you could never be sure when he would assume a rôle, to amuse whoever he was with. In Quinn and Axten's in Brixton, he pretended to be a floor-walker, clapping his hands at the sales-girls and directing mystified customers to inappropriate counters. On the train to Burgh Heath he wound a towel round his head and stuck his head out of the window pretending to be a Sikh, hectoring the porters on the platform. In a tea-shop he loudly demanded a Sally Lunn sandwich (a Sally Lunn was a kind of cream bun) to tease a pretty waitress. Many of his jokes were for the benefit of female company, and his flirtatious ways brought out the coquette in my mother, who flirted back. You couldn't walk across the room in front of him, she told me once, without Cecil managing to touch you. Years later, on his death-bed, Hicks, by now a frail old man, was visited by his elder son, Douglas, who was puzzled to notice him staring at the ceiling with a faraway smile. 'What are you thinking about, Dad?' Hicks replied, 'Cunt.' Douglas, taken aback, said, 'That's a funny thing to be thinking about at a time like this.' His father whispered, 'I'm always th-th-thinking about it.'

When told of this deathbed conversation long afterwards by my father, I heard it with interest but no real surprise. It seemed to confirm what I had always dimly realised about this big, bluff, red-faced man in plus-fours who had been Uncle Cecil to my brother and me during our 1930s boyhood. He and his wife ('Auntie' Ada) lived by then in another part of the suburban sprawl, in a newly-built terraced house in Carshalton. John and I were the same age. His brother Douglas was at least five years older and in the days when my friendship with John was in its prime, Douglas might as well have been a grown-up. In those days in that house in Nightingale Lane there was a stronger sexual dynamism than existed at home. Sex was, as it were, nearer the surface. John reported seeing on the clothes-line in the garden a large washable rubber condom hung out to dry, causing excited speculation as to its use and effects. I could not possibly imagine anything like that on our clothes-line in New Malden, nor could I imagine making such a sensational discovery there as John and I made in a wardrobe: copies of La Vie Parisienne, hidden rather perfunctorily, with a text, of course, frustratingly in French. The pictures, however, which showed the first naked breasts I had ever seen, had no need of an interpreter and filled us with wild excitement.

Moreover, it was an open secret, and a stimulus to further lewd speculation, that an elderly but vigorous man known as Uncle Jack, or 'Nunks', who would sometimes be at the house when our family paid a visit, was really Cecil Hicks' father. Uncle Jack had the manner of an Edwardian gentleman: well-fed, elegantly dressed in a faintly old-fashioned manner, sometimes smoking a cigar. He had a sprightly young wife, about thirty years his junior, indeed more or less the contemporary of Auntie Ada and my mother, who with only a little persuasion would accompany herself at the piano in 'My Heart is Like a Singing Bird' – the Hicks had one of the new 'mini-pianos', a little low instrument you might expect to see in a cocktail bar but which fitted conveniently into a suburban sitting room, with an octave or two fewer than normal. Nunks himself, on Sunday afternoons, was often called upon to sing, in his hearty, quavering baritone, songs like 'Father O'Flynn' or 'The Minstrel Boy'; or to recite a dramatic monologue, such as *My Little Jacob Strauss* or *Kissing Cup's Last Race*. Uncle Cecil would sit enthralled during these performances, imperiously shushing John and me, who often spoiled things by giggling.

In contrast to Uncle Cecil's boisterous manner, his wife Ada habitually presented to the world an air of pained resignation, broken now and then by a tired smile, as he joked and showed off to their friends, or brought out his toys. Toys were something he had a lot of, though they were never openly admitted to be such. Some of the best times for us were when Cecil Hicks would get out his collection of toy theatre sheets. He was the one who introduced us to the Victorian toy theatre, or so-called Juvenile Drama, and to Robert Louis Stevenson's essay on the subject, 'A Penny Plain and Tuppence Coloured', and he was responsible for our visits to the last of the authentic publishers of toy theatre plays, Mr Webb's shop in Old Street, or the Misses Pollock's in Hoxton, the two aged spinster daughters of the original Benjamin Pollock. Uncle Cecil's enjoyment of the sheets of posturing characters and romantic scenery was both intense and contagious. Poring over a particularly prized set, his coloured sheets of Webb's *The Miller and his Men,* which someone, perhaps Uncle Cecil himself, once called the *Hamlet* of the Juvenile Drama (the hyperbole would have been typical), he would gloat over the Bohemian costumes, the villains brandishing pistols and the demure early Victorian heroines. As we bent over our penny-plain sheets, surrounded by boxes of water colours, he would read aloud a caption or stage direction, relishing the extravagance of it all: 'Grindoff, 2nd Dress . . . Banditti c-c-carousing!'

Of course he had a proper toy theatre, built by himself, but we never got as far, or not then, as producing a play, possibly because it was an experience Stevenson had warned us about in his essay in *Memories and Portraits*: no child, he wrote, would twice risk 'the tedium, the worry, and the long-drawn disenchantment of an actual performance'. (Among those who did in fact take this risk were Charles Dickens, Winston Churchill and countless others, including, in later life, myself.) However, for Uncle Cecil's benefit, David, John and I would set up the opening scene of *The Miller and his Men; or, the Bohemian Banditti*, with its view of old Kelmar's cottage, strips of blue-painted cardboard to represent a lake, and a distant view of the fateful mill. The grown-ups, back from the pub in good humour and tolerant for a while of the impending boredom, would sit and watch while we put an appropriate record on the wind-up portable gramophone (the Hungarian Dance from *Swan Lake* struck the right note of stagey romance), raised the curtain and carefully pushed Lothair, 1st dress, on his metal slide from one side of the stage to the other. Lothair, the hero, is in the act of poling his way across the lake as the play begins, and we would seize the chance of a sound-effect – a glass of water into which one of us would blow bubbles through a drinking straw.

Later, after supper, perhaps as a reward for such diversions, and if he were feeling more than usually content with life, Uncle Cecil would let us cajole him into bringing out another of his special possessions, a collection of toy soldiers, a complete troop of the 17th/21st Lancers ('The D-D-Death or G-Glory Boys') which he would set up in parade ground formation on the specially cleared dining room table: only John was allowed to assist him in this coveted exercise. Then the soldiers would be admired, inspected, squinted at from every angle, or perhaps Uncle Cecil would bark out one or two arcane commands – and they would all be put away again into long maroon-coloured boxes lined with tissue paper, leaving me to nurse a secret, shameful wish that they could have been sent into a proper toy soldier battle, stormed at with shot and shell like their real historical counterparts. I was still madly keen on toy soldiers and harbouring romantic feelings about warfare that were fuelled by *The Charge of the Light Brigade,* one of the texts which, like *The Revenge,* my father would read to me.

Uncle Cecil's *penchant* for military display struck a sensitive nerve: soldiering was glamorous, and in the narrow hallway of the house in Nightingale Lane, armed with walking-sticks or toy rifles, we enthusiastically practised the Shoulder Arms, the Present Arms and the Slope. We played a game of Attack and Defence, crawling up the stairs or round the shrubs in the back garden, or better still on Burgh Heath, where we went for picnics. There never seemed to be anyone about and we were in sole possession of acre upon acre of open countryside. Uncle Cecil could play the fool as much as he wished. I have a photograph of one of these expeditions to which he had brought a new toy – a large bow and a quiver of arrows. In the picture, he is posing as Eros. The point would not have been lost on him.

Uncle Cecil had formed his own cricket team, officially the Epsom Cricket Club's Third XI but usually known as Cecil Hicks' XI. The team was made up of cronies like my father and other reliables whom he called 'boon companions' – the sort of phrase he would take a fancy to and perhaps get slightly wrong (to me he would speak of his son John as 'your erstwhile playmate'). John and I were the team scorers; Saturday after-noons in the summer were spent in little huts overlooking the pitch, breathing the musty, creosoted smell in the summer heat, inscribing neat little ticks and other symbols in the Eleven's scorebook – finishing the job with the simple arithmetic that gave bowling and batting averages, the number of maiden overs and such other statistics as were requested afterwards in the tea-tent or the pavilion. The outings always ended, of course, in a local pub, an anti-climax for the scorers, who had to spend the evening sitting in a car park drinking fizzy lemonade and eating Smith's Crisps or meat pies; while inside the Eleven celebrated its victory or, more usually, consoled itself for its defeat.

Uncle Cecil himself was far from being a notable player but called himself a 'useful all-rounder'. It was the occasion he enjoyed, with a club tie round his plump waist keeping his baggy trousers up, a cap with some sort of club colours, all the paraphernalia of the game. Meanwhile my father, too, seldom distinguished himself, was always low down in the batting order and unreliable in the field. When, as infrequently happened, he was put on to bowl, I was uncomfortably aware than he cut an awkward figure, with an ungainly, hunched-up action, partly the result of a broken collar-bone in young manhood, and a slow pace that brought out the most lethal stroke-play from opposing batsmen.

On only one occasion, by some miracle, everything seemed to go right for him. It was late in the afternoon. Hicks' XI was being trounced, as usual. Sent in at number eight or nine, my father quite suddenly began to clout the ball soundly, scoring a four, a two, a three, another four. Though the frowsty smell of the saloon bar must already have been in their nostrils, the watchers in their deck-chairs began to pay attention, and nowhere was the excitement more lively than in the score-box. His confidence growing with every ball, my father scored an unprecedented 34 before being caught. He returned to the pavilion amid prolonged applause. Hicks' XI still lost, and the miracle never happened again, yet my father remembered his fifteen minutes of triumph for the rest of his life.

Although I was no good at the game either, the friendliness and good humour of those Saturday fixtures and the long summer afternoons, often on peaceful, rural pitches, worked their alchemy. I longed to play better. I would even practise batting strokes in my bedroom in front of the wardrobe mirror with the bat my father had bought me before we left Brixton – from a little old craftsman, in a tiny terraced house smelling of linseed oil, near Brockwell Park. But when I was faced with the realities of the game – the unexpected speed and abruptness of the deliveries, the hardness of the ball and the likelihood of being hit in the face – then my ardour melted rapidly away. At Maiden College in summer we played cricket once a week. Self-consciously I would take my beautiful well-oiled bat to the ground in my father's heavy leather cricket-bag, and, with sickening certainty, score a duck. Not only that, my failure would be compounded in the field, where I dropped every catch that came near me and my throw-ins seldom came near the wicket-keeper.

It was at Maiden College that I realised I was even less cut out to be a participant in sporting activities than I was to be a spectator. Football in the winter was even worse than cricket. The rules mystified me, I couldn't dribble the ball or kick it straight, couldn't run and couldn't tackle. If I were tackled in turn I was, literally, a pushover. I could work up no competitive feelings about playing the game and the very word football became a synonym for cold, discomfort, tedium and mud.

Instead, out of the blue, I was smitten with music.

It happened indecisively at first. But I conceived the idea of taking violin lessons. The three-quarter size 'Stradivarius' inherited from my grandfather was now in the possession of my Uncle Joe, and he had taken it to some expert in London who had duly pronounced it more or less valueless; yet my uncle hankered wistfully after the thought that he might have an instrument created by the master of Cremona. It was therefore with a certain reluctance that he agreed I could borrow it.

Peter Greaves' father, a keen pianist, said he would teach me. My mother was enthusiastic. And so, every Sunday morning, I took the Stradivarius round to *The Two Poplars* (owT ehT sralpoP) and had a lesson. My mother gave me half-a-crown to give to Mr Greaves each week and he would place it on the picture-rail in their sitting room, out of reach of their children, his objective being to line up his half-crowns until they reached all round the room.

The lessons were rudimentary affairs. Mr Greaves was uninterested in teaching musical theory. His idea of a violin lesson was to get me to play a tune while he accompanied me. We played 'Ah! che la morte' and Handel's 'Largo', and after a few months got as far as Haydn's 'Gypsy Rondo', with Mrs Greaves joining us astride her 'cello. Then we had the audacity, not to say impertinence, to attempt the last movement of one of the Beethoven violin sonatas, at about half the right speed. It was an extraordinary idea, especially as Mr Greaves had no great knowledge of violin technique, nor, I think, of the questions of theory he glossed swiftly over during our lessons. In consequence my information about these things was sketchy: I was vague about accidentals, key signatures and note values, though he seemed to believe I should have picked up the important points by some non-verbal means. 'Don't say "that note",' he would exclaim, 'say "G".' 'G.' 'It's an F,' said Mr Greaves testily, 'EGBDF, Every Good Boy Deserves Favour, Eat Good Bread Dear Father, now, try it again, let's play!'

For a time my initial keenness provided momentum enough for me to practise often in the front lounge. But my patience was on the short side. When I made a mistake I developed the peculiar habit of punishing the instrument rather than myself, and did this by removing a single strand of horse-hair from the bow, which in consequence began to grow mysteriously thinner. Once I was so enraged by a stubborn passage in the Haydn that I rapped the bow smartly on the lid of our Boehringer and broke it in half. I forget how I explained this singular event to my mother but she unquestioningly bought me another from the music shop in New Malden, and practising was resumed.

Meanwhile she had bought some music for us to perform together, with a part for my father. It was a song called 'An Old Violin', which had an obbligato accompaniment for me to play. Once or twice my father was persuaded to try singing it: 'Up in the garret, away from the din, Someone is playing an old violin. Tenderly, pleadingly, so the notes fall, Just for the love of the music, that's all . . .' Of course I was the 'someone', and at that point in the music I would come in with the first four bars of

Beethoven's 'Minuet in G'. My father needed little encouragement to make an early departure for the Maiden Manor.

Although there were times when I thought I might be beginning to make the right sound, more and more often there seemed better things to do than practise on my own in the chilly sitting room. Mr Greaves' line of half-crowns never did join up, or if they did, I had no hand in it. I nursed a secret grievance against him, though, because Mr Greaves somehow managed to gain possession of my broken bow, and I learned from Peter Greaves that his father had found a new use for it. He had set off at a new tangent and become the conductor of an amateur orchestra in Surbiton; and to make a baton he had thriftily trimmed both ends off my much-abused bow. I resentfully thought I would have done the same thing if only it had occurred to me in time. The idea of being a conductor appealed to me. Now and then, especially if we had been to an Astaire-Rogers movie or a backstage musical at one of the Odeons, I indulged fantasies in which I waved a baton in front of a dance band, turning to smile coolly at an imaginary camera. Sometimes these fantasies grew into charades played with my brother, when we re-enacted the plot of some film musical, with David performing, solo, an approximation of the dance routines.

However, for the time being, my formal musical career went into suspense. 'An Old Violin' was put away in the piano stool and the phony Strad returned to its case. It wasn't long before my uncle prudently reclaimed it, and back it went to Carshalton Beeches.

David and I remained at Malden College for just under two years. By then my father, suspicious of the results, or lack of them, began looking round for something else.

He pondered the idea of a school in Wimbledon, one of the more genteel suburbs, where there was no lack of schools to choose from. For boys there was Rutlish, over in South Wimbledon, and up on the edge of the Common there was King's

College School. Neither was a boarding school (though King's took a small number of boarders) but both had a certain prestige. King's was a Headmasters' Conference School – officially a 'public' school – and socially it was desirable, having the correct old-grey-stones appearance, with its prominent Gothic Revival chapel complete with ivy, and the boys wearing straw hats in summer. It even had a cadet force. The date of its foundation was 1829. But Rutlish, founded in 1895, wasn't all that far behind, and its upper-middle-class aura was enhanced by pictures in the local newspaper of dinner-jacketed Old Boys dining, all smiles, in a smart London hotel, or by generous reports of a visit to France by a group of forty Rutlishians in the summer holidays.

There was also Wimbledon College, but that was run by Jesuits and so out of the running. King's being financially out of reach (£40 a term), my father decided on Rutlish. There was something about the name that suggested a good, sound, old-fashioned education. Good schools, after all, generally had single-word titles, and, like King's, Rutlish also had crenellated red brick, with an expanse of lawn down to the road. Later, I learned one of the masters had shot himself on that same lawn, which might have caused my father to change his mind, but at the time none of us was aware of this sensational fact.

The headmaster of Rutlish then was a certain Mr Varnish. Varnish of Rutlish – a name difficult to take seriously, but in some ways curiously apt. He was a somewhat pedantic man who believed in doing what he could to tighten up the pupils' slovenly standards of speech, and he invented a system by which the boys were supposed to monitor each other's pronunciation and grammar. Each boy was issued at the beginning of each week with a fixed quantity of black marbles. If you heard someone offending the rules of correct spoken English you were supposed to hand him a black marble. There were penalties for boys who finished the week with more marbles than Varnish considered desirable, and rewards for those who managed to get rid of their entire stock. Needless to say, the system collapsed soon after it had been introduced, having been proved hopelessly unpractical, an invitation to, at best, licensed priggishness and at worst, wholesale corruption and intimidation.

My father would have approved of Varnish's aims, if not his method, but he never had the opportunity of hearing about it. One day in the late summer of 1935 he called on Varnish to discuss the possibility of our enrolling as Rutlishians. It didn't seem to occur to him that he might take David or me with him. Varnish said he would have us, but can't have been over-keen, because he urged my father to consider a new school on the point of opening on the Kingston Bypass, and much nearer to our house.

In fact, the numbers at Rutlish had become temporarily and uncomfortably swollen to accommodate boys who were waiting for the new school to be ready. It was these short-term 'lodgers', incidentally, who were the principal targets of Varnish's campaign to defend the King's English – Cockneys and other bumpkins whose parents had joined the rush to the suburbs. Varnish couldn't wait to get rid of them. More than likely, he lumped us in this category too: the new school, obviously, was the one for Johnny-come-latelies like us.

There had been a good deal of comment on it in the local newspaper, the *Wimbledon Borough News,* but my father, no follower of parochial events, hadn't heard of the place. It was called Raynes Park County School. Nor had he heard of the headmaster, though the *Borough News* had written about him, too. This was John Garrett.

Eight

RAYNES PARK ITSELF, lying between Wimbledon and New Maiden, was one of the suburban communities that grew suddenly as travel to London by rail or road became easier and cheaper. In many ways, a typical suburb – an invention on the part of engineers and administrators. A century earlier there had been no such place as Raynes Park, only a farm owned by a family called Raynes, whose sheep grazed the soggy meadows from Cannon Hill northwards to Coombe Lane. Across their land galloped the local hunt, and at the farmhouse at West Barnes, local gentlemen met to ride a two-mile steeplechase or set off over Cannon Hill Park to shoot partridge, pheasant, hares or rabbits, or wildfowl on the modest lake known as Bushey Mead.

Unlike many of their neighbours the Raynes clan welcomed the arrival of the railway. The London and Southampton, later the South-Western, line from Nine Elms to Woking was laid down in 1837 by the engineer Joseph Locke, and opened in May the following year. Thirty years later the branch line to Kingston-upon-Thames was opened and a new station built where the line divided. The Raynes gave some of their land to accommodate the station, and the railway company acknowledged their gift by naming the station Raynes' Park. It was opened in 1871. Houses and shops soon followed.

In 1935, as now, the station was the most conspicuous thing

about this suburb within a suburb. Perched on a viaduct some thirty feet up, an earthwork to escape the flooding for which the Raynes estate was notorious, the station was of elementary design. Between its two platforms express trains sped to Winchester, Portsmouth, Salisbury, the West, thundering straight past Raynes Park, an insignificant place with no real identity other than what was convenient for the purposes of local government and the railway company.

Not all of the Raynes' land had been built over. An area about a mile or two square had become sports and recreation grounds and a slightly bigger patch had been made into a golf course. Not for long. In 1926 it had been sold for development, and now the brief little roads with their rows of identical semis had names that reflected their immediate past: Linkway, Greenway, Crossway, Firstway.

Close to this 'Golf Club' estate was another tract of open land, and this was where the new Raynes Park County School had been built. Until then, the site had remained farming land, and some of the boys who came to the school when it opened in September 1935 could remember the farm buildings and duck pond that had been there. Now, in one corner of the space given to it by the Surrey County Council, stood the school building, mainly of red brick. It had cost slightly over £25,000 to build and another £2,500 to equip, and it had been designed by the county architect: a square lay-out, with a small paved quadrangle in the centre hardly more than thirty yards across. A corridor ran round the inside wall of the quad, and off this were classrooms, cloakrooms, a large gymnasium, staff room and offices. Upstairs were more classrooms, a library, geography and art room, and science laboratories. On the ground floor there was also a woodwork room, and on the side nearest the Kingston Bypass, the school Hall, with walls of panelled oak up to half-way, to be adorned in due course with the names of housemasters, cup winners, benefactors and The Fallen. The stage, at first no more than a platform behind an arch, was at one end: at the other, the kitchens, and above them, a flat for the school caretaker.

During inattentive moments the boys could gaze out from the classroom windows on the school playing field, where there was to be cricket in summer, and in winter, not soccer but – a significant choice – rugby football. There was also room for two hard tennis courts, laid down in the 1940s, and a small plot which soon after the school opened was given over to the school's own Scout Troop and known as the Scout Reservation.

From their Common Room, on the other hand, the masters looked out across a triangle of newly-laid turf to the long, low buildings of Bradbury Wilkinson's, who designed and printed banknotes for countries all over the world. Their pastoral-looking grounds were separated from the school by a narrow stream called Pyl Brook, flowing through a gully some fifteen feet deep with railings on either side. Across the main road but also within sight of the Masters' Common Room was Senior's Fish and Meat Paste factory. Now and then a faint savoury whiff of sardine, bloater or crab would steal across the school grounds: a hint of the paste sandwiches of lost drawing-room teas.

There were other factories in the near neighbourhood: Venner's (time switches), and on what had already become known as Shannon Corner there was Shannon's (office equipment), and Meeten's Motor Mecca for second-hand cars, on whose huge billboard a single giant M served as initial for all three words: M eeten's otor ecca. Away to the south-east, on the other side of the school, was another large commercial establishment, Carter's Tested Seeds. Their white stuccoed building, low-lying but with a wide flight of steps leading up to a grandiose front entrance, was surrounded by extensive seed-beds.

'The district of Raynes Park,' said the *Wimbledon Borough News* condescendingly, when Raynes Park County School was opened, 'has hitherto been notable only for its factories and sports grounds.' It was true. But there were two other schools already open on sites adjoining the new school. One was for infants. The other was for boys of eleven and upwards, like Raynes Park, but it was a 'Central School', providing a 'modern' education for those who hadn't passed, or hadn't tried, the entrance examination in English and Maths which you had to take to get into Raynes Park County School. There was fated to be a snobbish cultural gap between the two but rarely open hostility, probably because in those days school discipline was strict enough to prevent it. For instance, the back way into Raynes Park led from West Barnes Lane (once famous for the Raynes' large haybarns), which curved round to join the Kingston Bypass at Shannon Corner half a mile further west. The path from this road – no longer even faintly resembling a lane – bordered the Central School, and boys who used this entrance had to wheel their bicycles or walk along a narrow path between iron railings, with Pyl Brook on their left and, on the right, Bushey Central playground, a passage-way that could have been as fraught with danger as a frontier pass. Now and then stones, lumps of clay or snowballs might be thrown, and sometimes other missiles would arc over the high wooden fence, extended upwards by wire netting, which separated the two grounds. But most of the time, the two populations of boys kept to themselves.

Now, sixty years on, the two schools have become one. There is no dividing fence any more and the much enlarged buildings of the original County School block, and Bushey Central, are part of a huge educational complex known as Raynes Park High School. It is a comprehensive school and takes boys and girls of every intellectual level, around eight hundred of them, from those of potential university calibre to children who can barely read or write.

It was all very different in 1935. On 19 September that year only 160 boys arrived for the first roll-call. My brother and I paid our first visit a few weeks later, on one cold, wet Saturday morning in December. While my father sat about in a waiting room we were taken to a classroom and tested in Maths and English.

Supervising us was a master dressed as though for a round of golf, in plus-fours – trousers like tweed knickerbockers with long woolly socks over his narrow, spindle legs; and his crisp demeanour, breezy yet resolute, was in noticeable contrast to the general seediness of the staff at Maiden College. He was Gibb, the Second Master. As we were shortly to discover, he was quite unlike the headmaster, John Garrett. Gibb was tall, dry, efficient – level-headed Adjutant, you might say, to Garrett's romantic Colonel, and he strove to give the school 'backbone', adherence to a code of probity and honour, teaching the virtues of owning up, taking one's punishment, doing the decent thing. 'Well tried,' he called out earnestly to me once, as I struggled in, chest bursting with useless effort and last by half a length in the swimming sports. From Gibb, that was high praise. He was feared a little, but well-liked because he was fair and even-tempered and was to prove a kindly housemaster. Like Varnish of Rutlish, he was hot on correct standards of speech. He taught Geography and English Grammar, and took the latter subject to include pronunciation. He would go round the class making each of us say, in turn, '*How now, brown cow*' and '*Put coals on the fire*', grimacing at our nasal South London diphthongs and exhorting us to listen carefully to the BBC announcers and their faultless, dialect-free English.

On that first Saturday morning his brisk, soldierly character was a clear signal that, from now on, school and schoolmasters would have to be treated with respect. Another pointer to the same could be seen in the character of the Maths master, an unfriendly, red-faced man with a rasping, high-pitched voice and a way of talking out of the side of his mouth. His name was Courchée. I made a bad start with him by being unable to answer more than a few of the arithmetic questions he set us and was aware of him fuming quietly.

At the end of the visit we were taken, separately, into the Headmaster's study. David went in first, I took his place ten minutes later. There was John Garrett, sitting behind an extremely large desk in a well-carpeted office. I was bashful, and intimidated by this imposing man, with his big nose and fruity smile, and nonplussed by what I thought peculiar questions. If A equals B, and B equals C, what relation is A to C? My brain congealed. I blushed and mumbled that I didn't know. He chewed his smile with his front teeth and asked me if I had seen an advertisement which had something in it about a toucan. Could I repeat it? I managed to remember how it went.

> If he can say as you can
> Guinness is good for you,
> How grand to be a toucan,
> Just think what Toucan do.

In the picture was a toucan, which had reminded me of one of Rupert Bear's adventures when he had been kept an unwilling guest in the medieval castle of a toucan king. The advertisement Garrett had in mind showed a toucan, all orange beak and glittering eyes, coveting a pint of Guinness and looking, as a matter of fact, not unlike Garrett himself as he smiled indulgently at me across the desk. He asked if I was reading anything at the moment. I was. It was a book called *The Redhead from Sun Dog* – not, as Garrett may have assumed, a lurid romance, but a book about a ginger-haired vagabond cowboy by a prolific writer of formula Westerns called W C Tuttle. Garrett didn't ask for details. It seemed enough that I could remember the title. Had he asked, he might have learned it was one of my father's books, disturbed from slumber behind the glass-fronted bookcase in the dining room.

Shortly afterwards the three of us were sitting together in front of Garrett's desk – David, my father and I. At this point my father embarrassed me with a jovially intended comparison of our two personalities: while David, he said, preferred to keep to himself and stay away from trouble, I was different. If I saw a fight going on, I would be likely to 'go and ask if it were private'. Garrett continued smiling and I wondered wretchedly if he could possibly be aware this was flagrantly untrue. What made my father say it? Did he really think I was capable of 'wading in' to start 'throwing punches' as if in some simple-minded adventure movie? Who did he think I was? Had he, by some dreadful mischance, heard of the Taylor-Two fiasco? Or was he again deceiving himself that I would naturally aspire to the stereotype of the two-fisted male which David plainly was not and which he himself wanted vainly to be?

What with this pretentious character reference and my boorish reading matter, not to mention my stupidity at what I assumed to have been algebra (a subject absent from the Malden College curriculum), I was sure I had made a poor showing at this interview. My brother casually let fall the fact that he for his part had cracked the ABC riddle, and it also emerged that the hypertensive Maths master Courchée, though prepared to accept David, had recommended my rejection on grounds of mathematical incompetence.

However Garrett had liked my English paper. He thought it made up for the rest and was prepared to take us both. Many years later I had the odd experience of reading about this interview from his side of the desk. It was early in the school's development that Garrett formed his habit of keeping notes about his interviews with parents, entering them in plain exercise books in his small, neat handwriting. When I read it nearly fifty years later, the entry for that particular morning astounded me. It suggests we had somehow made a strikingly favourable impression, though possibly for the wrong reasons. 'Admit at all costs,' he wrote under our names, inexplicably adding 'Money.' He had underlined the word. 'Father wants both to go to Varsity.' (Was that my father's word, or Garrett's? And why had he never told us?) 'David wants to be a film star!' And another note says, 'Father. Alleyns.' My father, I suspect, had striven to convey an impression of affluence, goaded perhaps by Garrett's haughty accent and a wish to reassert his own membership of the officer class. Whatever the reason, we had been able to meet Garrett's criteria of social if not intellectual acceptability. We were in.

When the news was broken to the management at Malden College, it was frostily received. Russell Davies Senior made no attempt to hide his disapproval, describing Raynes Park as a 'glorified council school'. But the school Garrett had started was to become famous as a great deal more than that, a go-ahead place held up as an example of how even a state school could send boys to Oxford and Cambridge, and generally get itself talked about – light years distant from the comprehension of Russell Davies.

With the foundation of Raynes Park County School, the new suburban community was able to articulate the aspirations it nourished on behalf of its own children, and so of the future. But the idea of what a school ought to be like, especially a boys' school, current in our corner of south-west London at that time, was evidently as conventional as the architecture of our parents' houses. It was derived from the same cultural sources as the stereotypes invented by Frank Richards in *The Magnet* and *The Gem*, with their tales of ripping japes, comic disasters and moral crises behind the ivy-hung walls of Greyfriars and St Jim's. They bore only a sketchy resemblance to the real thing but visions of places like those fictitious public schools, and the kind of schooling they supposedly provided lay, I suspect, behind even the architecture of Raynes Park County School, with its four sides enclosing a central quadrangle. All we needed were cloisters and a chapel. My father said more than once, with a judicious manner, that it was a pity Raynes Park had no tradition. I am not sure he knew precisely what he meant. I dare say he would have liked a school which had things like Big Side, six of the best for offenders, forms called the Remove or the Shell, a Latin motto, cups for acceptable achievements and a system of trivial do's and don'ts enforced by prefects with tassels in their caps. Garrett's reply to this observation when my father daringly made it to him was that Raynes Park was creating its own tradition. And what he meant by that amounted to a cautiously updated, day school version of a conventional English public school. The basic syllabus was conventional also: English Literature and English Grammar, French, Latin (Greek was added later), Mathematics and Geography, and the science triad of Chemistry, Physics and Biology. We also had Art, Woodwork, and 'Scripture'.

It was to Garrett's credit that he should have been so successful in creating a school with a clear, positive identity in the surroundings of an uninspiring London suburb, but his ideas in this respect were not entirely original. He came to Raynes Park from Whitgift, a minor public school in Croydon, where he had been English master or, as he preferred to put it, Head of the English Department. In fact his degree was in History.

The Headmaster at Whitgift, called impressively 'The Master', was a certain Ronald Gurner. A survivor of the Great War, in which he had fought for four years and won the MC, he had published a book of patriotic war poems in 1917 and after the war several novels, two of them on school subjects. Later he set out his ideas on secondary education in a lively book, published in 1937, *I Chose Teaching*. He was a large, red-faced man and when he came to visit Raynes Park he reminded one of our teachers of a family butcher. Garrett respected him: he had worked under Gurner not only at Whitgift but also at the Strand School as a student teacher.

Gurner was an enthusiast for the day school. One of his novels, *The Day Boy*, fictionalised this enthusiasm, and I suppose Garrett absorbed many of his ideas, both theoretical and practical, especially his belief that you could reproduce the public school atmosphere, with the stress on school loyalty and kinship, in a middle-or working-class area. These ideas Garrett probably expounded to the men and women who appointed him, members of the Surrey Education Committee. One can imagine the committee, under whose aegis the school had been planned and built, being moved by, for one thing, Garrett's comparative youth: in September 1935 when the school opened its doors, he was thirty-three – young for a headmaster, though not unprecedentedly so, for more than one has been appointed under the age of thirty. I can picture him appearing for an interview and impressing the committee with his confident air, the resolute set of his jaw and, not least, by a decidedly Oxford air. This would have been taken as a guarantee of a whole series of necessary attributes: easy, sociable manners, intellectual authority, good breeding and no less important, 'correct' English. Those were the days of the Oxford accent – indeed its heyday. And Garrett certainly had that.

Even though I haven't heard it for more than twenty years I find it easy to remember his voice, with its stagey emphases, a way of speaking in italics. Listening to it now in my mind's ear, I believe I can detect the sound of his native West Country in some of those vowels, because for all his social polish and Oxford manner, John Garrett, like most of his pupils, came from a lower-middle-class family. His father had been a Warrant Officer in the army, serving in India. Once back in civilian life he had set up in business as a gents' hairdresser in Trowbridge.

Outwardly, almost all traces of Garrett's rather lowly upbringing had been wiped out in the course of his advancement from Trowbridge High School, a small, undistinguished day school for boys, founded around the 1880s, to Exeter College, Oxford. He went there as a History Exhibitioner in 1920. On his arrival, according to his friend A L Rowse, who was going through the same process of upward social movement, and was also from the West Country, 'his accent was *no good*'.

Rowse once wrote a poem about Garrett. It is in his collection *The Road to Oxford*, published in 1978, and it is called 'Trowbridge'. In the poem Rowse has found a copy of a book called *An Oxonian Remembers*, by some forgotten Oxford figure, and there is an inscription inside the cover, 'To John from Mother', together with Garrett's own book-plate with the legend *Coll:Exon:Oxon*. The discovery has brought back sentimental memories of Garrett the undergraduate ('How proud Mother must have been of her lanky son') living a quiet life in rooms facing down Ship Street, 'A sober exhibitioner, a barber's son,

Yellow corn-coloured hair, long of leg.' Rowse notes the drooping eyelid, giving 'a curious effect of collusion'. Then, passing through Trowbridge on a different occasion, he wonders where the Garrett family had lived, where the barber's shop had been, and he reflects on the family's extinction, with a 'Mother's son not one for marrying, And only I to remember him passing by.'

Nine

IT ISN'T DIFFICULT to imagine the effect Oxford in the 1920s must have had on the youthful John Garrett – a clever young man, only child of doting parents, and with an especially close bond with his mother, with whom, said one of the Raynes Park masters, he had a lifelong love affair. He had strong feelings, too, for Oxford. Rowse writes in the poem about

> . . . the years now dead
> When spring thrilled along the nerves and veins:
> In summer those shadowy watered streets,
> The Turl, the Broad and Brasenose Lane,
> The life so hurriedly lived, so much enjoyed,
> And now all over, folded and put away.

Garrett would have recognised Rowse's nostalgic dream. Newly arrived at this enchanted city, he was impressionable, gregarious, socially ambitious, and privately awed by the brilliance and *élan* of post-war Oxford at a famous period in its history, the springtime of (in Martin Green's term) the Dandy-Aesthete; and although Garrett was not a member of the inner circle and could claim no acquaintance with the likes of Harold Acton and Brian Howard, some of the lustre of such brilliant people must have been shed on him. He went down in 1923 with a second in History (Rowse: 'That was about right') and a number of friendships – like the one with Rowse – which he kept intact for most of his life and carefully tended for the sake of his career. Probably in a flippant moment, he once told an assistant master the only reason for going to a university was to make friends who would be useful to you in later life.

En route to graduate status, Garrett acquired the right vowel sounds and the italicised, *sforzando* delivery common among Oxford men of the period and said to have been derived from C M Bowra, later Warden of Wadham but then a young Oxford celebrity whom Garrett knew and in due course assiduously cultivated. In a celebratory volume published in 1974 after Bowra's death, the novelist Anthony Powell describes 'the Bowra delivery, loud, stylised, ironic . . . its echoes are to be heard to this day in the tones of disciples.' (This style of speech could be one of the things that distinguished Oxford from Cambridge, where the feverishly fashionable undergraduate Cecil Beaton noted in his diary in November 1922, 'I think it's rather a pose here to talk very quietly and softly and slowly.') At any rate Garrett's style of speech made him a popular subject for mimicry among the schoolboy wits at Raynes Park, where among our lumpen middle-class voices his sounded a note of effortless superiority. Later, we too began to worry about our accents, working diligently on our short O's and dropped G's. Garrett had passed that way before us.

So by 1935 he had long ago negotiated the barrier between Them and Us and taken his place among the speakers of RP, or Received Pronunciation. Accents were still important to him. In the summer of that year, when he was recruiting his staff, Garrett made sure the post of Art Master – who would be working three days a week at the school to leave time for his own painting – went to the twenty-eight-year old Claude Rogers, an artist with a bright future. As he approached him with hand outstretched in congratulations, Garrett exclaimed, 'I am *so* pleased, Rogers, that *you* are coming on my staff. You were the *only* candidate with a *halfway decent accent.*' Rogers was scandalised by this snobbery ('I wanted to kick him in the stomach,' he said many years later). But jobs were scarce.

Undoubtedly there was more to Garrett's choice than Claude Rogers' vowels, and the tones in which this Old Boy of St Paul's School addressed the small committee of school governors who with Garrett's advice made the appointment. Garrett would have enjoyed Rogers' enthusiasm for awakening in suburban schoolchildren some response to colour and design; but he also had an instinct for the right kind of intellectual connections. Rogers was a friend and former Slade contemporary of William Coldstream, then working at the GPO Film Unit in a group that included Benjamin Britten, Basil Wright, and W H Auden. By this time Garrett and Auden were friends. Garrett was the older man by five years: they had been introduced by a mutual friend, Nevill Coghill, Garrett's close contemporary at Exeter and a junior don when Auden, in turn, went up to Christ Church. Nobody seems to remember exactly when Auden and Garrett met, nor what the exact circumstances were, and I suppose it is possible, considering what has been written about Auden's sexual appetite, that the assumption of one of Garrett's Oxford circle was correct, and that they had had a brief love affair, with no special commitment on either side.

At any rate, one result of their meeting was the anthology *The Poet's Tongue*, by W H Auden and John Garrett, published in 1935 by Bell and Co. in two volumes. Bell were the publishers of a rather lightweight anthology Garrett had compiled and published in 1933, *Scenes from School Life*, consisting of extracts from the work of sixteen English authors, from Boswell to Beverly Nichols, all of them about school.

The Poet's Tongue was in a more serious league; but it isn't clear, and no one seems to remember, how the collaboration worked. The Preface is quoted now and then for what are assumed to be exclusively Auden's thoughts about poetry: Edward Mendelson in *The English Auden* (1980) doesn't even mention the anthology's joint editorship and Samuel Hynes in *The Auden Generation* (1976) says it is 'clearly the work of

Auden'. But I am not the only Raynes Park alumnus who can hear in certain phrases the occasional Garrettism, those echoes of a well-remembered voice: 'A great many people dislike the idea of poetry as they dislike over-earnest people, because they imagine it is always worrying about the eternal verities. Those, in Mr Spender's words, who try to put poetry on a pedestal only succeed in putting it on the shelf.' When I read that I remember Garrett's continuous pursuit of the apt quotation, and his insistence on our referring to living writers by their titles. (Later in this Preface there is a reference to 'E M Forster', *tout court*. Auden, this time, perhaps.) And 'eternal verities': that's very John Garrett.

There was a story in the school that the idea for *The Poet's Tongue* came to the two men during a conversation in a pub, with both of them scribbling down suggestions on the back of an envelope. No one knows who did the donkey work of collecting the anthology's 291 entries, nor who negotiated whatever agreement they had with Bell and Co., who are no longer in business. The anthology went into many editions, sometimes in one volume, and it was a standard text-book at Raynes Park and probably other schools as well. It is an exceptionally lively anthology, in which the poems are printed anonymously and in an entirely arbitrary order – alphabetically, according to their first words. The choice is eclectic and stimulating: ballads next to Shakespeare, the Bible next to a song by W S Gilbert.

Garrett's achievement in bringing out the book would have looked good on his *curriculum vitae*, together with his earlier anthology, and three small readers for schools which he had edited for a series called *The King's Treasuries of Literature*, published by J M Dent under the general editorial guidance of Sir Arthur Quiller-Couch. Garrett made selections from Dickens and Daudet (yoked together in one volume) and from Boswell's *Life of Dr Johnson*.

All of these earlier anthologies bear the imprint of Garrett's hand as his pupils would remember it, with their Introductions in the artificial *belle-lettriste* tradition of which 'Q' himself was a notable exponent. The Dickens-Daudet volume, the first in Dent's series, somewhat pointlessly argues the similarities between the two writers in their treatment of children and the working-class, and their 'bond in spirit and sympathy', the thesis well padded out with quotations ('Like Rupert Brooke he could see "the essential glory and beauty of all the people" he met . . . Where Daudet delicately etched, Dickens splashed paints', etc). A bee or two can be heard droning in the editor's bonnet (plus the odd well-rehearsed witticism) as he addresses his schoolboy readers, sometimes with scant relevance to the matter in hand, and in testy, schoolmasterish tones: 'From every magazine advertisements challenge us with their quack nostrums, and the patent roller promises to make us slim without taking exercise . . . *Lady Into Fox* has become a trifling miracle compared with *Monkey Gland into Lady*. Elderly aunts refuse to grow old, and the jazz floor has replaced the patience table . . .' etc, etc. Likewise, his prefatory remarks to passages from *The Arabian Nights* in his school anthology include a digression, prompted by a newspaper report that in the palace of King Ibn Saud an electric lift was being installed. Garrett affected to find this 'sadly indicative of the changing face of Asia [*sic*] today,' and rumbled on about 'the Western traveller, seeking relief from the tyranny of a syncopated civilisation' and now no longer able to find it, as ancient customs wither before 'the great god Speed'.

John Garrett's friendship with Auden had another consequence in addition to *The Poet's Tongue*. Auden was persuaded to write the Raynes Park school song. He also supplied a school motto. Parents and governors must have been taken aback when they learned that instead of something in Latin, Raynes Park was going to have a quotation from Karl Marx – to be exact, a line Marx had cited in his *Critique of the Gotha Programme* as suitable for a banner, and which Auden had slightly rewritten to make the last line of *The Dog Beneath the Skin*, the first of his

three plays with Christopher Isherwood. That play was produced at the Group Theatre in January 1936, but it had been
published a few months earlier. Garrett had reviewed it in the
July 1935 issue of T S Eliot's literary quarterly *The Criterion*, a.
notice one can now recognise as another fine example of the
Higher Balderdash. There is no question of summarising, still
less analysing, the plot or ideas in the play, but instead a
succession of hifalutin compliments:

> When Macaulay praised Milton he disparaged Boswellism,
> but himself went one better. It would be hypocrisy as idle to
> disguise the enthusiasm one feels for this play . . . Didacticism
> and entertainment have here become perfect bedfellows . . .
> The story is simple but sufficient, and all the better as a vehicle
> for satire in that its familiarity is calculated to divert but not to
> instruct . . . the work of a dramatist who is also a poet . . .

(A critic in *New Verse* said rather more accurately that Auden
was 'not a dramatist but a poet interested in the theatre'.)

The play's final line, which gave Garrett his motto, was 'To
each his need, from each his power.' Whatever they may have
thought of the source of this axiom, parents as well as boys
regarded it as succinct and pertinent.

As for the school song, there was nothing second-hand about
that. It was custom-made, a genuine original Auden poem, and
a scoop for Garrett to be proud of. It was to be one of the
school's major selling points, often reprinted in school publications and sung by the boys *en masse* on the first and last days of
term, on Speech Days and at House Suppers. The first verse ran:

> Time will make its utter changes
> Circumstance will scatter us,
> But the memories of our school days
> Are a living part of us.

There were five more four-line stanzas, with a chorus repeated
after each:

So remember then, when you are men
   With important things to do,
That once you were young, and this song have sung,
   For you were at school here too.

I wonder how seriously Auden took the task of writing those words. Probably he considered it part of the poet's journeyman duty. The artist Rupert Shephard, who succeeded Claude Rogers as Art Master and had worked with Auden at the Group Theatre, used to say that Auden would have dashed off the Raynes Park school song in an evening. 'If you'd ever seen him at work,' said Shephard, 'you'd know he was terribly fluent. I can remember occasions at the Theatre when we were rehearsing *The Dance of Death*. Rupert Doone would say, "It's a bit thin here, Wystan", or, "We could do with a few more words at this point", and Auden would oblige.' In the case of *The Dog Beneath the Skin*, incidentally, that sort of ad hoc composition was evidently ineffectual. In his memoir *Drawn from Life* (1983) the Director of the Group Theatre, Robert Medley, said the play's principal fault, its confused, chaotic finale, 'could not be remedied by Wystan scribbling new lines on the back of an envelope.' He implies that the same is true of the succeeding plays, *The Ascent of F6* and *On the Frontier*.

However, having acquired the words, Garrett now needed the music to go with them. Casting around for a composer who would deliver a simple, rousing tune, he approached Thomas Wood, a Fellow of Exeter whom he had met again in the summer of 1935 at a College Gaudy. Wood's life had been a lot more varied than the average musician's: he had travelled far and wide with his father, a Master Mariner, and even shipped aboard a tramp steamer at the precocious age of eight. He had studied under Stanford at the Royal College of Music and during his later travels had become especially keen on Australia: he was credited with the responsibility of popularising *Waltzing Matilda* outside the country.

Aside from music and travel, Wood's prevailing passions were the British Empire and the sea, a fact that can be surmised from the titles of such compositions as *Master Mariners*, *Merchant-men*, and *Forty Singing Seamen*. Another of his interests was the supernatural. He had once seen a headless ghost on his staircase at Exeter while carousing with friends over cocoa, but since he suffered from congenital cataract, with one-tenth normal vision in one eye and rather less in the other, it is difficult to take the story seriously; nor to regard other than sceptically the eager account of the sighting in his autobiography, a breezy and stimulating volume called *True Thomas*, which he published in 1936.

Wood had also written a monograph on music and schools and was keen on the idea of boys singing together ('a jolly physical exercise . . . Could there not be sing-songs in every school?'). To Garrett he probably seemed just the man for the job he had in mind, yet it was in some ways an odd choice. Wood's rollicking, faintly Elgarian setting always sounded out of character with Auden's words and came to be disliked at the school. There were at least two attempts to replace it. One was by the French master, Frank Beecroft, who was also a gifted musician, and another was the work of a later Art Master, George Haslam, who not only wrote the music for a new song but, audaciously, new words too. They began:

> In early days of striving
> When childhood comes to end:
> In newer ways of living
> In making of a friend;
> Let this be our spirit, in word and in deed
> 'From each one his power, to each one his need'.

Serviceable enough, but not really a rival to Auden's. Neither this version nor Beecroft's was taken up seriously, and for all its disadvantages, the Auden-Wood original proved to have sticking power. The whole thing shows that writing words or music for a school song, should the task ever be necessary again, is no easy matter. Some of Auden's words used to provoke grimaces of disgust among the more senior boys, especially –

> Daily we sit down in form rooms
> Inky hand to puzzled head.
> Reason's Light and knowledge Power,
> Man must study till he's dead.

It was the second line that grated: not so much Auden, we felt, as Winnie the Pooh, but at least the verses contained one line he considered good enough to use again. Our third stanza ran,

> Man has mind but body also
> So we learn to tackle low,
> Bowl the off-breaks, hit the sixes,
> Bend the diver's brilliant bow.

The last image found a second and more durable home in one of Auden's best-known shorter poems of the period, written in 1937 and included in *Another Time*, published in 1940. It is No 26 in that collection ('As I walked out one evening'), and the ninth stanza goes –

> Into many a green valley
> Drifts the appalling snow;
> Time breaks the threaded dances
> And the diver's brilliant bow.

However, although the Raynes Park school song was included in Gavin Ewart's anthology of school songs, *Forty Years On* (1969), where it was conspicuous for its superior quality, it does not appear in Edward Mendelson's (by intention) definitive collection of 1977, *The English Auden*.

I think it is significant that at the time when Garrett cajoled the school song from him, Auden was interested in the phenomenon of the new suburbs, and alluding in his poetry to the suburban wasteland that he would surely have seen exemplified in Raynes Park and the neighbouring communities. He visited the school, though it's not clear when: it must have been some time before 1942, when his name appeared in Garrett's lost Visitors' Book, the contents of which were cited in the school magazine, *The Spur*, in December of that year. Had he been to Raynes Park to see Garrett's new school in 1935 while it was still being built? I think it more than possible: then, he could not have failed to see 'the areas of greatest congestion, the homes of those with the least power of choice . . . district of the bypass and the season ticket'. It could have been the new estates and railway lines around postal district SW20 that supplied him with a reference point for, for instance, *The Ascent of F6*, written in 1936. One of the themes of that play is that the climber Michael Ransom is offering a vicarious means of heroic achievement to Mr and Mrs A (A for average, no doubt) who follow newspaper and wireless reports of his journey up a mountain in Tibet from their cosy little semi, commenting on his progress with a mixture of envy, prurience and a kind of fatuous patriotism. When one of the climbers is swept away by an avalanche, Mr A tells the audience, 'He has died To satisfy our smug suburban pride.'

When I first read these lines I was horribly afraid they had been written with people like my parents in mind. The A's are the classic cowed suburban couple, yearning for a hero to inspire them, abjectly swapping their own unexciting experiences when Mr A comes in from his dull, repetitive job. 'Evening,' Mrs A is telling herself over the cooker as she awaits his return, 'a slick and unctuous time, Has sold us yet another shop-soiled day.' And when poor harassed A does arrive a few moments later, she greets him with what is meant (by Auden) to be a depressing synopsis of events since he left for the station that morning. To his hopeful inquiry, 'Has anything happened?' she returns a listless answer:

> What should happen?
> The cat has died at Ivy Dene,

The Crowthers' pimply son has passed Matric.,
St Neots has put up bright blue curtains,
Frankie is walking out with Winnie
And Georgie loves himself.

Many writers would have judged that to have been a day packed
with incident, however petty and pointless it may have seemed
to Auden and Isherwood. Mr A's news is even less riveting. All
he has to report is

The eight o'clock train, the customary place,
Holding the paper in front of your face . . .
The public stairs, the glass swing door,
The peg for your hat, the linoleum floor . . .
Then the journey home again
In the hot suburban train
To the tawdry new estate.

In the Preface to *The Poet's Tongue* Auden, presumably with
Garrett's approval (he wouldn't have dared disagree), had
written a parallel passage: 'Only when it throws light on our
own experience . . . as we see, say, the unhappy face of a
stockbroker in the suburban train, does poetry convince us of its
significance.' Thus does the idea of the suburbs, and of money-
making occupations, come to Auden's (and Garrett's?) mind
when he wishes to suggest gloom, anxiety, frustration.

Mr A, of course, is surely not a stockbroker. More likely a
stockbroker's clerk, or even something in linoleum. And the
word linoleum in A's speech piques my curiosity further. I find
myself wondering, could it possibly be that Garrett had put the
word into Auden's head, talking about the sort of parents he
had to deal with? Had he by any chance mentioned my father's
occupation? No, I suppose these speculations are too fanciful.
Yet the A's dumb despair ('Give us something to be thankful
for,' pleads Mrs A as Ransom sets off on his symbolic journey)
embodied a prevalent attitude towards suburban life. It arose
partly because of what the developers had done to the innocent

countryside of the Home Counties: the Mr and Mrs A's, no less than the Vaughans and countless other couples in search of quasi-pastoral contentment, suffered guilt by association.

Sixty years ago the middle classes, to Garrett and his circle, were the great reservoir of philistinism, blinkered appeasement, unthinking patriotism and English bloody-mindedness. To be laid against them were their supposed intellectual limitations and their bovine acceptance of the tawdry aesthetic standards wished on them by the jerry-builders who had created the new housing estates. The word 'suburban' no longer has the pejorative force it had in Garrett's time. Now, not even the architectural environment seems so objectionable. Raynes Park itself has become a far from undesirable address, certainly not those parts of it which were thought *démodé* in the 1930s, the Victorian villas and terraced dwellings put up in the great building boom of a hundred years ago. Those houses, now fetching extravagant prices, have acquired a patina derived from other things besides the weather. What's more, the semi-detacheds of the twenties and thirties, which were looking shoddy by the forties, are coming through the bad taste barrier, often to be restored to their original style, or a version of it, with stained glass, model galleons, gnomes lurking in the gardens and china ducks in flight across oak-panelled walls.

Mr and Mrs A must have lived in some such place. She speaks of 'the six small rooms'; among them, 'The parlour, once the magnificent image of my freedom, And the bedroom which once held for me The mysterious languors of Egypt and the terrifying Indias.' 'But you all live in such horrid little houses!' John Garrett once exclaimed to a group of boys who had never thought of their parents' homes that way. But he was only echoing received opinion about the bourgeoisie and their boring habitat. 'Along the North Circular and the Great West roads,' wrote Louis MacNeice,

> Running the gauntlet of impoverished fancy
> Where housewives bolster up their jerry-built abodes
> With *amour-propre* and the habit of Hire Purchase.

And 'How beastly the bourgeois is! Especially the male of the species,' wrote D H Lawrence in a text I remember discovering with puzzlement. 'Touch him, and you'll find he's all gone inside, like a wet meringue.' Could it have been us he was writing about?

Ten

I SUPPOSE MOST of the boys at Raynes Park County School must have realised John Garrett was different from the grown-up men we already knew. Only later did we find out that on the dais in Hall every morning, in his MA gown, was a fringe member of the country's intellectual *corps d'élite* – with his Oxbridge background, an itch to get into print, and (temporarily as it turned out) leftish sympathies.

Nowadays probably his homosexuality would be obvious but to us innocents it was not. All we knew was that he walked like a bit of a cissy: chin up, arms loose at his sides but hands turned outwards, wagging his shoulders as he proceeded along the school corridors, moving with quick, alert steps, his approach often advertised by the sound of that peremptory, barking, upper-class voice with its italicised rhythms. Disapproval he would indicate by means of a short, sharp exclamation, something between a cough and a gasp, while abruptly turning away his head as though someone had shown him something faintly disgusting, or broken wind in his presence. As A L Rowse remembered in his poem, there was something peculiar about one eye. Sometimes it seemed to open wider than the other one as if a muscle somewhere had given up. His clothes were elegant and looked expensive: he favoured the sort of single-colour woolly ties fashionable among intellectuals of the day – ties in which to be photographed by Howard Coster (which later on

Garrett was), and to set off suits our fathers and uncles, in their conventional clerical greys and dark blues, would never have dreamed of wearing. One of Garrett's, I remember, was a greyish-lavender tweed, with which he wore a plain, dark mauve tie. That combination used to fascinate me, with its luscious contrast of colours. It was an object-lesson in style.

Nobody among the people at home either looked or talked the way he did. In our house it was considered in some way daring – 'modern' would have been my mother's way of expressing it, modernity being a prized attribute – that Garrett did not live in a house, like everyone else, but in a flat. When in due course she and my father were invited there to sherry one Sunday morning, it was as if they had been summoned to the Mayor's parlour. It seemed right that the road he lived in was called Grand Drive – known as *The* Grand Drive, until during the twenties the arrival of a row of extra large houses, downhill towards the road's better end, changed the local geography and for some reason the road signs. It was in one of those newer houses that Garrett lived.

In spite of his modest start in life, Garrett had the knack of being able to convey an impression of social distinction, the poise of a man used to better things than our dusty and monotonous suburban streets with their endless terracotta tiled roofs, narrow grass verges and spiky, immature little trees. Most parents were as much in awe of him as their sons were. His social superiority made a difference, and it is obvious from the notes Garrett kept about them at those first interviews that the Raynes Park parents represented a fairly average cross-section of the middle classes of South London.

As time went on, these notebooks assumed more and more the character of a confidential school diary in which Garrett put down his thoughts on boys and their parents and sometimes on the staff as well. His observations were occasionally scandalous, even possibly actionable. 'Mother deaf, perfumed, and chic' . . . 'Unattractive youth. Pimply, greased, long hair, & common' . . .

'Mouldy, unimpressive gent. Worms? . . . Dark. No personality. Left son's future too late.'

I can see Garrett writing down these observations, in his small, neat script, as the nervous parents talked on, often no doubt all too revealingly, about a matter close to their hearts: a son's future. Now and then Garrett registered other qualities than a candidate's academic potential. 'Boy with charming smile, well set-up. Only child. Admit if possible' . . . 'A blue-eyed, fair-haired child who must be admitted,' Garrett told himself. As they came into his daunting presence, no doubt for those questions about toucans and algebraic logic, he regarded them like specimens, sometimes with an almost literary detachment: 'A good man with kindly eyes' . . . 'Enormously fat youth with legs like beer bottles' . . . 'Beastly looking, wizened son of a hideous elderly father' (not admitted) . . . 'Husband six foot and very broad, and handles flowers as tenderly as babies.' I have often thought Garrett would have liked to write a novel. (He certainly liked the idea of literary journalism and wanted to write for the *New Statesman*, according to V S Pritchett, who remarked to me once, 'The trouble was, like all schoolmasters, he couldn't write.')

I have in my possession one of those panoramic school photographs that used to be taken once a year, with everyone in them – a custom that seems to have died out: nowadays every pupil is photographed alone, in colour. My picture of Raynes Park is in black and white and it was taken in the early summer of 1937, when the school was not quite two years old. In the centre of the group is John Garrett's confident, smiling figure, leaning forward a little. He is wearing a double-breasted light grey suit with a cream shirt and a patterned tie which I remember as yellow in colour. Lined up all round him are five rows of boys, 188 of us – and that, plus the day's absentees, made up the school's entire strength. There are fourteen masters, from Garrett himself to the PT master, an unpopular man called Sweeney who is dressed in a fashion appropriate to his rôle, tweed jacket with white trousers and shoes, and a white silk scarf bunched around his neck. The School Secretary Mrs French, wife of a local dentist, is also in the picture, as well as four women in white overalls who were the kitchen staff: today they would be called Dinner Ladies, a term which would have excited Garrett's contemptuous amusement. Their leader, a grim-faced woman with coiffed grey hair brushed stiffly upwards, was a Mrs Brown: she seemed not to like schoolboys. Then there is the Caretaker, fat, pink-jowled Mr Sugden, who was brought in like Pierrepoint the hangman to assist at the school's infrequent canings: it was his job to hoist the victim over his back while Garrett or Gibb wielded the cane. Shortly afterwards, Sugden came into some money, in consequence of which he resigned and bought a sweet-shop half a mile or so away called The Gem.

On the day of the school photograph, it is June. We must have been having a heat wave: the grass is cropped close and already looking a little scorched. Most of the windows on the school's western façade are wide open to let in the summer air. Seven of the boys in the photograph, sitting to the left of the row of masters, are prefects, the first to be appointed. I can't remember the names of many of the boys but random events and exploits come back, sometimes with unexpected clarity after more than fifty years. That boy in the back row: not expelled exactly, but asked to leave. Later he joined the RAF and became a fighter pilot: his Spitfire was shot down and he was posthumously awarded the DFC, whereupon his distraught mother came to the school and made a scene in the course of which she smacked Garrett's face. I wonder if his face somehow invited this treatment: there was another mother who slapped it and for a similar reason, believing he had under-estimated her son's potential. All that particular boy seemed to want to do, in Garrett's opinion, was play with model aeroplanes, and when in later life he became a highly-placed executive in British Aerospace, I suppose that vindicated to some extent his mother's impulsive action.

A boy in the next rank in front died in hospital of some wasting disease within a year of the photograph being taken:

leukaemia, perhaps. He is smirking, and so is his neighbour, a boy with a curious, braying laugh, famed for the extent and sophistication of his sexual information and the size of his penis. He not only knew all about birth control and was rumoured to have been seen walking with a girl, he also used to bring hand-written pornographic texts to school, and organized fellatio sessions after hours with another boy, whom I can see eight places to his left. That one was somebody Garrett seemed to have taken the measure of, describing him in his notebooks as 'flirtatious'.

Another boy in the same row had a father who beat him ('throttles him and carries him up to bed & then says he's conquered him,' says Garrett's note) and who before long had a mental breakdown and died young. Yet another boy, not far away, was shy, cowed, broody and withdrawn: he too suffered a mental collapse, became schizophrenic and died in hospital after a careless nurse or doctor had given him an overdose of insulin.

There they all are, the bullies, the rowdies, the lazy, the conceited, the clever, the obscure, the knowing and the naive, and the small number – no more than about a dozen – who were going to be killed in the war, then only two years ahead. One of the boys in the rank and file had moved as the camera reached him: his face remains forever distorted and unrecognisable. And meanwhile, there we stood or sat, in June 1937, in our school blazers with their brand new badges on the breast pocket. At first the blazers had been adorned with a conventional badge: a shield divided into four with the initials RPCS, one in each quarter. Garrett wanted something more unusual than that, and so the shield was abandoned in favour of a small chromium emblem like a brooch, two parallel lines with an arc over the top and a bolt of lightning whizzing through the middle. It looked up-to-date or 'modernistic', and used to puzzle people in the street. Once, a man on a 72 bus asked me if the badge had anything to do with the British Union of Fascists, whose emblem showed a similar bolt of lightning inside a circle. I think he was hoping I would say yes, but I'm not sure what he would have replied if I had. In fact the design was meant to be a pictorial representation of the school's location next to two aerial roads, with a railway bridge beneath which the electric trains sped to and from London.

The idea that Raynes Park might have entertained some Mosleyite connection would have caused indignation in the Masters' Common Room. There, the prevailing political climate was left-wing. The average age of the staff was unusually low: around thirty-three – Garrett's own age in 1935. Most of the masters in the school's early days were from Oxford or Cambridge. Pawky jokes about 'the other place' were part of the stock-in-trade of the Headmaster's Notes in the school magazine, which was called *The Spur* – yet another reference to the school's location. 'The title derives, of course,' Garrett explained in the first number, published in October 1936, 'from the situation of the School on the Merton Spur of the Kingston By-Pass Road.'

That same opening issue shows how Garrett's ideas for the management of a boys' secondary grammar school were falling into place. 'Man has mind but body also,' he quotes from Auden's school song, in a report on the school's first Open Night which included a gymnastic display: 'A large audience watched them leap and run, perform prodigious feats on the apparatus, and contort their bodies into shapes that were fantastic to the eye but beneficial to the constitution.' It can be seen that Garrett cultivated a certain joke pomposity of style for *The Spur*, a kind of donnish humour that probably struck some of the parents, at whom the magazine was principally aimed, as rather impressive, others as horribly affected: 'Considering the brevity of our tenure, the grounds have done the School credit,' says another paragraph. 'The brave impertinence of the crocus, the grace of daffodils and narcissi, and the blaze of golden yellow and white tulips, which constituted our Spring show, was entirely due to the generosity of our neighbours, James Carter & Co.' Yes, Garrett would surely like to have written a novel, and what it would have been like is all too clear.

However, his literary pretensions helped to give *The Spur* a distinctive character that now makes it seem very much of its time, with its rosy-tinted accounts of school activities: the first rugger fixture, against a XV from Garrett's former school Whitgift, described as 'an interesting match in every way . . . we came through it beaten soundly, but by no means disgraced', its cricket fixtures ('we were badly beaten . . . but by no means disgraced'), and the growth of the school library, whose stock speedily increased but whose premises were evidently misused now and then ('too many idle loungers make it a meeting place for hatching crime and rebellion'). The advertisements, too, between which the school reports were sandwiched, fill out the picture of a community of boys doing what were then, half a century ago, deemed acceptably boyish things: someone had managed to sell advertising space to Bassett-Lowke Ltd, makers of model railways and ships, to Cadbury's ('I break up every day', grins a youth wearing – quite inappropriately – an Eton collar, both thumbs up, 'A Block of Cadbury's Milk Chocolate of Course!' – the price, fourpence a quarter-pound), to Hamley's of Regent Street, to Gunn and Moore, maker of hockey sticks ('will not sting, will not break, and will give a better ball control because of its perfect balance . . . Seven Models from 7/6 to 22/6') and Bassett's Original Liquorice Allsorts ('From Fags to Prefects – we all have a weakness for Bassett's Allsorts . . . jolly good value').

Garrett was also diligently extending the school lecture list, later to become one of his more spectacular achievements. Soon there would hardly be a member of the Auden circle who had not turned up to talk to the boys, but at the time when the first *Spur* was published there seems to have been a strong preference for men of the cloth: boy audiences had sat through the addresses of two Bishops and a rank-and-file clergyman ('a talk on books and his debt to them'), but we had also had Councillor Drake, JP, a member of the Governing Body, on 'The Changing World', and the architect Basil Ward, whose talk sounds as if it must have reinforced Garrett's views about the suburbs, because he 'gave us seriously to think about the kind of houses with which we are fast despoiling what remains of our countryside.' Garrett's mentor Ronald Gurner came from Whitgift to talk of 'the purpose of schools, and did much to lay low the wretched heresy that the sole object of a secondary education is to equip a boy to earn his living.' Suburban parents, please note.

So far it must have seemed the school was developing along predictable lines, even if it was already showing signs of ideas beyond its social station, with the emphasis on Oxbridge, the choice of rugger instead of soccer, and sporting fixtures with only the 'right' schools. A sign that something different might be happening came when someone gave the school some money which Garrett decided to spend on pictures to be hung round the rooms and corridors. One day I was summoned to go after school to an art shop in Kensington, driven by one of the masters in his car. I helped to load it up with a collection of reproductions which were put up in all the classrooms: Canalettos, Monets, Van Goghs, Botticellis, Constables and Renoirs. Boys were silently initiated into the world of the great masters.

One public school feature Raynes Park didn't have was a Cadet Force. However, there was a school Scout Troop, and I asked if I could join.

A huge mistake: the Scoutmaster was the one man I feared among the staff, the flinty and disagreeable Courchée. 'This is a very serious step, you know, Vaughan,' he told me, out of the side of his mouth. I should have smelled a rat. But it was the regimental ring of 'the 19th Wimbledon', suggesting something like the 17th/21st Lancers or the 2nd of Foot and so pandering to my naive feelings about military glory, that helped to propel me into this foolhardy decision. I came to regret it, especially when I put on my Scout uniform for the first time, even more so when in due course I had to endure the discomfort and misery of a Scout camp in Cornwall. I had seen Baden-Powell's *Scouting for Boys* and been rather impressed with his drawings of cheery

Scouts, dressed for the Siege of Ladysmith in corduroy shorts and slouch hats, using their Scout staves to leap across streams and improvise stretchers, or defend themselves against attack by swearing louts. I suspect Courchée was responsible for the Raynes Park version of this free-and-easy costume: the 19th Wimbledon turned up for school on Mondays dressed in thick dark blue serge and coarse grey socks, an outfit that itched abominably and was unbearable in summer.

Worse still, the unfriendly and pompous manner adopted by Courchée seemed to poison all the troop's activities. I swiftly lost interest. It revived, though, with the news that Courchée was leaving to become, Heaven help them, Headmaster of a school in Cumberland. My relief was short-lived. His replacement as Maths master and as Scoutmaster was even worse, a glowering, morose and lonely man called Raynham. Everyone went in fear of him. His Maths classes were conducted in an atmosphere frozen with terror, the class tense as whippets. Raynham did something Courchée was never known to do: he strode into school on Mondays dressed ready for the evening parade, ludicrous in his knee-length shorts, shirt crusted with badges and a whistle hanging on a clean white lanyard. On top of all that, his academic gown – and God help anyone who sniggered.

Raynham, a large and ponderous individual, was unpopular in the Staff Room too, where he came to be known as The Granite Crusher. Yet after school hours, when the Scouts were mustering on the patch known as the Scout Reservation, he would attempt to modify his grim and sarcastic manner with stiff jokes and a steely grin: all in vain – the memory of those hushed, inhibited Maths periods was too fresh. Nor did he improve his standing by letting it be known that in his rôle as Scoutmaster he would like to be known either as 'Skipper', or, preferably, 'Tiger'. Later in the evening of a Scout parade, he would cast over his shoulders a heavy woollen blanket with a tiger's head design sewn on the back and, by way of further explanation, the word *Tiger* below.

No wonder my enthusiasm for Scouting melted away, soon after I had enlisted in the 19th Wimbledon and been posted to the Falcon patrol – whose patrol 'cry' was 'Hic, hic, hic'. The patrol cries were one of the barmier things about the Scout movement: they were meant to enable members of a patrol to signal to each other while tracking something. Most of the cries were animal noises, as the Falcons' was supposed to be, but the Rattlesnake patrol, which would have been unpopular had there been one in our Troop, were instructed in the Scout Handbook to 'rattle a pebble in a small potted-meat tin'. I doubt if many people, let alone rattlesnakes, would have been taken in for long.

On enrolment, like everyone else, I had publicly taken the Scout Promise, swearing before the entire Troop to 'do my duty to God and the King' and to 'obey the orders of my parent or Scoutmaster *without question*'. The Scout Handbook contained this earnestly italicised instruction, along with the Scout Motto, *Be Prepared* (for what? against whom?), and a check-list of the moral qualities held essential in a member of the movement: A Scout smiles and whistles under all difficulties, A Scout is clean in thought, word, and deed, etc. The homiletic prose of this code had been rendered into verse to make it easier to remember:

> Trusty, loyal, helpful,
> Brotherly, courteous, kind,
> Obedient, smiling, thrifty,
> Clean in body and mind.

Or, as another, more lyrical version had it, 'Clean as the rustling wind.'

That was an extremely hard rule to keep, and it was getting harder all the time. At the end of my first year I had been promoted from Form 1b to 2a, where the thirty-odd boys on the form register included a particularly knowing group, among them Fred Lucas, the boy with the champion penis, and another boy of I think Swedish extraction called Tullberg, with a tanned complexion and curly blonde hair, Lucas's partner in a number of sexual escapades.

The atmosphere in 2a was humid with sex, vibrant with sexual curiosity. It was a boy in that form who was discovered during an Art lesson painting his penis bright blue. Claude Rogers, ambling among the desks with hands in pockets, perhaps sucking some boiled sweets he had confiscated, observed the event and, unperturbed, drawled, 'Put that away.' The boy sheepishly obeyed. Another youth claimed to be on the verge of perfecting the legendary feat of auto-fellatio. No one believed him and he refused to give a demonstration. Meanwhile the prevalent spirit of anarchic sexual experimentation had of course spurred me on in private to ever more heroic feats of masturbation, and my guilt over these activities and the lascivious thoughts that went with them was intensified by heavily fingered passages in my copy of *Scouting for Boys*. In this famous publication, Lord Baden-Powell, the Chief Scout – a lean, brown, wizened, manifestly incorruptible man, a kind of super-Raynham – had issued crisp warnings about the dangers of self-abuse: it could turn you blind or send you mad, and chronic masturbators, he warned, were reduced to incoherent, blushing confusion at the 'mere sight' of a pretty girl. Apparently the only cure for self-abuse was self-control and cold baths, either first thing in the morning or, it was implied, whenever the urge came upon you. In the case of most of the boys in 2a observance of this rule would have resulted in a more or less continuous traffic to and from the gymnasium showers.

Anyway, neither of Baden-Powell's remedies was available to me, and so I would sit guiltily in the lavatory masturbating over my copy of Baden-Powell's master-work and the thought of encountering a pretty girl in the street. After all, you never knew. A boy in the form had claimed that one night, as he was walking home through a thick fog along Amberwood Rise, a nude girl had emerged from the murk of some suburban close and said

'Fuck me', disappearing into the darkness before he could gather his wits and obey this curt instruction. Another boy spread the word that a girl called Peggy on one of the counters in New Malden Woolworth's would do it with anybody: my friend Leander Richardson and I made an early reconnaissance one afternoon after school, both of us dry-mouthed with excitement. We failed to identify through our covert inspection of the staff which one might be Peggy, nor should we have known what to do if she had in some way identified herself for us. Nevertheless, the excursion was an exciting addition to one's sexual mythology and good for a few lurid fantasies afterwards, hence not entirely wasted.

This sort of behaviour was the very thing 'Tiger' Raynham was knitting his brows over. So much so that he instructed one of the assistant masters, a certain Mr James, who had been induced to join him as Assistant Scoutmaster, to lecture 2a on the subject of what he called *smut*. This seemed to mean telling dirty jokes, the collection and passing-on of which comprised one of the form's principal pastimes. These too, with all their feebleness, not to mention anatomical inaccuracy, contributed heavily to our sexual lore, though we didn't understand how Raynham and his assistant had got to know about it. Mr James found his rôle as moral propagandist uncomfortable. His embarrassment was plain as he blushingly enumerated the consequences of passing on the latest story: one of them, I recall, was that you would be insulting the other boy's mother, an argument that left me, then as now, entirely baffled. Needless to say, the lecture, and the parallel one Raynham was understood to be giving to another group of boys at the same time, had no effect on 2a's raunchy and deplorable behaviour.

In any case, Raynham (later to become a supporter of Moral Rearmament) was swimming against the tide. The lewdness in 2a was not exactly helped by the activities of our form-master, a tall, ungainly man with terrible teeth, just down from Cambridge. He was friendly and popular. Everyone knew him as Sam. He would set us some work – perhaps a brief composition or a comprehension test on some story he had read us (he liked Saki and P G Wodehouse) – and then the action would begin. As he sat behind his standard-issue Surrey Education Committee desk, left hand propping up his chin, right hand somewhere out of sight in his trouser pocket, his right arm would begin to wag rhythmically, faster and faster. Now and then he would straighten up clumsily, sit back, adjust position, not losing momentum. At first it seemed inconceivable that a grown-up man was doing in public what I had been doing privately and it was some time before I realised what he was up to. But even I could hardly doubt the explanation as Sam's behaviour became more flagrant. His face would become flushed: sometimes, he would look at us, sometimes out of the window, then, at the moment of climax, apparently oblivious of our glances and the sly grins exchanged, his face would be transfixed in a snarl of sexual crisis . . . then he would be fiddling about below the desk, trembling a little and shifting in his chair and, as we supposed, somehow cleaning himself up.

So regularly did these classroom incidents occur that, after a while, we ceased to take any notice of them, although a boy in 3a once propped up a large mirror behind Sam's chair, so that if he should get going, the front row would be in an advantageous position to confirm what by now we had all realised to be the case, that he was, as the current expression went, *rubbing up*, or *tossing off* under the desk. When Sam came in and saw the mirror he grinned conspiratorially and put it against the wall out of harm's way. Fifteen minutes later, he was masturbating just the same. Perhaps our effrontery only enhanced the element of exhibitionism that I suppose formed part of Sam's pleasure.

On yet another occasion, as he neared climax or, for all one knew, attained it, the door opened. In walked Garrett. Stifled giggles spread through the class: masters were expected to stand when the Headmaster entered. Sam stumbled to his feet, bending forward, face mottled, one hand in trouser pocket, trying to cover things up, smiling desperately and gradually straightening as Garrett went on talking to him. We couldn't hear the conversation, conducted in a low murmur. Garrett looked puzzled, vexed.

Many years later I learned that this young master had been Garrett's homosexual lover. The relationship had begun well, but Garrett had grown tired of Sam and been hugely relieved when, soon after the war began, he had left to join the RAF. 'At last,' he confided to a colleague, 'I have got *rid* of that *albatross*.'

We boys were innocently unaware of whatever sexual tensions there may have been between members of the staff, or for that matter between members of the staff and some of the pupils. We weren't shocked, only mildly amused by what Sam was doing. It was the same with the PT master, Sweeney. He was an ex-NCO from the Army Physical Training Corps, a crop-haired, straight-backed, hard-faced little martinet with the voice of a drill-sergeant, not so much loud as penetrating, made to carry across some vast parade-ground in Aldershot or Wrotham. Sweeney was another case where Garrett's flair for picking the right people had let him down. He never quite fitted in. His clothes marked him out for a start. While other masters wore 'sports' jackets and flannel or corduroy trousers, or occasionally suits, Sweeney came to school in white trousers and shoes, and a white pullover with a silk scarf tucked inside the collar in lieu of a shirt. Nobody liked him much, and nobody liked PT much, even though there was enthusiastic support for an after-hours activity called Voluntary Gym, in which you could swing on the ropes, or clamber up the wall-bars or the window-ladder without Sweeney's nasal bark to hound you on. Unpopular with the boys, he didn't get on with the rest of the staff either: one day he abruptly stopped turning up for tea from the trolley in the Staff Common Room and it was believed he had taken offence at something, nobody knew what. Gibb was deputed to go and have an avuncular chat, but Sweeney remained distant, and ceased to appear at Morning Assembly.

Many and various were the excuses used in the attempt to finesse your way out of a daytime Gym class. Most often tried was the plea that you had forgotten your PT kit – baggy blue cotton shorts and plimsolls. But when a boy called Symes gave this as his excuse once too often, Sweeney boiled over: he ordered him to do PT nude. The sight of Symes climbing and descending the window-ladder, all anus and scrotum, drove the rest of the class into paroxysms of embarrassed mirth. Sweeney bridled. 'What's the matter with you? I've seen 'undreds of dickies in my time. You'll see 'undreds, too, afore you're done.' The remark became famous, but his rebuke only made the giggling worse. Dickies! Squaring his shoulders, Sweeney ordered every boy to remove his shorts immediately: the rest of the period was performed in a state of nudity that soon became unremarkable, at least to the boys. But Sweeney went further. He took to ordering us to strip off, regardless of whether anyone had forgotten, or 'forgotten', his Gym shorts – then, raising the stakes further still, he would send us to do PT outside, nude, in full view of such passers-by as there may have been on the Kingston Bypass on a summer afternoon.

We tolerated Sweeney's actions, as children generally do tolerate the eccentric and inexplicable behaviour of adults, assuming they have reasons peculiar to adulthood which have yet to become clear. But, some twenty years later, I heard that Sweeney, by now PT master at a small private prep school in Wimbledon, had been sacked for interfering with a pupil in the garden: with this information, his fondness for putting the Raynes Park boys through nude PT classes took on a different hue.

In the light of one's adult knowledge of sexual behaviour, its huge variety and even absurdity, and in the light also of what has been written about the sexual idiosyncrasies of English schoolteachers, it is hard to believe there was anything especially out of the ordinary about the staff of Raynes Park County School. Cecil Day Lewis, a close friend of Garrett's, once remarked in conversation how extraordinary it was that no member of the Education authority, no parents, no school Governor, no one at all had apparently noticed that John Garrett himself was 'queer' – that this man who had charge of three or four hundred innocent schoolboys was, as would have been said (or whispered), 'pansy'. Day Lewis was making the common error of believing all homosexual men must be pederasts: however, I also doubt whether the people he believed so negligent saw anything amiss in Garrett's 'camp' mannerisms (a word which probably hadn't been invented then, or at least hadn't penetrated to the south-western suburbs). My own father and mother were much like their neighbours in remaining mystified by the subject, even when it stared them in the face in our own family circle. In our suburban environment it was known there were some men who were 'nancies' or 'cissies', who behaved in a more or less effeminate way, but the idea of homosexual activities, let alone homosexual love between men (still less women) wouldn't, I am sure, have been allowed to enter their thoughts.

Perhaps this attitude was repressive, probably it was the cause of much secret misery. But it was also part of the conformism of suburban society – a respect for convention Garrett liked to flout. His Oxford aesthete manner, with a dangerous hint of nameless vice, was one way of doing that. He had managed to win for himself a licence to shock, performing his intellectual pirouettes for the benefit of awed school parents. The old game of astonishing the bourgeois, after all, was much in favour in the kind of circle Garrett frequented. Indeed the contrast between his exotic *persona* and the local landscape of factories, sports grounds and semi-detached villas was largely responsible for the character of Raynes Park County School and the celebrity it achieved.

In his notes of meetings with parents there are indications of the way Garrett kept his own private life separate from normal school proceedings, despite the entries that indicate an appreciative eye for boyish glamour. One boy, some ten years old, had been having problems of glandular development. 'Testicles wouldn't drop. Penis a button,' Garrett wrote wonderingly. 'Injected with 25 doses of pregnant woman's urine. Result, 14½ age development. Penis phenomenal and hirsute growth unique. Doctor delighted but bewildered.' (I wonder how Garrett came by this information?) That he shared the doctor's astonishment, and possibly conceived an exaggerated faith in chemical remedies in such cases, is suggested by a note a few days later concerning a boy whose mother had consulted a doctor about her son's homosexual tendencies. Somehow she had brought herself, I suppose in all innocence, to discuss the problem with Garrett. He informed her, 'In my opinion there is ample evidence for vigorous action to prevent him developing into a homosexual – or at least to be sufficiently maladjusted sexually to make normal married life a gamble.' Garrett recommended her to a certain Harley Street endocrinologist, who presumably got busy with his hypodermic. I remember the boy well – a big-bottomed youth, tall for his age, with an ingratiating manner. He became a prison doctor.

All things considered, the place was comparatively free – remarkably so in the circumstances – of sexual scandal. Garrett may have entertained fantasies that the school harboured sexual coteries of the kind that flourished in public schools and I dare say at Oxford in his day: he once said in my hearing that a certain small boy with pink cheeks and an innocent air had 'caused a flutter in the amorous dovecots of the school'. I pondered this observation. What amorous dovecots? What was an amorous dovecot, anyway? If there were any, their existence was hidden from me and my friends, but some of the masters must have been aware of them, for (unknown to any of us until years later) a rhyme was invented by one of them:

> Have you heard of the wonderful school
> They've built on the Kingston Bypass?
> They say it's no place for a fool,
> But it helps if you've got a nice arse.

Likewise if there were any sexual scandals, they were efficiently hushed up. There was one incident, out of school, in Wimbledon: a group of boys had been enticed into an empty house for some homosexual escapade. Fred Lucas, I recall with no surprise, was one of them. Certain boys were summoned to Garrett's study and questioned. None of them would tell the rest of us exactly what had happened: a man was said to have been arrested. Perhaps it was the same man who had assaulted another boy in the Wimbledon Baths: the story had reached Garrett, who duly logged the incident in his notes ('man mouthed his parts', he recorded distastefully) and informed the police.

Garrett was a man with a tidy, perhaps slightly obsessional mind, and liked to keep lists and build up archives, all entered in blue ink in his small, neat handwriting, the letters seldom cursive but carefully separated. He kept an exercise book which he had labelled *Castigation!* The exclamation mark was his, as though astonishing himself, or as if when writing it down he assumed, like a character in a charade, the magisterial mien of the sterotype dominie. He had established three types of corporal punishment: in ascending order of severity you could be caned, beaten, or thrashed. Caning meant four strokes, beating meant six, and thrashing – well, the sky was the limit, theoretically at least. Garrett or Gibb would wield the cane, and the School Caretaker, the overweight, baby-faced Sugden (sometimes known, as at a public school, as the Porter), would hold the victim. Every time a boy had the cane used on him, on whatever scale of magnitude, the fact was entered in the Castigation Book, along with the reason. Sometimes Garrett would add a note to record how a boy withstood the experience – 'squealed and sobbed', 'behaviour totally worm-like', 'took it very well', etc.: interesting to speculate how Garrett himself might have behaved had the tables been turned. The first boy to get the cane at Raynes Park was a tough egg called Reed, who got six strokes for a total of five separate crimes – the fifth, and doubtless the crowning offence, being defined, none too precisely, as 'sloth, idleness, and anti-social stupidity'.

Garrett's system was to hold caning sessions at no fixed

intervals, saving up the victims so that the whole business could be despatched at one go. An uncomfortable, even cruel system for the victims as they waited day by day for the summons, when mass sentences would be carried out on two, three, or even five boys, one after the other, for crimes listed, again in teacher-speak, as, for instance, 'idling in the lavatory without permission', 'hooliganism', 'appalling and degrading manner in class and out', 'taking another boy's bicycle', and (surely a miscarriage of school justice), 'Saying "I thank you" in tones of Arthur Askey at end of Lord's Prayer yesterday.'

The heaviest punishment ever meted out was part of a Raynes Park *cause célèbre*. A group of boys had forced open the locked door of Garrett's personal notice board. On a list of those whose work at a school Open Night had been specially commended but from which their names had been omitted, they inscribed the words *Bloody Wangle*. It seems a mild comment, but fifty years ago it precipitated the school into a condition of crisis: it could hardly have been worse if a member of staff had rifled the Tuck Shop till or a boy had exposed himself to one of the cooks. A hunt to discover who was responsible failed to identify the culprits. Garrett threatened to place the entire school in detention: still no one owned up. The school was duly assembled in Hall and made to stand silent and unmoving for three quarters of an hour. At last the two boys who had done it were tracked down and made to confess, whereupon Garrett gave them what must have been the worst punishment he ever administered: twelve strokes each. Even then his wrath was not assuaged. A prefect, who knew who had done it but hadn't given them away, was also punished – even though he had tried to persuade them to give themselves up. The morning after the thrashing, Garrett swept on to the platform at prayers, his Oxford MA gown billowing in his wake. He glared at the school and announced in tones of the Last Trump, '*Clayden is no longer a prefect*.' Public disgrace. The silence in the school hall was palpable.

The week in July 1938 in which these events took place always seemed to the boys who were there at the time one of the most melodramatic in the school's history. Now it seems not only absurdly exaggerated but a product of Garrett's instinct for self-dramatization, yet the *Bloody Wangle* incident was burned into our memories as the supreme example of disobedience, rebellion, and cowardly evasion of condign punishment – what's more, of betrayal of the schoolboy code which insisted that the guilty should own up and *take their medicine*. What made their crime even worse was that the two boys had actually defied, if not defiled, the Headmaster's own law, by writing their *graffiti* on Garrett's personal notice board, where nobody but John Garrett himself ever wrote anything. The episode demonstrates not only Garrett's liking for the rôle of school despot but also his enthusiasm for reinventing the public school ethos for a suburban day school.

These values went without challenge. Garrett's response was not considered too extreme, either by the boys or the staff, who stood behind him on the platform in their gowns, with brows thunderously knit, like the Judges of the Secret Court.

Eleven

THE SURREY EDUCATION Committee allowed John Garrett to appoint his own assistant masters. No one had to appear before a full Board – the usual custom – and with one or two exceptions he chose well. Most of the masters were friendly, popular, and good at their profession, with degrees from the 'right' places. Also, like Garrett himself, they were all young: none had reached forty.

Rupert Shephard was twenty-eight when he succeeded Claude Rogers as Art Master. He was a tall, bespectacled man, mild of manner, and he came to Raynes Park after a teaching job in West Ham. After that, Raynes Park seemed to him the quintessence of suburbia, the masters 'men of culture and good breeding', dashing out at weekends along the Kingston Bypass in fast cars to play golf – whereas West Ham had been 'on the edge of factories and stink'.

One fast-moving colleague he probably had in mind was Tom Cobb, a tall, permanently sun-tanned, athletic-looking man who taught French and German and gave the impression of private affluence. He was well-connected: his middle name was Powys – later in the school's history, he was able to arrange for a group of boys to be evacuated to Powys Castle in mid-Wales to escape the German rockets, the V2s. He smoked Balkan Sobranie cigarettes, wore sporty clothes and owned a white open-topped DKW roadster. His wife had been a member of the Women's

League of Health and Beauty, founded by Prunella Stack: we had seen them on the Gaumont-British News doing formation gymnastics in well-cut shorts and radiant smiles. Mrs Cobb had had her share of adventure, having worked as an assistant to Jasper Maskelyne, the Variety theatre illusionist – she was the one he sawed in half. Apparently it irked Cobb that she had refused to give away the secret of how it was done, and later the marriage foundered: perhaps Mrs Cobb's reticence about her stage act was a contributing factor. Cobb was a man whom one vaguely suspected to have had broader, more interesting experiences than the other masters. I discovered later that he had been among the archaeologist Louis Leakey's team of diggers out in Kenya when significant discoveries were made relating to the early history of man. Later, after the war, Cobb left England and went to run a hotel in the Austrian Alps.

In 1936 he was Form Master to 1b. One day he stood in front of the class and said there was a Civil War in Spain and it was an event we should all know about: people were being shot and bombed, and Englishmen were going out to fight against some other people called the insurgents. There was a Spanish boy called de Cossio in the form, one of the few foreigners in the school. Cobb told him to stand up and tell us what was happening in his native country, and what it meant. De Cossio knew nothing, only that the rebels had captured San Sebastian: it was that day's news.

No doubt the mood in the Masters' Common Room was grim – and the mood would have been shared by Garrett, who always had the week's *New Statesman* prominently displayed and now and then used to read some of it out to us. Yet when the school ran its own imitation General Election in 1936, it was the National Government 'candidate' who won the contest by a handsome majority, probably a reflection of our parents' opinions, and doubtless something of a disappointment to the masters. It would have particularly disappointed Alan Milton, the dashing and universally-liked young History master, with openly left-wing views, who set up a special notice board called

The Pillory, on which he pinned newspaper cuttings he considered to exemplify dishonest or biased reporting.

Another notice board carried reviews of new films, taken from the *Statesman* or *World Film News*. One of *World Film News'* founders was Basil Wright, who had become a close friend of Garrett's and was another frequent visitor. Periodically, he arranged showings of films we weren't likely to catch at the local Odeon: boys were marched in form order to the Rialto cinema in Raynes Park to see the latest production from the Post Office Film Unit or the Gas Board, often promotional films like *Meet Mister Therm* (doubtless the work of one of Garrett's friends), with a song in it that we came away singing:

> Meet Mister Therm
> He'll make your life a pleasure,
> And double all your leisure
> So, meet Mister Therm!

What we had thought of as *going to the pictures* was, we learned, cinema. Films, the masters told us, were an art form of our own time. We had special showings of Pabst's *Kameradschaft*, Wright's own *Night Mail* and, later, Pare Lorentz' *The River*.

To be on John Garrett's staff was a good thing. From the Staff Common Room, with its atmosphere of an Oxbridge JCR, Raynes Park masters went off to spend evenings dining or drinking in Soho or Fitzrovia or at a favourite bar in Cecil Court. Their jaunts to the West End sometimes lasted into the early morning. Once, Alan Milton and Frank Beecroft appeared at Prayers in full evening dress having had no time to go home and change. Garrett was not entirely pleased, but he too was a frequenter of first nights and 'important' parties; he was writing reviews for *The Criterion* and being seen at Glyndebourne. To Basil Wright he seemed an important, even, he said, a seminal figure in the documentary movement that was one of the Thirties' main achievements – a kind of explorer from the Oxbridge-educated classes, reconnoitring in the suburban wasteland, whose people 'crawl out daily to their dingy labours' (Auden again), and discovering that there was salvageable 'material' there: he meant us. And it is true that he took an interest in recording, more or less objectively, the sociology of the school.

For the Art Master, the twenty-eight-year old Claude Rogers, the appointment at Raynes Park proved a turning point. It wasn't only because he had been hard-up that he was glad to get the job; Raynes Park also had seemed very different from the other schools he had written to. He had never taught before and he had been trembling with nerves before he went in to take his first Art Class. Uncertain how the job was supposed to be done, he had worked out a series of questions to ask the boys to find out about their experience of art. Question One: Write down the names of any three pictures hanging on the wall at home. None of them seemed to have any, or if they had they couldn't remember what they were. Then he asked which posters or advertisements they liked. 'It was all the comic ones. Bisto, Guinness.' (Claude used to drop his r's.) 'I vealized you had to start absolutely fvom scvatch. Almost anything you could show them would be a vevelation.'

Claude Rogers, a short, round man with a high-pitched voice, was not the stuff of which the great schoolmasters are made. Art lessons, always double periods lasting eighty minutes, took place in more or less continuous uproar, only exceeded in decibels and misbehaviour in the Woodwork lessons, with an amiable, shock-headed young man called Guerrier who was totally unable to keep order and had a none too secure grasp of his subject. There was no obvious reason why he should have done – he had a Modern Languages degree from Oxford: perhaps we were the only school in England to have a Balliol man teaching carpentry. However, Claude Rogers' inability to keep the class in order must have been even more obvious than Guerrier's, because the Art Room was immediately above Garrett's study. Complaints came from Geography and Chemistry along the corridor, and so Claude thought up a system of his own for keeping the boys in order but without making the lessons absurdly repressive, which in his opinion would have been quite contrary in spirit to the work in hand. So he announced that for each period there would be one forbidden activity: one week there'd be no talking in class, the next no sweet-eating, then no walking across the room without permission, and so on.

It didn't work. Garrett's patience snapped, and he told Claude he would have to go. The solution he'd thought of, a rather odd one, was to combine the posts of Woodwork and Art teacher, so saving money and ridding himself simultaneously of two incompetent disciplinarians. At this point, through Claude Rogers' friend William Coldstream, news of Garrett's plan came to W H Auden's ears. Auden had recently made a marriage of convenience with Thomas Mann's daughter Erica so that she could acquire British citizenship and so be given permission to leave Nazi Germany. With his well-known fondness for organising his friends' lives, Auden had the idea that other English homosexuals should make the same sort of deal with other German women: why not Garrett? When he asked him, Garrett was outraged and flatly refused. 'Wystan,' he fumed, 'wanted me to marry some *chorus* girl.'

Hence, Auden wasn't best pleased with Garrett, and when he heard of the plan to dump Claude Rogers, he at once took Claude's part. With the Coldstreams, they met for what was said to have been an uproarious evening at the ABC in Soho. Auden told Claude not to worry – *he* would have a word with Garrett. He added melodramatically, 'I know enough to see him in Hades.'

Whatever Auden said to Garrett after this encounter, it did the trick: a few days later, Garrett stopped Claude in the school corridor. 'Ah, Claude,' (Christian name this time) 'I've been thinking things over. I really think we can't do without you. We shall have to find a way round this problem.' He would keep him on, but there was a condition. Garrett insisted Claude should make a point of attending Morning Prayers. Since Claude and his wife Elsie lived in Chiswick and he was no early riser, he heard this instruction with foreboding: nevertheless, he duly turned up for nine o'clock Assembly, but the result was quite unexpected. 'As soon as I took my place,' he said, 'I was absolutely fascinated by the scene in fvont of me. All these little boys in their blue blazers and their pink faces, stvetching back to the othev end of this vevy large hall.' He put it all into a picture called *Boys at Prayers*: it mystified the pupils when he presented it to the school and for many years it hung in the hall; then it was vandalised, restored, and at length given a safer home in the Headmaster's study.

Claude Rogers had a similar experience when Garrett told him he should stay to School Dinner, a midday ritual to which Garrett attached a lot of importance: parents were always asked at preliminary interviews to make sure their sons would stay, and Garrett required a convincing excuse for their doing otherwise, stating in his prospectus that: 'This is the only way of attaining in a day-school something of that continuous community life which is a valuable feature of the English tradition of education . . . it is a necessity if boys are to profit from the continuity of environment afforded.' Masters too were expected to attend School Dinner, and in order to get to know the boys socially they had to put up with the overcooked meat and vegetables, soused in lumpy gravy, routinely provided by the kitchen staff of four unsmiling women in white overalls. Considering the menus on Merton Spur, occasional escapes to Soho would have been essential: mince, thin as gruel, sliding over scoops of grubby-looking mashed potato; overcooked brown stew or liver, with slushy cabbage or carrots; beef sausages, the skin roasted to a glistening, greasy carapace; all these appeared with awful regularity, as did, to follow, jam slice with thin custard or sago pudding dressed with a pale streak of stewed plum.

Probably all this was no more unappetising than most English institutional fare of the time, but it so happened that the food at Raynes Park County School would be helped down with draughts of water for which brightly coloured bakelite beakers were set round the tables – and it was these that transformed Claude Rogers' lunchtimes. He would sit there doing his best to engage the boys around him in conversation, but with his visual sense vibrating at those splashes of vivid red, green, blue and yellow. More than one painting emerged from this. One of them was exhibited at Agnew's in their Coronation Exhibition of 1937 – a picture with the coloured beakers in the foreground, boys at table, and a master's face, almost certainly Garrett's, almost obscured by a large vase of flowers, perhaps as an act of revenge.

Teaching at Raynes Park drove Rogers back to what he considered his true métier as a painter. He had flirted with abstract art, but now began to paint what he saw in front of him: boys in class, at prayers, at School Dinner – and this, he decided, was what he really wanted to do. His enthusiasm growing, he organised an exhibition at the school, to try to convey to the boys and parents and anyone else what contemporary English painting was like: he borrowed works from Duncan Grant, Vanessa Bell, Roderigo Moynihan, Victor Pasmore, William Coldstream and others, and for security's sake hung them in the Masters' Common Room. Boys were allowed to enter at fixed times, and view the paintings in the fug of stale tobacco. Other local schools sent parties of pupils to inspect the pictures, and the *Wimbledon Borough News* sent a reporter, who wrote some jocular remarks about modern painting.

Claude Rogers was popular with the boys, who thought his habits eccentric but endearing, and enjoyed the double-period Art lessons in all their chaos and noise. Powder paint was our medium, mixed in the sort of tin pans our mothers used when baking tarts. When you didn't use too much water, it was possible to produce a satisfyingly thick paste of vivid colour. Also, my father had the bright idea of offering the school a large quantity of small squares of brown linoleum – samples of something or other, which had been gathering dust in his office in Old Bailey. Claude took them gratefully, and boys were soon set to work producing lino-cuts, often at the expense of badly gouged hands and fingers.

But his sojourn at Raynes Park didn't last long. In 1937, he, Pasmore and Coldstream set up the School of Drawing and Painting in Fitzroy Street, which later moved to become the Euston Road School. While it was getting established, Claude worked at a few portrait commissions and Garrett kept his Raynes Park job open for him, with Rupert Shephard as stand-in. But Claude finally resigned in June 1938. He died in 1977. His last gift to the school had been a portrait of Garrett, painted in 1950. It shows him in a blue suit and waistcoat, with wide lapels and a red woolly tie quite loosely knotted with a soft shirt. He has that familiar look – expectant, quizzical, with a jovial, well-fed, optimistic smile and what Rogers described as 'those debauched eyes'. It catches him well.

Claude Rogers was one of those who saw no special merit in John Garrett's ambition to create at Raynes Park a 'public school' atmosphere. The 'material' he had to work with, he would say, was naturally intractable, and in any case, the boys had their own culture.

Quite so, but in that culture there were already elements of what Garrett wanted, derived at second-hand from our parents' ideas of what had made England (not Britain, in those days) great, and from the books and boys' weeklies we read. Raynes Park boys tended to take *The Magnet* or *The Gem*, or the more raffish publications of D C Thomson of Dundee like *The Hotspur*, *The Pilot* or *The Wizard*, the last-named being devoted exclusively on its first appearance to school stories. This was its main selling-point: they might be schools for footballers or for practical jokers, or just ordinary boys, but schools they were, and not all day schools either, even though they had an indefinably 'common' feel about them compared with Greyfriars, St Jim's or Rookwood, the public schools featured in the stories that flowed without stint from the pen of Frank Richards.

All these fictitious places were bastions of the old principles of fair play and patriotism, and they influenced the way we behaved. There comes to my mind an episode that took place one night after school in the late thirties. I think it must have been November because the evenings have drawn in and a festive end of term seems near. Two boys have fallen out and are having a fierce, flushed argument: one is Simmonds, a slim, freckled, romantic boy always out on some Dawn Patrol of his own imagination, and the other is Hambrook, stocky, phlegmatic, dark, and slow-moving. Simmonds proposes settling the argument with fisticuffs – but 'properly', according to the rules, in the Gym with boxing gloves.

Instead of scoffing at him, Hambrook agrees. Someone is sent to the Staff Room to get Alan Milton, the embodiment, with his international hockey cap and zealous, open manner, of English decency and pluck.

Milton (with reluctance, it's said) stops what he is doing, and after a longish interval during which the antagonists' tempers cool somewhat, he arrives at the Gym. He has removed his jacket and donned gym shoes, as though such a serious matter required at least an approximation to the correct outfit. This is Raynes Park, and Garrett's 'school day' is far from over: there are boys all over the place – in school societies, in the library, some at their desks doing their homework, others just 'messing about'. From this rump of the normal daily population, a small group of boys has collected, but to their disappointment, Milton locks the gymnasium doors, and we have to deduce what we can from the thumps and muffled gasps audible now and then through the curtained glass panes in the double doors on the corridor. Milton doesn't want any barracking to interfere with the course of schoolboy justice.

Of course it emerged later that the fight was entirely indecisive, but the incident shows how we tended towards a Harry Wharton code of honour: at Greyfriars the argument would have been settled in a roughly similar fashion behind the Fives Court, whatever that might have been. But whatever the chosen arena, it would have been unsportsmanlike of Hambrook to decline the challenge: he was probably a *Magnet* reader too. As for Simmonds, I have a later memory of him, returning to the school some months after leaving. It is 1940, the first school Open Night of the war. Simmonds has been one of the first Old Boys to enlist, and he turns up in full uniform, resplendent as, of all things, a private in some Highland regiment, with khaki tunic buttoned to the neck, a kilt, a sporran, and a dagger in his sock. I observe him sitting in the cloakroom surrounded by admiring cronies, leading them in a chorus of 'Here's a toast to the next man that dies.' I am glad to say Simmonds survived the war.

At school, you didn't cheat and you didn't sneak. If you knew someone had done something wrong, it wasn't up to you to tell the masters. There was a Latvian boy, Zolmanis, fat, rich, rather unpopular and a butt for chauvinistic scorn. More than once he scandalised the rest of the form by openly naming some offender to the form master – and expecting to be applauded for it. (When the war started, Zolmanis disappeared back to Latvia and was never heard of again: oddly, we missed him.) Fights had to be equal: 'Two on to one – not fair' was a playground rule. And if two boys had a fight, an audience would quickly assemble and form a ring so that the fighting could be watched and any fouls discovered. But if one of the contestants wanted a temporary truce, he could cry 'Faynites!' and the appeal would be respected.

There was also a tacit agreement that you didn't 'disgrace' the school uniform, which you were expected to wear all the time when you went out, even at weekends. If you were in your school cap and blazer you didn't lark about on buses or in shops. If you saw a master outside the school, you raised your cap to him. Within limits, in or out of school, you were expected to look tidy, and would have been told off if your shoes weren't polished or your shirt-tail were hanging out.

Playground games were then much as they are now. 'He' (or

148

'It') was the most popular, and preferred to ball games: football was seldom played in the gaps between lessons, and certainly not rugger. Occasionally there were other diversions, such as Grandmother's Footsteps, or a game known as Chariots: two boys linked arms, while another boy held on behind them with a fourth riding piggy-back. This precarious group would then run races with others similarly arranged.

Every now and then, crazes swept through the school like minor epidemics. There were the standard, sometimes seasonal ones, like conkers, fivestones or marbles; there were paper pellets fired with elastic bands, spinning tops, pocket mirrors to reflect the sun and cigarette cards for collecting or flicking. Then there were others, newer and more transitory: the Yo-Yo, for instance, whipped on by the *Daily Express* in a special Yo-Yo column ('Next week: how to make your Yo-Yo "walk"'). The *Express* also popularised the idea of the 'doodle', a drawing idly executed on any handy piece of paper while you were waiting for something. Leander Richardson reported having seen in his father's newspaper the headline, 'This is a photograph of the Prince of Wales's doodle.'

As crazes do, these came and went, enjoying a brief popularity like the catch-phrases on comedy programmes on the wireless, which were followed eagerly and discussed in the morning, with imitations of the likes of Claude Dampier, Stainless Stephen, Tommy Handley and Arthur Askey. 'Children's Hour' had an avid following, though in our house this couldn't compete with what was on the National Programme from London, namely the BBC Dance Orchestra.

Garrett preferred to make us aware, if he could, of superior values. In 1937 he launched the School Play: always Shakespeare, and the producer was always the debonair, well-liked French master, Frank Beecroft, although for reasons of his own Garrett refused to have Beecroft's name printed in the programmes, perhaps wanting the credit for himself. The first production was *Julius Caesar*, with two girls, daughters of some of Garrett's friends, brought in to play Portia and Calpurnia, one of them with the ominous name of Sandra Molestova. There was also a score or so of junior boys dressed in sacking as the Roman mob, surging in through the audience in an unconvincing Cockney mêlée shouting, 'Caesar! Caesar! Caesar!' *Hamlet* followed, this time with boys in the women's parts – Ophelia and Gertrude and ladies of the court. I was one of those, attired in grey *crêpe-de-chine* with a pink stand-up collar and sash, and with one line, shared with all the other extras: 'Lights! Lights! Away! Lights!' But, this being Raynes Park County School, the production was reviewed in the *Daily Telegraph*: Garrett, presumably, knew the paper's theatre critic; it was presented in the paper as though for mere county school boys to act in Shakespeare was an unheard-of phenomenon.

Next we had *Twelfth Night*. Rupert Shephard, who had worked in the Group Theatre, was pressed into creating the stage designs and was puzzled to overhear two members of the troupe asking coolly when the *Statesman* review would be appearing. What's more, they weren't joking. The review went in a few days later. *Macbeth* was next, with my brother as Lady Macbeth (I played Third Apparition, my hopes for a good part frustrated again). There were the usual reviews, and this time a news story with photograph, in the *Evening Standard*.

What these productions had to commend them, it is hard to say. Photographs in the corridors at the school showed lines of boys standing stiffly, under garish lighting, in fudged-up Elizabethan costumes, with wrinkled tights and the worried, vacant look of guests who have arrived too soon at a fancy dress party. My memories of the verse-speaking are that it was often poor and in too many cases scarcely audible, as our South London accents struggled with Shakespeare's mighty, incomprehensible images. The reviews, preserved by Garrett in a large scrap-book, give praise in such guarded and at times condescending terms that it seems fairly obvious that critics like Raymond Mortimer and Rosamund Lehmann were merely doing Garrett a favour.

Garrett was a brilliant manipulator of his friends and acquaintances: the list of his achievements in that respect is awe-inspiring. By the time he had been at Raynes Park for six years, not only had he managed to cajole or persuade a formidable number of prominent people to come and give lectures free of charge to selected groups of boys, but also to eat the terrible School Dinners, sitting on the stage with Garrett at what he was pleased to call High Table, with one or two masters and chosen boys who were expected to profit by, and who knows, contribute to the sparkling conversation. Meanwhile, in the Hall below, the lumpen life of the school went on as usual.

The distinguished visitors included (to choose a few at random) John Lehmann, Stephen Spender, Louis MacNeice, Arthur Calder-Marshall, Michel St-Denis, Nevill Coghill, Dacre Balsdon, A L Rowse, Rupert Doone, Robert Medley, Benjamin Britten, Father D'Arcy, George Lansbury. Some came to lecture, others merely to have a look round, talk to John Garrett and some of the boys. Some came to divert us in other ways. Michael Redgrave, appearing in *The Beggar's Opera*, came to sing some of Macheath's songs. Sybil Thorndike gave a one-woman Shakespeare recital, moving from side to side as she hectically assumed one character after another.

Other schools had local politicians or retired generals to give away the prizes. Not Raynes Park. We had Sir Richard Livingstone, Lord David Cecil, and (surely Garrett's crowning act of persuasive skill) T S Eliot, who not only presented the prizes but then came again on another occasion, to speak to a small group of Sixth Formers. Afterwards there were questions. Charles Honeker, a timber merchant's son who was one of the intellectual stars of the school, asked the great man what he meant by a certain line in one of the poems. Eliot gave his standard answer: 'It means whatever you want it to mean.' Honeker, blinking nervously: 'I'll tell you what you meant by it' (scandalised giggles). Eliot listened politely to Honeker's exegesis, then gave a long and incomprehensible reply, as though talking to himself.

The visitors included musical as well as literary people. The violinist Elizabeth Lockhart came, sometimes with Stephen Spender's wife Natasha Litvin, to give violin and piano recitals.

Garrett wasn't particularly musical, but he took these events seriously, ostentatiously closing his eyes and wearing on his face an expression of strenuous appreciation. As a rule, a boy would be picked to hand the soloists a large bouquet when the recital came to an end. Once, he chose me. I had instructions to go up to the platform on Garrett's signal, and hand over the flowers, bowing from the waist. I sat through the concert growing more nervous by the minute, disliking the idea of being stared at and disliking almost as much the fact that there was a large, showy bouquet under my chair, which I was afraid would label me either a cissy or a toady. There came a moment when with a flurry of arpeggios the two women reached the end of whatever they had been playing, and Garrett turned round to direct a noisy *OH!* or *AH!* at someone sitting behind me, searching the Hall with his gaze, clapping as he always did, long and slow, his hands coming together and exploding like cowpats falling on wet grass. Misinterpreting this as the dreaded signal, I picked up my bouquet and strode forward, scarlet with embarrassment, marched up the steps and thrust the flowers at Miss Lockhart. 'But I haven't finished,' I heard her say. Having no other choice, she took the flowers nevertheless, and I returned to my seat, grinning sheepishly. It was a bad moment, but Garrett evidently excused my gaffe, because a few weeks later he sent for me and once again gave me the job of handing over a complimentary bouquet. I have forgotten who the recipient was to be this time: it might have been Natasha Litvin on her own, but whoever it was, I made precisely the same blunder and proffered the flowers before the end of the recital. This time I was not forgiven. I wasn't asked again, and I was extremely glad of it.

Sometimes I wondered innocently why Auden himself never appeared at the school. Of course I knew nothing of his rift with Garrett and he seemed a conspicuous absentee, though he did at some time pay a private visit and had left his mark in the form of a signature on a copy of the school song. There was also a cigarette burn he had allegedly left on the Blüthner grand piano Basil Wright had presented to the school.

There was a tiff, too, between Garrett and Cecil Day Lewis, for a long time one of the school's loyal supporters. At least once a year he would arrive to give a reading of his poetry or to sing from his repertoire of Irish or Scottish folk-songs, or German *lieder* with Frank Beecroft as his accompanist: Garrett had good reason to be grateful for Beecroft's talents. Once, after some important school occasion, perhaps a performance of a school play, Garrett and Beecroft, with Day Lewis and Rosamund Lehmann, repaired to a friend's house near Wimbledon Common. Whisky was brought, records were put on, and Garrett, in a state of tipsy euphoria, seized Rosamund Lehmann round the waist. 'Come on, you great big beautiful bitch,' he cried, 'dance with me!' Together, they glided across the parquet while Day Lewis glared at them in a jealous rage. His anger lasted many weeks, much to the chagrin of Garrett.

Day Lewis had peevishly turned his back on him, but things were patched up in time. Indeed, in July 1941 Day Lewis made handsome amends. He and L A G Strong, the Anglo-Irish novelist and poet who was another Raynes Park supporter, together dedicated their *New Anthology of Modern Verse* 'To the Staff and Pupils of Raynes Park County School'. Strong, as did Basil Wright, later became a Governor of the school. He was another of Garrett's Oxford acquaintances and was brought in to judge the school's poetry-recitation contests, for which an annual prize was given for the best recitation in front of the entire school. (Prefiguring later developments in the careers of all three of us, this prize was won successively by myself, Derek Cooper, and Robert Robinson.) Strong, a courteous, friendly man, had been at Wadham College and had also taught in Oxford, at Summer Fields School. He had known Cecil Day Lewis as well as another Oxford poet, Day Lewis's Wadham contemporary and a classical scholar of the college, Rex Warner. Rex joined the staff of Raynes Park in 1940 to teach Classics and to apply himself to the activities of what was called the Alpha Class, a group of high-fliers who met to discuss philosophy, politics and the history of culture. Rex Warner was another of Garrett's plum acquisitions, and indeed the last, although we nearly had another Thirties poet on the staff, George Barker, who asked Garrett for a job. He was turned down. Somehow, he failed to satisfy Garrett's criteria.

Twelve

MORNING ASSEMBLY AT Raynes Park was an occasion
Garrett choreographed into a carefully worked-out ceremony.
Gibb, the Second Master, would be the first member of staff to
make an appearance, standing alone on the platform at the end
of the Hall, crow-like in his gown, hymn-book clasped in both
hands, surveying without a smile the entry of files of boys, who
had assembled form by form in the corridor at the opposite end
of the Hall, and whose sparrowish chattering ceased as they
came under Gibb's scrutiny. Juniors proceeded to the front,
seniors stayed at the back, with the Sixth Form, when eventually
there was one, along one side. They had chairs to sit on.
Everyone else had to sit on the floor. Prefects were lined up by
the door through which, when all were assembled, the masters
would enter, filing on to the stage in their gowns – which, of
course, they wore throughout the day when they were teaching.
They remained standing on the platform in front of their chairs.
Then, when Gibb or the Prefect of Hall had shouted for silence,
the double doors to the staff corridor would open again.

Enter John Garrett.

He too wore his gown, but unlike the other masters he also
wore his 'square' (he always used the Oxford term for what we
thought was a mortar-board), removing it again when he
reached the table in front of the staff and faced the school.
Sometimes you could predict from his manner, or the glare he

directed at his audience, what the tone of the morning announcements would be, after we had sung a hymn and heard him say a prayer, followed by the Lord's Prayer. Sometimes – rarely – he had nothing to say. Usually he had a word of reproof, praise or advice. Once he devoted the morning speech to telling us that lunch at school ought to become more of a social occasion than it was: not merely a matter of bolting the food and making a beeline for the playground. We were to make conversation: 'Be witty!' he exhorted us, while the boys looked blankly back. No doubt he hoped the epigrams would fly back and forth that day across the trestle tables as we remembered his words over deep-fried beef sausages.

Morning Assembly was also the time for announcements about serious matters: lists were publicly read out of boys who had bad reports, or there might be some grave warning about misbehaviour on local public transport, or boys might have been reported not to have raised their caps when meeting a master in the street. Business over, we sang another hymn, with Beecroft, as always, at Basil Wright's Blüthner. Then, donning his 'square' again, Garrett would stride out, the masters following, with Gibb at the rear. Prefects supervised our departure.

Garrett spent most of his time in his study, but had the habit of roaming the school during the day: his brisk figure would be seen through the opaque interior windows of the classrooms as he passed by. When school was over, he would have another look round, appraising the 'school day': the school's community life was expected to go on after lessons were done. The Science master, Frank Halliwell, wrote down and kept something Garrett said in his opening speech to the assembled boys, on the school's first day in September 1935: 'I want you to regard your school, from the very beginning, as a place to which you like to come and in whose friendly walls you like to linger.' Out-of-class activities were encouraged: the Art Club, the Stamp Club, Mock Trials and debates, Voluntary Gym and the Gardening Club, and during the war, the Pig Club. Every boy was expected to stay to School Dinner (witty repartee at the ready) and before

afternoon lessons began, there were more things to do: gramophone recitals, play rehearsals, the Train Club, the printing
press.

During his after-school patrols Garrett would sometimes stop
and engage any stray boy in conversation. Once he found me
sitting alone in 3a's form room, long after everyone else had
gone. I was doing my homework. To my dismay he came in and
began questioning me about my school life. Why hadn't I gone
home? Who were my best friends? What did I like doing? What
was I interested in? When I mumbled something in twelve-year
old embarrassment about being keen on heraldry (it was because
I'd read Conan Doyle's adventure novels of the Hundred Years
War, *Sir Nigel* and *The White Company*), he pronounced his
headmasterly verdict that the important thing was to be
interested in something, it didn't appear to matter what. Then,
with an italicised commendation of my having stayed behind to
do homework (though it was only because I hadn't wanted the
fag of taking my books home), to my relief he was gone.

Other boys had similar encounters. The story got round that
one boy in the Fifth Form had been asked some very personal
questions. Did he masturbate? The boy, whose name was Page,
was mystified. Commonly known, Garrett translated, as tossing
off. Page, who played drums in a dance-band and later left
school to become a jockey, blushingly admitted that he did.
When? Garrett next wanted to know. Well, said Page, *you*
know, when I feel like it. Well, don't worry, he was told, it's
only a habit you get into. The conversation puzzled Page's
contemporaries: none of us would have wanted to be interrogated by the Headmaster about our private habits. For a long
time I believed Garrett was behaving in a 'progressive' manner,
having convinced himself the conscientious teacher should take
an interest in the emotional problems of adolescent boys.
Perhaps I was wrong; perhaps Garrett's interest in Page's erotic
life was a prurient one.

Of course there were boys with whom Garrett can only be
said to have failed dismally. One was Roy Barnes, expelled from

the school, later awarded a posthumous DFC. Another was Fred Lucas, the louche, rebellious, licentious boy, famous for cheeking the masters and flaunting his individuality through such activities as the after-school sexual larks of which he was usually the star. Garrett caned Lucas more than once, and he was often in disgrace: finally he was expelled, written off as beyond reclaim. John Petit was another, a boy with strong opinions he could express with conviction, author of many brilliant English compositions but chronically untidy and incapable of conforming to school rules. Such things as school uniform and punctuality concerned him not at all. Garrett didn't beat him, but harried him with a special disciplinary régime – Petit had to report daily to the Second Master to have his uniform inspected and to make sure he was on time. No use: Petit's appearance, unpunctuality and rebelliousness were as bad as ever and he was summarily suspended. His response was to stage one-boy raids into the school premises during school hours, leaving threatening messages addressed to Garrett, like some schoolboy Zorro. That was no way to win Garrett over and he expelled Petit forthwith. Unknown to Garrett, Alan Milton visited Petit's house and talked to his widowed mother, then managed to get him an introduction to the Editor of the local newspaper. Soon, though, Petit was called up and joined the RAF: his friends at school lost touch with him.

There were others, boys with whom for one reason or another Garrett had little sympathy: a languid, dandyish boy called Mason, who had played Osric in the school production of *Hamlet* and later went into Fleet Street, annoyed Garrett by daring to sell his first book while he was still at school. It was an anthology of animal verse, published by Pelican, no mean achievement for a 16-year-old suburban schoolboy. Garrett might have been expected to applaud his initiative, but Mason had made the mistake of not informing Garrett what he was doing. Hence, the Headmaster lost no opportunity of pouring scorn on the modest little anthology, reserving his most scathing criticism for the About-the-Author note at the back, where

Mason listed his 'likes' as, 'The idea of flying, and chows' and where it was also stated that he had compiled the collection while studying for School Certificate exams. Garrett read this out to an audience of Sixth Form boys with a loud snort of contempt.

However, Garrett's brilliance as a headmaster was attested by more than one of his former staff, who would speak of his firm control of staff meetings, his clear decisions and sympathetic understanding of their problems. As a class teacher he himself was not too effective. The subject he taught in the school's lower reaches was Religious Instruction: he was devout in his own private life, went to church regularly and told one close friend later in his life that his unfulfilled ambition was to have taken Holy Orders. He presided over Morning Prayers at nine o'clock every day in the School Hall with what appeared to be genuine piety. But his RI lessons were not memorable, consisting of readings from the Bible with brief disquisitions on their meaning. It did not surprise me to read later of a boy being given six strokes in June 1939 for 'reading a novel in my RI lesson'.

In the late summer of that year the cartoonist David Low published a drawing of a typical English holidaymaker with a handkerchief knotted round his head to keep off the August sun, dozing in a deck-chair. Behind him, unobserved, an avalanche was on the point of crushing him, his chair and his newspaper and sweeping the pieces away. Low's complacent Englishman snored on. It might have been a picture of the Vaughan family's annual holiday that summer: a fortnight in Sandown, Isle of Wight, with the Fol-de-Rols on the pier, the Sandown Regatta where we won a competition for making animal noises, and the usual coach-trip to Alum Bay and the Needles. Our holiday was taken as unconcernedly as always. My father's newspaper, the *Daily Express*, had repeatedly told us there would be no war; and, after all, the previous autumn's war-scare had blown over, thanks to Mr Chamberlain, of whom my father approved.

I had seen Alexander Korda's film of Wells' *Things to Come* and knew exactly what to expect if, as my father used to say knowingly, the balloon went up. The film had scared me stiff. I was decidedly put off by the crudely optimistic vision of the distant future, when a pair of lovers in silly little tunics were propelled into space in order to found a new civilisation; but what got to me most was the opening five minutes, in which Bliss's music marched to a grim crescendo and the sky over London was hidden by a locust-cloud of stiffly-moving black bombers.

At the time of the Munich crisis we had been issued with gas masks. Each day we were supposed to wear them for ten minutes at a time in order to get used to them. They were awful: uncomfortable, hot, sweaty and rubbery. But as we turned and looked at each other wearing these pig-like snouts, distress turned to hilarity. When you began to snigger, the rubber vibrating against your face made a farting noise. It was worse when we looked at the master, sitting at his desk with his mask on, a super-porker trying to glare sternly at us and only able to communicate by signs or muffled shouting, like a wasp in a bottle.

It was hard to take seriously these preparations for global war, especially when the *Express* ran a competition to find the best portmanteau name for the respirators ('gask' was one short-listed suggestion). Then the newsreels ran their pictures of Chamberlain waving his piece of paper at Croydon Aerodrome and talking about 'Herr Hitler', with Halifax nursing his withered arm behind him. The audience at the Tolworth Odeon (now a Marks and Spencer's food store) applauded enthusiastically, and commemorative mugs were manufactured with the Prime Minister's face on them, wreathed in quotations – 'I am in my heart a man of peace' and 'Out of this nettle, danger, we pluck this flower, safety.'

The following twelve months, during which our arch-enemy became just plain Hitler, was a peculiar time. Something made me change my behaviour: was it world politics? I doubt it. More likely it was something in the air at home: my father's increasing boredom with his family and his wife, his nightly escapes to the smoky, chummy atmosphere of the pub, located conveniently by the railway station he came home to every evening. For whatever reason, I became one of the form's problem boys, responsive with subjects I liked, bored and inattentive with everything else, and showing my boredom by what must have been an insufferable act in class, wisecracking and finding opportunities for facetious display. My reputation slumped. I was repeatedly carpeted at the end of term, my name humiliatingly read out at Prayers on the list of boys with bad school reports, and summoned to Garrett's study for a dose of his awful brand of scorn and cold rage. None of it made any difference. My reports were as bad as ever, but were shrugged off by my father, who seemed to have other things on his mind.

Now I had my first attack of migraine. I was on the hockey field one day. All at once, there was a tiny empty space in the universe where the ball had been, and unless I looked directly at it, the curved end of the hockey stick wasn't there either. There was an area of nothingness, always just beyond the immediate line of vision, and it got gradually bigger. Then it began to twitch, in a peculiar herring-bone pattern, and gradually spread out into an arc, a 'C' of visual chaos that made it impossible to see what was happening anywhere but right in front of me. I went home, scared, my skull pierced by a headache sharp enough to split it in two. 'Liverishness,' said my father owlishly. 'What have you been eating? Try to avoid fatty foods. I get spots before the eyes, too.' In any case, the whole thing had gone away by that time: he told me to forget about it. But it came again a week later, then two or three times a month, then sometimes in mass onslaughts of four or five a day, one after the other, so that I had to accept it as a recurrent burden I could do nothing about. Sometimes a master would notice my stricken expression, my face yellow with nausea, and send me to the School Secretary, Mrs French, who would give me what she probably gave the masters for their hangovers, a tumbler of Bisodol. Now and then

Garrett would see me sitting miserably in her office and invite me into his study to sit in his armchair, giving me the *New Statesman* to read.

Migraine, surely one of the classic psychogenic afflictions, was doubtless my self-inflicted punishment for delinquency in class, or maybe it could be explained in psycho-analytical terms as a wish to banish something from my sight. For whatever reason, migraine plagued me until I left school, then more or less abruptly stopped. Had all this happened now, in the 1990s, I should probably have been marked down for the Child Guidance Clinic, and perhaps the reasons for my anti-social behaviour would have been unearthed, though I cannot imagine it would have made any difference to the way life went on at 'Wayside'. The fortnight we spent in Sandown in 1939 was the last family holiday. When we came back, the balloon did indeed go up. We listened to Chamberlain's broadcast on 3 September, and within a few hours we were making for Devon, where my mother probably felt her roots were. There had already been a false alarm air raid warning within a few minutes of the despondent and resentful speech in which Neville Chamberlain declared war, and I fully expected the roar of high explosive and the crash of falling buildings to pursue us down the road to the West.

From that journey I remember only the general air of misery that enveloped our Wolseley saloon like a personal raincloud. Nobody knew precisely where we were going but we ended up in the quaint-sounding village of Budleigh Salterton, and rented a house a mile or so from the beach. Having unloaded us and our baggage, my father turned the car round and set off back to London. He was an improvident, unthrifty person, and had no savings he could raid for this emergency. The move was made possible because my mother had saved £60 from her housekeeping allowance. My mother, my brother and I spent four or five miserable weeks at Budleigh Salterton: our friends were hundreds of miles away, the weather was bad and there was nothing to do. There was a cinema that seemed to show only films we'd already seen. My mother tried her best to spend as little as possible.

I bought a map of Europe and stuck it on the wall of my bedroom, then made some tiny flags and lined them up along the French frontier, in the hope that I could start moving them about, like a boy general, as the fighting became serious and the regiments surged to and fro.

Nothing happened. Although the newspapers now and then reported 'movement' on the 'Front', the opposing Maginot and Siegfried Lines remained intact, as far as I was concerned disappointingly so. From the newsreels, it looked like a very hygienic sort of war. There was film of *poilus* being moved about underground on little trolleys, rushing speedily to man their strongpoints. Occasionally there would be pictures of British troops swinging along poplar-lined country roads singing 'South of the Border' and grinning round their Woodbines, giving the thumbs up. More encouraging still were pictures of the Fleet, massive broad battleships in line astern ploughing grimly through the waves, undoubtedly taken in peacetime but newly significant, for we had thrilled to the *Daily Express* headline of 4 September, 'Fleet Begins the Blockade.' Perhaps it was all going to be all right – the blockade had worked before. What was more, my father reassured us, now Winston Churchill was First Lord of the Admiralty again, and we had a man of iron, far preferable to a Birmingham businessman with an umbrella and a Strube moustache.

When he drove down at weekends to see us – not every weekend, because he had 'things to do' in town – my father brought news of what was happening in London. But as the war's deafening silence lengthened and the dust collected on my miniature campaign flags, we three evacuees grew more and more impatient. News reached us that Garrett had worked out an emergency plan, with masters holding tutorials in their houses. Boys who hadn't been rushed off to various private hiding-places, like us, had been formed into small groups, and would make their way from one master's house to another for an hour's lesson, and in spite of extra homework, I envied them. It was certainly preferable to exile in South Devon, where my mother's £60 was dwindling. My father capitulated. Back we came. Almost at once my brother and I went down with chicken-pox, but even that was better than perishing of boredom in Budleigh.

As for the war, it was beginning to seem like some huge mistake. The tutorial system was soon abandoned, the school was reopened with brick shelters in the grounds, and an air-raid drill prepared and practised just in case. None of these events, great or small, did anything to improve Vaughan P W's view of the world, and with School Certificate looming, I was still the form wag, at least in Maths, in which we were taught by a polite, flustered young man of Quaker persuasion called Robinson. Somehow I managed to put out of my mind the imminence of this big exam which everyone but me seemed to think important, chattered inanely through Robinson's classes, dreamed my way through Geography and Science, and failed abjectly in the Mock Exam. The worst school report I'd ever had ('His dismal failure' . . . 'Lazy and ineffective term' . . . 'Extremely unpleasant attitude in class') and another of those *mauvais quarts d'heure* in Garrett's study did somehow convince me something had to be done. Piqued by the things they had said about me, I determined to pay them out. And then, all of a sudden, the war became serious again: the Blitzkrieg shattered the drawing-room calm of the war's first nine months, the fool's paradise that came to be known as the Sitzkrieg, frontiers fell like playing-card houses, governments caved in. John Ellis, a lanky, ironical boy who was one of the few who went home to lunch, was instantly surrounded when he came back to school for an account of what he had heard on the wireless lunch-time news. Holland had fallen, then Belgium, the Germans had over-run Denmark, and Norway was next; German tanks were in sight of Paris and the British Expeditionary Force was scrambling for the Channel. And 5a was taking School Certificate.

*

The school broke up shortly afterwards. The masters must have wondered if Raynes Park County School would ever have another Morning Assembly. The Battle of Britain started, and we had our first air raid. My father had dug a large hole in the back garden and built an air raid shelter, rather like a narrow dug-out on the Somme, so far without the mud. It was half in and half out of the ground. There was just enough room for two bunk beds, one on top of the other, and a couple of old fireside chairs. There were sandbags on top and a sacking curtain, and one morning they had been left undrawn when the siren started its stomach-curdling *glissandi*: hence I was able to catch the briefest possible glimpse of a brilliantly painted German fighter, yellow and green, like some huge mad parrot, strafing the Kingston Bypass with its machine guns cackling. When the All Clear sounded, I ran over to see the bullet-holes in the concrete where I'd bicycled to school for the last four years.

Up above, the air battles had the excitement of a war film. You could watch the vapour trails as the pilots swooped and dived and climbed away, and you could hear in the distance the screaming of engines and the tapping of machine guns. I never saw a plane brought down, but each day the newspapers gave the score, almost as though it were some international sporting contest – with the British, of course, winning, the numbers (as was later admitted) being artificially improved as a prop to national morale.

A prop was well and truly needed when the Luftwaffe changed its tactics. One weekend afternoon, defying the sirens, we had gone for a swim in the Surbiton Lagoon. While we changed to go home, the sirens sounded: the pool cleared like magic and with my father and an uncle, we scorched down the Bypass and made it home before anything happened. It was all unpleasantly quiet. Then the humming of engines, a thin whistling, and an explosion, then a couple more, while we sat tense in the gloom of the little dug-out in the garden. When it was over, I bicycled out to have a look. Bombs had fallen less than half a mile away: a house in South Lane, on the way to New Maiden and my mother's 'village' street, had been abruptly demolished. Dust hung about, ambulance bells sounded.

My father was proud of the shelter he had created, and for the benefit of visitors was pleased to run through the details of its construction – how many spits deep, how many planks of timber were under the sandbags on its roof, how he had taken maximum advantage of the house as a means of deflecting blast, etc, etc – but when the night raids started the dug-out began to show its inadequacies, being cold, cramped, and far from dry. Curiously, however, the sounds the neighbours would have heard most often from the Vaughan family shelter were not moans of discomfort and panic, but hearty laughter. As shelter reading I had taken two books by 'Beachcomber', the name under which for many years J B Morton wrote his comic column, called *By The Way*, in the *Daily Express*. I giggled helplessly in my corner, and my parents, more irritated than amused, demanded the reason: eyes streaming with tears, hardly able to get the words out, I would read to them from the adventures of Lady Cabstanleigh, Mr Justice Cocklecarrot or Big White Carstairs ('Trousers Over Africa'), while the sirens ululated and the ack-ack guns begun to rumble. Soon the whole family was laughing uncontrollably.

Even Beachcomber's lunatic invention was in vain when the afternoons grew shorter and the raids longer. My father converted the small room downstairs, the one nobody had known what to do with, into an indoor shelter. A local builder was called in to remove the floorboards, dig down into the foundations and set up more bunk beds. The walls and ceiling were reinforced with timber props, and now our shelter looked more businesslike, further proof that my father had entered the spirit of the times. His office had been moved from the Old Bailey to Staines, and he drove there every day. In the glove compartment of the Wolseley he stowed a gleaming leather holster containing a fully loaded service pistol. My Uncle Alf, the family's arch fixer and now a Quarter-Master in the Royal Army Service Corps, had got it for him. My father would take it out and show it covertly to passengers – should there be an invasion and the balloon go up again, and if he met any parachuting Germans, who were said to have dropped over the Low Countries disguised, improbably, as nuns, there were, he declared grimly, 'six rounds in the chamber, and one up the spout'. The last round, he indicated, would be for himself, because they'd never take him alive. I couldn't take these cinema heroics seriously. I knew he wasn't a particularly belligerent man, really: his was more a kind of Tory truculence, but it was in harmony with the Dunkirk spirit of defiance that possessed us in the suburbs in response to Churchill's thunderous, lisping rhetoric. And as he weeded the garden or attacked the steadily diminishing Sunday joint, my father would repeat some of the Prime Minister's best phrases. 'We will fight on the beaches', and 'Some chicken, some neck!', he would declare, with an excited, falsetto catch in his voice. 'Let 'em come! We're ready for 'em!'

All the same, you still had to get to school. I had strict instructions not to take the bus any more but to walk, in case 'something happened', and I would set off early to be in time for Prayers (put back to nine-fifteen as a concession to the times), plotting which house or garden I would dive into for shelter. I nursed apprehensive memories of the yob pilot in that green and yellow Messerschmitt screaming along above the road with its guns chattering. I managed to get to school every day without being shot at, but there was a special humiliation waiting for me, of the kind that can make a fourteen-year-old's heart heavy with resentment. I blamed Garrett for it. My school report for the previous term had been equivocal ('I hope the improvement has not been too late') but evidently it was assumed I had failed the exam, and I was not promoted to the Sixth Form but relegated to the Upper Fifth, a kind of lumber room for misfits and dolts, most of whom were going to leave as soon as they could manage it.

How trivial my disgrace seems now. Not at the time: I felt it keenly, the ignominy of failure, of having been passed over, the panicky sensation of being borne away on some path in life one hadn't chosen. My old classmates were drifting away from me. If I met them they would give lordly accounts of the privileges and pleasures of life in the Sixth, but I had been bundled away into the Upper Fifth, forced to start all over again with dreaded Maths, incomprehensible Physics and tedious Geography.

There were three weeks to wait until the results came through. Then we were summoned to the Hall, and Garrett read the lists aloud with measured solemnity, pausing now and then to make a comment, while I sat in misery, my heart beating urgently, expecting the worst. But when he came to my name, Garrett's voice took on an incredulous tone: in three subjects I had failed, but in the rest I had been given Credits, and they had decided to let me through. I had made it. Jubilant, I emptied my desk in the Upper Fifth classroom and went to the school library, where the Sixth Form worked, feeling like a Duke in exile who had been pardoned, and was now triumphantly reunited with friends and allies.

Of such private tragedies and triumphs are our schooldays made. Most of the time, the adults in charge know nothing about them. They have forgotten how sharply disappointment can bite and can no longer understand the terrible poignancy of a school failure.

Thirteen

FOR THE ARTS Sixth, Garrett had a special eye. We were his favourites, considered most likely to collect honours in the sort of sphere he understood, the ones who always attended talks by visiting celebrities, were organised into trips to the theatre, and had the best masters. Even our quarters were privileged: they were in the Library, out on a wing and set apart from the rest of the school.

Each boy was allocated a shelf for set books and grammars: Whitmarsh and Jewkes' *Advanced French Course for Schools*, Smith's *Latin Dictionary*, Caesar's *Commentaries*, Trevelyan's *English History*, Hugo's *Ruy Blas*, Beaumarchais' *Figaro* plays, *The Oxford Book of French Verse*, *Antony and Cleopatra*, *Henry IV Part One*, *Victorian Narrative Poems*, and, of course, *The Poet's Tongue*.

We affected the rôle of intellectal élite: superior, snobbish, grand, no more than glimpsed by other boys who came to the Library as deferential visitors, book borrowers, supplicants. In the changed atmosphere of the Sixth Form, masters were more friendly, you were expected to work without supervision and show signs of independent thought. My accomplishments in that respect were negligible, but I had other matters to concern me. By this time, aged fifteen, I was being overwhelmed by music: it was like some incurable viral infection. 'Some people are more ear-minded than others,' Aaron Copland once said, and for better or worse I was one of those. I could hear a whole orchestra in my head. I moved about the school and around the suburban roads on my bicycle, with the sounds of Beethoven, Mendelssohn, Brahms and the Russian classics reverberating in full score around my brain, the orchestral colours richer and more glowing than they have ever been since.

One Saturday afternoon I went to a concert at the Queen's Hall, still unbombed. On the programme were *Scheherazade* and Grieg's *Piano Concerto*, and the concert began with the overture to *Russlan and Ludmilla*. I have long since forgotten who was conducting but I shall never forget my excitement when the music started. A live orchestra! Not the sounds I had heard filtered through our wireless or on the wind-up gramophone in the front room. This was the real thing. I was electrified by the sibilance of the strings, the emphatic tympani and the spicy timbres of the woodwind. And the Hall! The music seemed to fill the great austere space above the heads of the audience and the musicians, and for these men – in their afternoon dress, with short black jackets and striped trousers, a uniform long gone out of fashion – I began to feel an ungovernable envy, their movements so casual as they assembled on the platform, yet when the baton came down, able to perform in such concentrated, ravishing synchrony.

We couldn't affort treats like that very often and in any case we were nervous about being caught in the middle of London in an air raid. So my brother and I persuaded my mother to buy a better gramophone, an electric one played through the wireless set and called a Radiogram. The first record we bought was of an orchestra conducted by Constant Lambert, playing Tchaikovsky's *Romeo and Juliet* Overture, probably an entrée to classical music for thousands of adolescents: the label told you it had been recorded in the Kingsway Hall. Every now and then, in quiet passages, you could hear the murmur of traffic outside, the occasional bleep of a motor horn. Then I advanced from Tchaikovsky and bought Toscanini's recording of Beethoven's *Seventh Symphony* and the *Violin Concerto*, with Heifetz. I played both sets obsessively, loudly, over and over again, indulging in transports of romantic exhilaration: it was music that made you want to storm the barricades of prejudice and philistinism and I wanted everybody to hear it. Up went the volume control, and Beethoven's thrilling climaxes spilled out over the Kingston Bypass.

It was around the time when I was starting to explore the mysteries and delights of the string quartet that my musical progress suddenly shot off at a different angle. My attitude to music was not only naively enthusiastic, it was also possessive, arrogant and snobbish. Only 'classical' music was any good. Then one day, another boy talked me into listening to the music he liked. Until then, I had scoffed at it, for what he liked was jazz. I bought 'China Boy' by a band calling itself MacKenzie and Condon's Chicagoans – a misleading name because 'Red' MacKenzie, vocalist and virtuoso of the comb-and-paper and the kazoo, though he may have been somewhere in the studio, didn't play a note on that recording or any of the other three from the same session in December 1927. Next, 'Royal Garden Blues' and 'Jazz Me Blues' by Bix Beiderbecke and his Orchestra, an absurd name for a seven-piece traditional jazz band, but I soon got used to the idiosyncrasies of jazz record labels.

My opposition had collapsed. Now the orchestra in my head was a jazz band. In no time, two men became the twin pillars of my jazz pantheon: the cornet player Bix Beiderbecke and the clarinettist on 'China Boy', Frank Teschemacher. Both were white, and both were dead. Bix had died of drink in 1931, aged only twenty-eight, Teschemacher had been killed in a motor accident a few months later, January 1932, when he was even younger – not quite twenty-six. Both events filled me with a passionate, retrospective regret that their inventive fluency had been untimely cut short, and that they had been victims of a system that favoured crass 'commercialism' in popular music at the expense of the jazz improviser's authentic creative energy. A crude simplification of the facts, but it suited my need for lost heroes to venerate.

I began to collect as many records of both of them as I could afford. Teschemacher was harder to collect than Bix: he only seemed to have made about half a dozen 'sides' as we called them in the days of 78s (now they are 'tracks'). His tense, nervous style of improvisation and the hard, acrid sound of his clarinet epitomised a school of jazz – the music of 1920s Chicago – with a pounding, driving rhythm that could cut through the smoky, gin-soaked air of a speakeasy liable at any moment to be shattered by the rattle of tommy-guns. Teschemacher was a true product of the city, and as I found out later from his friend, the cornet player Jimmy McPartland, he was also the brains of the band, the one who had originally filled the heads of his friends at Austin High School with his own zeal for hot music and supervised their conversion from members of the school orchestra to partners in one of the most exciting groups to emerge in the first flowering of white jazz. Teschemacher was also the one who created the arrangements they used on their records and decided on the order in which solos were to be taken. But it was the sound of his clarinet that was so enthralling – harsh, astringent and far from the suavity of the orchestral clarinet-playing I'd been listening to. Teschemacher's sound was not gruff or 'dirty' like, say, Pee Wee Russell's but reedy, pungent, vinegary, and venturing sometimes into a daring atonality. Now and then I wondered disloyally if this represented not bold innovation but carelessness or studio nerves. That choked grace-note, for instance, in his solo in 'Indiana' – was it really nothing but a squeak, swiftly covered-up and possibly due to a dodgy reed or an ill-cut mouthpiece, but a squeak just the same? It didn't matter. His solo in 'China Boy' took my breath away, starting on a hectic, staccato descending figure, then swerving into a downward glissando and jumping up to six repeated quavers that sounded slightly off-key. Bad tuning? An unreliable clarinet? I didn't care.

But if Teschemacher was the Shelley of jazz, Bix was the Keats of 'the good music' (I had no difficulty adopting the tone of aggressive cultural crusader that was one of the hallmarks of the jazz fan in those days). The Bix Beiderbecke legend had most of the necessary features of my romantic view of art: a young genius forced to prostitute his talent for the benefit of the rich ignoramuses in control of popular culture. Another exaggeration: but when you heard his solo – pure gold – rising from the surrounding wasteland in the Paul Whiteman Band's 'Lonely Melody', it was easy to surrender to the version of Bix's career romantically put forward in a novel popular among fans at the time, *Young Man With a Horn*, by an American writer, Dorothy Baker. Published eight years after Bix's death, this book chronicled in a laconic manner the life of a Bix-like figure called Rick Martin, driven to drink by the pressures of making a living, unable to play the kind of music he wanted. The novel has been credited with having initiated the Bix legend. When a film was made of it in 1950 (prudently retitled *Young Man of Music*), with Kirk Douglas as Rick, the scriptwriter, Carl Foreman, turned the hero's dilemma into a search for an impossibly high note, straining after which almost, but not quite, killed him. Kirk Douglas' trumpet (not cornet) was ghosted off-screen by Harry James, a formidable technician who was an habitué of the instrument's extreme top register and had long since, we thought, sold out to commercialism. Rick's girl friend was played by Doris Day, another absurdity. The film ended, as I remember it, with the voice of Rick's long-time buddy (black in the book, white in the film) telling us, 'Rick had learned to be a human being first, and a musician second', whatever that may have meant – but the crowning irony was that the part was played by Bix Beiderbecke's close friend Hoagy Carmichael, whose autobiography *The Stardust Road*, which came out in 1946, was one of the few authentic jazz texts available to English fans of the period.

It seemed necessary to protect Bix from such betrayals. Somehow one seemed personally involved with him. If you put your ear as close as possible to the sound-box of a wind-up gramophone, or the loudspeaker of the electric record-player, you could almost believe you were in a Columbia or an Okeh Studio in the Depression, so vivid would be the sound of Bix's cornet, so clean the attack on each note and so glowing the sound. As though striving to wipe out the few years since Bix's death, I would strain to catch some echo of the man himself, some faint extraneous noise: someone shuffling his feet, perhaps, clearing his throat or giving a murmur of satisfaction after one of those Bix solos that had printed themselves on my musical memory, and are there to this day.

Being a jazz fan in the 1940s was still unusual enough to mark you out as a rebel against the cultural status quo. It was enjoyable to astonish and annoy parents, relatives and for that matter the staff of Raynes Park with this new obsession. I can still see in my mind's eye the pained surprise with which my grandmother reacted to a Duke Ellington record called *Take It Easy* on the other side of Teschemacher's *Shimme-Sha Wobble* – the very names were enough for her. Cootie Williams' growling trumpet, smeared blue notes and 'jungle' rhythms left her and both my parents cold. Their bafflement was paralleled by the faintly scandalised reaction of my schoolmasters, whose tastes and opinions had previously been immune to challenge. They seemed to accept the jazz cult, shared among only a few boys in the Sixth, with much the same grudging indulgence as they had observed earlier crazes for the potato gun or the Yo-Yo.

I am fairly sure John Garrett would have disliked jazz, and wouldn't have understood it: his tastes in music were oddly conventional – and not only in music. First regarded as a privilege, attendance at his English classes was becoming a bore. Although he had read History at Oxford, he took the Arts Sixth in English, and conducted us through the books prescribed by London University for what was then called Higher School Certificate. Garrett's method was to read aloud a prepared essay of his own on the set book or author before us; from this miniature lecture we were expected to take notes. If we were working on a Shakespeare play he would read it aloud to us, although sometimes he would distribute the parts among the boys. We had the pocket-sized, skimpily annotated New Temple Shakespeare: he had the Arden edition, and thus was able to outwit us in all questions of interpretation. But he never dwelt upon such interesting matters as textual conundrums, nor did he attempt to analyse any of the set texts or discuss their wider meaning.

Garrett belonged to the grand old Oxford Eng-Lit tradition of enthusiastic admiration, expressed in jewelled prose. His notion of the right approach to, say *Antony and Cleopatra* was a review by Ivor Brown or Lennox Robinson or, especially, Harley Granville-Barker, whose *Prefaces to Shakespeare* he also read aloud to us, declaiming certain passages in a voice turgid with approval. 'Not move pity and admiration to the full? Was Bradley colour-blind or tone-deaf? I have read these last scenes score after score of times, and each time some new beauty, sequestered long, is discoverable.' Who was the theatrical pundit of the thirties who, if I have remembered them correctly, wrote these words? Who wrote that each time he read the last act of *Antony and Cleopatra* he found 'the sense ached with its leaping loveliness'? What tosh it all was. No, John Garrett was not brilliant in the form room in spite of his manifest qualities as an organising headmaster.

As a personal counsellor he was better. Once, when I was in a lower form, I had written a story that was commended by the English teacher: the custom was that you had to take the work to Garrett in his study so that he could endorse the master's approval. When he had initialled the much-coveted 'Commended Work' which the master inscribed in your exercise book, Garrett would inscribe your name on a list displayed behind glass on his personal notice board. My story was a supposed eye-witness account of the execution of Louis XVI, the result of reading Baroness Orczy and seeing the film *Marie Antoinette*, in which Robert Morley's performance as the luckless king had touched my adolescent heart. (I learned years later from Sheridan Morley that among the actors this film was known as *Marie and Toilette* because of the immensely long time it took them to put on their period wigs and makeup.) When Garrett read my composition, he proffered a piece of advice: start a writer's notebook, he said, get used to putting things down in it – anything, descriptions of what you see or of what you feel, get into the habit of writing, of using words. My enthusiasm kindled, I did as I was told and bought a notebook: I got under way with a lame description of a thunderstorm in our suburban streets, the end of which was signalled by the sound of the Wall's Ice Cream man ringing the bell on his tricycle and shouting *Wallsee*! (a vanished street-cry of our century), which I recall characterising ornately as 'a message of hope'. I no longer possess this early attempt at descriptive writing, which for a very long time was the only piece the book contained. It was later on that Garrett's well-meant advice bore fruit, and I became as compulsive a keeper of notebooks, lists and commonplace books as Garrett himself.

At home, my brother and I started a poetry-reading circle. A small group of us would meet at weekends, each one bringing three or four poems he'd liked, which he would read aloud: then we would talk about them. Mostly we read the new poets published by Faber and Faber: it was at one of those meetings that someone read a poem by Stephen Spender that began 'Last night I slept with the statue of Apollo': it caused my brother to remark, 'I dreamt I felt his marble balls.'

I doubt if we were the only boys at Raynes Park to bring an interest in literature home with them. The masters, the small talk and school gossip all encouraged a respect for books and writing and it all helped confirm Raynes Park's reputation as a 'literary' school.

Sir Kingsley Amis, who also grew up in South London in the 1930s, once wrote that, in his local environment, 'There was no local pundit, no opener of my eyes to the magic world of the imagination, and I would as soon have expected to fall in with a Hottentot as with a writer.' At Raynes Park we had every expectation of falling in with writers. Not only was there a steady stream of literary visitors, there was, from 1940 on, the presence in the school of the novelist and poet Rex Warner, who in many ways conformed to a 1930s stereotype of The Author – tall, tweedy, baggy-trousered, pipe-smoking, with strong features and a deep voice. By the time he arrived at Raynes Park he had already published two novels, the first of which, *The Wild Goose Chase*, a Swiftian allegory couched in gracefully Augustan prose, had been warmly received. His reputation was consolidated by his next book, *The Professor*, a fable showing up the inadequacy of an old-fashioned humane liberal when faced with the realities of Fascist violence. He brought out his third novel, *The Aerodrome*, in 1941, probably the book for which he is best known, a parable this time of the evils of all forms of totalitarianism, whether from right or left.

In 1937 Rex Warner had also published his first volume of poetry, dedicated to C. Day Lewis, a contemporary at Wadham College. The best poems are the ones about birds ('Lapwing', 'Dipper', or 'Curlew at Sunset') but there are also some In-Letters-of-Red political poems which when I first read them seemed to me stirring stuff:

> Come then companions, this is the spring of blood,
> Heart's heyday, movement of masses, beginning of good.

It could have been this very poem, called 'Ode', that Cyril Connolly parodied in 'The Condemned Playground'.

> M is for Marx, and movement of masses,
> And massing of arses, and clashing of classes.

When Rex brought out a revised and enlarged edition of his *Poems* in 1945, 'Ode' was one of the poems he discarded.

While he was at Raynes Park, Rex Warner wrote another book, which could be regarded as 'the' Raynes Park novel, since it contains material clearly derived from his life there.

The book began as the outline for a film Rex was asked to prepare by Basil Wright. At the time, there was a fashion for 'limbo' stories in films and plays: one thinks of *A Matter of Life and Death*, *Thunder Rock*, *Johnson Over Jordan*. The film of what became Rex's fourth novel would have been Basil Wright's only non-documentary film, but it was never made.

Instead, Rex's outline was published as a novella in 1943, and dedicated to Wright. The title is *Why Was I Killed?*: a subtitle describes it as a 'Dramatic Dialogue'. It is more a series of such dialogues, each one of which seeks justification for the death in action of an unknown soldier, an event briefly described in the opening pages. In them, a group of sightseers in a cathedral has gathered around the fallen soldier's tomb. Each is visited in turn by the spirit of the soldier, whose first-person narrative this is, in the hope that they will give an answer to the question posed in the title of the book. There is a representative of the ruling classes called Sir Alfred Fothey, who mouths conventional concepts of Duty, Patriotism and Honour. There is also a cynical, Blow-You-Jack aircraft engineer who sees the war as a means of feathering his nest, while he remains safe from call-up in his reserved occupation. Either of these characters could have stepped out of an Auden-Isherwood play, stablemates of Sir James Ransom or Destructive Desmond. Another of the group round the tomb is a Man from Spain, who has few doubts over the necessity of sacrifice in a just cause. But it is a woman who has lost both a husband and a son in the war whose words, giving the lie to Fothey's, have the most conviction:

> I hate these ideals which are only mentioned when it is a
> question of persuading men to kill each other. I have only to
> look into my heart to find something finer than all of them.
> You may talk of 'duty to one's country', loyalty', 'sacrifice',
> even 'duty to one's fellow-men', but to me these are
> meaningless and hypocritical words when I see the kind of
> actions to which they lead, and when I compare them with
> the duty which I feel and love, the duty to what is best in my
> heart and to the joy and love and beauty in all the universe.

It is curious that the character of the woman's missing son, a fighter pilot who has been shot down and killed and 'posthumously awarded some decoration or other' has the same surname – Barnes – as the Raynes Park boy I have mentioned, who was killed in similar circumstances and awarded the DFC, and whose mother smacked John Garrett's face. When I questioned Rex Warner about this more than twenty-five years later, he remembered nothing of that boy, and denied there was any connection. But the similarity remains.

There is also a character called Captain Wallace, clearly based on Alan Milton, the Raynes Park History master. Wallace makes his entrance in a chapter describing the boyhood of Bob Clark, the aircraft-factory worker present in the book's opening tombside scene. Wallace is a master at Clark's school, and, Milton-like (one thinks of his attempt to rescue the 'disgraced' John Petit), he goes home with him to try to persuade the boy's mother and father to keep him on at school. He thinks young Bob should go to a university; Bob's father wants him out earning a wage. This time it is Suburban Man versus the Auden generation, and the whole situation is very Raynes Park, except that – contrary to what happened to real Raynes Park boys – Wallace fails to make Clark *père* change his mind. The man has only one interest, and that is a sterile one – collecting garden gnomes and other plaster fauna, which cram his miserable little patch of a front garden with its 'grey and dirty' soil. He is obtuse and narrow-minded and a thoroughly unsympathetic character, even though, as his embarrassed son explains in extenuation, he has been out of work. Unsympathetic, too, on the whole, is Captain Wallace (unlike Milton himself) whose rank is never explained, and whose enthusiasm and eupeptic grin do not make up for his failure to understand the Clarks and their lower-middle-class background. Their house, called Hopedene, must have been like dozens of mean little semis Rex Warner would have passed on his way to school every morning to teach Latin – passed, but evidently not regarded with much sympathy, even though he was a popular man at school and a kindly teacher.

Milton, a man of strong principles who was much loved by the boys at Raynes Park, did not deserve to be depicted this way.

Later, Vice-Principal of the University College of Rhodesia, he led its resistance to attacks by Ian Smith's illegal regime, also preventing its academic isolation. Afterwards he became Pro-Vice-Chancellor of the new University of Ulster and its first Emeritus Professor.

When the book came out, Rex apologised to Milton for what was taken to be an unflattering portrait of a colleague. He insisted it wasn't meant personally. Milton took it all in good part: Rex was not a person against whom one could bear a grudge. This tall, broad-shouldered, ruggedly handsome man was nevertheless oddly unconfident before an audience of boys, with a habit of nervously patting himself with his hand or with a book, either on the top of his head or the back of his thigh – a habit he gave in *Why Was I Killed?* to the blustering, bogus patriot, Sir Alfred Fothey.

Probably it was inevitable in all the circumstances that sooner or later Raynes Park should have supplied the raw material for someone's fiction. It surprises me that it only appears to have happened once. Is John Garrett, I sometimes wonder, in some novel somewhere? After all, he knew a lot of writers and we had earned ourselves a place on the cultural map by the early 1940s, even if it was only a small corner. Once, in 1941, I was one of a group of Raynes Park boys who were asked to make their way to the now-defunct Merton Park Studios, about two miles down the road towards Tooting. Our job was to help with the incidental music for a Ministry of Information short they were finishing. This had been fixed up by the Art Master, George Haslam: Rupert Shephard had left in 1939 to spend all his time painting – in the event, he spent a good deal of it in a drawing office. Haslam had some connection with Merton Park, and later left the school to work there.

The film they were completing on this occasion was intended to promulgate the nation's war aims: our role was to represent Britain's youth – off-screen. Also present were some girls from a local secondary school. This ad hoc choir assembled in a large, cluttered barn of a studio to sing a song composed by Richard

Addinsell, something of a celebrity as composer of the *Warsaw Concerto*, a kind of instant Tchaikovsky concerto: it had been composed for a film called *Dangerous Moonlight*, in which the German actor Anton Walbrook played a Polish concert pianist turned RAF pilot. Our song wasn't the kind to achieve anything like the fame of the *Warsaw Concerto*, but I find I can remember to this day the words (and the tune – a tribute to Addinsell's talents). The sturdy, well-meaning sentiments in them would be expressed differently now.

> Tom, Dick and Mary,
> We're all on the job!
> Jack, Joan and Judy,
> Bill, Bess and Bob!
> Life's our adventure
> And we're on our way,
> All set to make a world for freedom
> One fine day!

Raynes Park at war began to change. One or two of the masters had joined up, but two were conscientious objectors. Alan Milton was one. Garrett tried to talk him out of it, but failed. Then he got A L Rowse to 'have a word' during one of his visits to the school: that was also in vain. Garrett had to put up with Milton's non-conformity. Sam, with the bad teeth and baggy trousers, joined the RAF, and Gibb the Home Guard, in which he was rapidly promoted to Captain. Part of the gardens became allotments and the school bought a pig, looked after by the boys, who formed a Pig Club. A school squadron of the Air Training Corps was mustered, with the Head of the Science Department, Frank Halliwell, as Commanding Officer, assisted by the PT master, Sweeney, who caused a sensation by turning up on parade, not in his usual white gear and silk scarf, but in the uniform of a Pilot Officer.

Somehow it seemed all the most boring boys were in the ATC, the ones who'd been Patrol Leaders in the Scouts or had become peculiarly officious prefects. Some of us in the Sixth Form, perhaps infected by Milton's example, stayed out. Instead, we did gardening, helping to grow vegetables which, more than likely, finished up on the Headmaster's table. Pressure was put upon us to join up: Garrett made speeches at Assembly, declaring the importance of doing one's bit while eyeing the Sixth Formers lined along one wall who were not in uniform. We gave in. We were issued with uncomfortable serge uniforms all too reminiscent of the itchy clothing still worn by the 19th Wimbledon Scout Troop, and attended twice-weekly parades. These were spent on Aircraft Recognition and Principles of Flight, but mainly on drill, to which for some reason great importance was attached: while Halliwell or Sweeney rapped out orders, we would march around the playground succumbing all too often to fits of helpless giggling, stumbling around the tarmac snorting with suppressed laughter. It was the absurdity of it all: the sense of everyone involved behaving out of character, the ridiculous forage caps, with Sweeney wearing his right in the centre of his head, giving his face a pinched, narrow look. How could you take it seriously?

One answer came when they sent us on a trip to a neighbouring airfield for a short flight in a Tiger Moth. Issued with parachutes and flying helmets, we lined up outside the hangar waiting for the summons to walk out to the plane, with the packed chutes bumping the backs of our knees. Suddenly it was my turn. With racing pulse I clambered into the rear cockpit. The pilot waved. We were rushing along the take-off strip: I tried to think of Biggies and Algy as the engine roared and the ground fell diagonally away. 'Anything particular you'd like to do?' yelled the pilot. 'Want to go anywhere?' 'I'd like to go above the clouds,' I shouted back. We duly did. For the first time I saw that expanse of solid-looking cotton wool stretching away without limit, a rare sight for civilians in those days. 'Take the stick,' yelled the pilot, 'try moving it gently from side to side.' The Tiger Moth rocked alarmingly: all at once the air beneath us seemed even more insubstantial. Then the pilot took over and we banked down into that huge fluffy white pillow and were flying down through skeins of thick mist. Within five minutes we were on the ground again and it was all over.

It was more exciting than the air raids, which by this time had become more tedious than frightening. Hours were spent sitting in the school's brick shelters with masters trying to continue lessons in the dim light. One morning the siren wailed at about nine o' clock. Rex Warner, on his way to school, became aware of the sound of a bomb, as he crossed the road on his way to the school's back gate – that sound like an express train coming at you head-on from the sky in a spine-chilling crescendo. Remembering what he'd been told to do, he lay flat on the ground, then realised he was actually lying on a level crossing, hardly a prudent place to lie down, bomb or no bomb. Next to the crossing was a small tobacco kiosk. Like a rugby forward diving for the goal-line, he hurled himself into the shop, grabbing the elderly proprietress round the waist as though in a tackle. There was a huge explosion, and the two of them, tangled together on the floor, were showered with chocolate, boiled sweets, broken glass and packets of war-time cigarettes, Ark Royal, Gold Flake, Senior Service. The bomb, though close, was a small one, but it had landed almost at the spot on the level crossing on which Rex had been lying face down. From then on, the tobacco-shop woman regarded this broad-shouldered schoolmaster as the man who had saved her life, and she would keep cigarettes on one side for him when they were in short supply.

That the main characteristic of war was boredom was a truth we had learned. There were air raids when absolutely nothing happened, yet the school was obliged to march outside to the shelters by the playing field and sit in the damp, smelly half-light while our teachers improvised quiz games, spelling bees and general knowledge tests. Garrett's policy was business as usual. Poets and dons and progressive clerics came to lecture, school plays were produced, Day Lewis sang. The play-reading circle, open to parents, continued to meet once a month, and the Sixth Form discussion group, The Partisans (by invitation only: beer provided) met once a week. Garrett accepted one or two women on the staff, stipulating that the boys should address them as 'Sir'. This rule reinforced the general feeling that this dilution of the teaching staff wasn't quite right: proper schools didn't have women teachers.

An opportunity to see for ourselves what a proper school was really like came when Garrett organised reciprocal visits with a public school, Aldenham, in Hertfordshire. The school play in 1941 was *The Taming of the Shrew*. As part of the arrangement between the two schools, the entire production was taken to Aldenham and performed in the school Hall. We stayed the night, sleeping in dormitories and being shown round by lordly boys who explained to us some of the school's unwritten laws: only Sixth Formers were allowed to walk beyond that grass verge, only boys of a certain seniority were allowed to have the bottom button of their blazers undone, only prefects could have their towels around their necks between five and six pm, etc, etc. If this was what we were supposed to be imitating, it didn't seem such a terrific idea. Also, the place was shabbier, seedier-looking than Raynes Park: the furniture was scuffed, old, heavily carved with initials – another practice presumably sanctified by custom and one that would have been frowned on along the Kingston Bypass.

The boys were polite enough but there was an indefinable feeling of being condescended to that soured this attempt at *entente* across the class barriers. One of our number overheard one of the Aldenham boys imitating us. He was talking in an exaggerated Cockney voice to a grinning audience, like a comic servant in a play. It was a bad moment for those of us who were trying to suppress our short O's and A's and other tell-tale signs of what would shortly be called non-U speech. What was more, I was trying to overcome a private handicap I had inherited from my father: the dropped R, otherwise known as the English R, a mild form of dysphasia exhibited also by Field Marshal Montgomery, Graham Greene, Professor C E M Joad and, for that matter, Claude Rogers. I suffered all the tortures of adolescent embarrassment after I had publicly recited at the Verse Speaking Competition a poem by Gerard Manley Hopkins, *Binsey Poplars*, which ended with the line, 'Rural scene, rural scene, sweet especial rural scene.' Determined to escape from the stigma, I would bicycle to school practising trilled R's and trying to manage sentences like *Round the rugged rocks, the ragged rascals ran their rural races.*

By 1942 Garrett's aim to establish an Oxbridge link for Raynes Park was well and truly realised. My brother David, who left in 1941 to go up to Wadham, was one of twenty or so boys who by that time had got places at an Oxford or Cambridge college, an unprecedented achievement for any state grammar school, let alone one that had been going for a mere seven years. Then Garrett dropped a bombshell. He informed us one morning at Prayers that he had been appointed Headmaster of Bristol Grammar School and had handed in his resignation.

He was to leave at the end of the Christmas Term. Moreover he would be taking Frank Beecroft with him. Many boys felt let down, abandoned. So, after all, none of it had been serious! The Headmaster thought his advancement more important than the school's. But who cared: as the term went on, time was running out for me, too. I had taken Higher Certificate and was idling about as one of a small number of boys in the Third Year Sixth, acquiring the reputation, Garrett told my brother, of a desiccated aesthete. It was decided that my brother would leave Wadham and I would go up in his place: the Warden, C M Bowra, agreed to take me even though I was barely seventeen and younger even than that in terms of intellectual maturity.

Having not much else to do, I directed the House Play, choosing the last act of *The Ascent of F6*, for, with its sideswipes at suburban values and nose-thumbing at conventional patriotism, it vaguely represented my own view of the universe. It also conformed to my tastes in reading: I bought Penguin *New Writing* and the *New Statesman*, possessed some of the Faber poets, including Auden and MacNeice, and understood less than half of any of them. However, it was enough to be seen reading these books, or carrying them about.

Politically we veered to the left, stimulated by my father's sternly Tory views. He was an Air Raid Warden, but had improved conditions in the local ARP Post by setting up a bar there. It was curious that he always seemed to be on duty on Sunday mornings about midday, when he would don his blue battledress and blue beret, and with gas-mask and tin helmet over his shoulder, march off to the Post. Sunday dinner would be eaten around two o'clock or later, when his spell of duty had come to an end: invariably it ended with political arguments, when my father, red-faced and barely keeping his temper, argued strenuously with my brother and me over something in that day's *Sunday Express*, while my mother sat in uncomfortable silence opposite him. Feeling the need for a positive gesture, I wrote to the local Secretary of the Young Communist League asking if I could join. A letter came back setting up a rendezvous at Morden Underground Station: my vis-à-vis would be recognisable, he said, by his red tie and brown jacket and he would be carrying a copy of *The Communist Manifesto*. When the day came, I lost my nerve and didn't go, comforting myself instead with books like *Guilty Men*, *The Lion and the Unicorn* and *In Letters of Red*.

As my last term, and Garrett's, went on, he grew sentimental about his approaching departure. 'Will the daffodils bloom when I am gone?' he asked stagily of a boy who was helping him pack his books. The last school event of term was the Carol Conceit. I went home with the Latin words of the hymn in my head: *Adeste Fideles*. I too was full of nostalgic thoughts of the preceding seven years, but excited by the prospects opening before me – my own rooms at Wadham, freedom from constraint and the genteel suburban surroundings of 'Wayside'. But on the following day, the last of term, Garrett staged his most memorable piece of school theatre. After he had given his final speech to the assembled school and we had sung hymns, the

School Song and Parry's *Jerusalem*, he announced that he wished to say a personal goodbye to every boy in the school. We were all to file out through the masters' entrance, where he would be standing.

The ceremony began. The bloods of the Sixth Form were inescapably reminded of the scene in *In Which We Serve* when Captain Noel Coward had shaken hands personally with each member of his destroyer's crew who had survived a catastrophic torpedo attack. Gradually, Garrett broke down, and by the time he got to the Arts Sixth, he was sobbing. When my turn came, I found it hard to look at him: his face was convulsed with grief.

Fourteen

OXFORD IN JANUARY 1943 was slowed down, muted, ticking over, shabby and dimly-lit for the black-out. Its student population was small, and so was its population of dons. The joke of the day, not a very good one, was that the only people still 'up' were cranks, crooks, and crocks: that is, those who had been able to avoid being called up through madness or eccentricity, guile, or genuine ill-health.

There were stories about how you could dupe the army doctor who examined likely conscripts when you were summoned to a room in the Town Hall to have your medical examination. One theory was that if you could convince them you were 'an active homosexual' they were certain to disqualify you. I didn't hear of anyone who had actually tried it, but one man I knew had prepared for his medical by drinking three cups of strong black coffee, masturbating four times in rapid succession and swallowing ten aspirin. With his heart thumping almost audibly, he was graded C3, Unfit for Service. Another had actually been called up and then let go again, after convincing the army he was crazy: 'I told the psychiatrist, "I wake up screaming".' That seemed to have done the trick.

But the cranks-crooks-crocks jest wasn't entirely true. For one thing there were certain University faculties, such as Engineering, Chemistry or Medicine, whose members weren't in any of these categories but were excused because they were deemed to be doing, actually or potentially, work of national importance. Then there were the 'cadets' – the World War Two equivalent of young hopefuls like my father. This time they were probable officers-to-be who had got places on short University courses, although technically they had already enlisted in the Army, the Navy or the Air Force: they lived in college at government expense for six months, dividing their time between service training and academic work with the emphasis on the former. They weren't given degrees. But part of the deal was that when they were demobbed, assuming they survived the fighting and hadn't proved themselves hopelessly stupid, they were more or less guaranteed a place at the University so that they could take a full degree course.

And there were a few people like me, who had been able to slip in through being too young to be called up. The objective for us was something called a War Degree. You could take it bit by bit and it wasn't classified: no firsts, seconds, thirds, or fourths – either you passed or you didn't. But there were three conditions: the first was that you had to pass a series of four exams called sections, and you could take them piecemeal, in any combination of subjects, one at the end of each term. The second condition – harder to fulfil – was that you had to be a resident member of the University for five terms. It meant that somehow you had to put off being, as they rather fancifully put it, called to the colours. There was always the slim possibility that 'the authorities' (that mysterious, unattractive power that directed everything from ration books to road signs) might put off sending for you if you had one last exam to take. It had happened – but it was getting more and more unusual: all around me undergraduate careers were being abruptly halted, in some cases for ever, as the buff envelopes arrived with their curt instructions and warrants for free railway travel.

Then there was the third requirement for a War Degree, and that was that you had to serve the equivalent of four more University terms in whatever branch of the services you ended up: this plus your five terms in residence would add up to the nine of a conventional degree. After that, as long as you'd passed your four sections and if you had a mind to, you could put BA after your name. You could even convert it to MA, not by taking another exam, but in the time-honoured Oxford way, by paying the appropriate number of guineas (twenty, if I remember correctly) to the University Chest.

These bargain basement degrees must have seemed ludicrous and even somewhat disreputable to some of the older dons, but then there was very little that the war hadn't pushed out of place in some way. The University precincts themselves must have seemed uncannily quiet and empty to anyone who'd known Oxford in peacetime. True, the population was slightly enlarged by the presence of evacuees from other establishments: the Slade School of Art had set up shop somewhere, and Westfield, a women's college of London University, had taken over St Peter's Hall. Keble College was occupied by women civil servants: the few remaining Keble undergraduates were living in Wadham, where, as in every other college, there was plenty of room. Instead of being squashed, two or even three to a room, which became the norm when the war was over, nearly every member of the college had a room to himself. After being given my brother's old room in the back quad, I moved soon afterwards to a large room near the porter's lodge, with windows on the main quad on one side and out on to Parks Road on the other. It had a separate bedroom and another small room where coal was kept.

Shabby and ill-furnished though this set was, I was delighted with it. It was close to the mainstream of college life, and the only snag was my scout, a ferocious, moustachioed, stocky man in black boots and a blue suit with a watch chain stretched across his belly, by the name of Tom Butcher. As a senior scout he supervised the dishing out of breakfast, standing over a cauldron of kedgeree with a large turnip watch in one hand: he had no sympathy with an eighteen-year old's deep need for sleep and, on the stroke of nine, closed the cauldron lid with a clang and locked the Hall door. No breakfast. I was self-consciously aware of my inexperience at dealing with servants and felt that with the right kind of public school insouciance I should have been able to deal with this and other examples of Tom's thinly disguised hostility.

I went to few lectures after I heard a fellow-undergraduate, David Dean, remark urbanely that as far as he could see, the usefulness of the lecture as a means of instruction had been largely superseded by the invention of the printing press. I regret my attitude now. Some famous men were to be seen mounting the dais at the Taylorian Institute or the Schools building: C S Lewis (endlessly giving a series called *Prolegomena to Renaissance Poetry*), J R Tolkien, A J P Taylor, Nevill Coghill, C M Bowra himself. The only lectures I attended with any diligence were those by a woman don on phonetics, which helped me to cure at last my inherited problem with the letter 'r', for which I had been ridiculed at school. Armed with new information on the physiology of speech I was able to work out how to trill an 'r' convincingly, and would walk and bicycle round Oxford trilling quietly to myself. This achievement proved invaluable in due time.

Most of the famous University activities had been put on hold. Sportsmen were not being awarded Blues, but the Boat Race was rowed, not on the Thames in London but on the Isis, Oxford's own stretch of the Thames, with its own name. The University Orchestra had been replaced by something called the Musicians Club. (I joined it for a while, playing extremely badly at the back of the second violins.) The OUDS had been wound up temporarily, their substitute a quasi-OUDS called The Friends of the Oxford University Dramatic Society. One of their productions, by Nevill Coghill, earned a place in theatre history: *Measure for Measure*, done in Christ Church Cloisters in June 1944 with Richard Burton as Angelo – the first of his performances to get him noticed by a wider world. Among the others in the cast were the novelist John Wain (he was then usually known as Barry Wain) as Claudio and the antiquarian Roger Lancelyn Green as Elbow.

A few undergraduates were around whose flamboyance or cleverness recalled Oxford's dandyist period. One was Peter Brook, who started the Oxford University Film Society and with Gavin Lambert (now novelist, screen-writer and film critic) actually made a film: it was of Sterne's *Sentimental Journey*. They gave a party in Magdalen that was evidently too disorderly even for war-time: it resulted in one undergraduate's premature departure and another's rustication. One of the few remaining Oxford 'exquisites' was a certain Frederick Hurdis-Jones, who lived in Oscar Wilde's rooms in Magdalen: a bullet-hole in one window-pane, said to have been made when a college philistine fired a pistol at Wilde, had been lovingly preserved. Moreover Hurdis-Jones carefully modelled his behaviour on his predecessor. When Peter Brook produced Wilde's *Salome* in 1942, Hurdis-Jones played Herod. There was also a story that, as he made his way along the High for coffee one morning, cane in hand and dressed to kill, a woman stopped him and demanded to know how he had the effrontery to look the way he did. 'Don't you realise,' she shouted, 'there are men out there fighting for you?' Hurdis-Jones was unmoved. 'Fighting for me?' he replied languidly. 'My dear, they're *dying* for me.'

This seemed like the Oxford I'd been expecting.

What had I been expecting? Some kind of magic, I suppose. A temple of the arts, populated by intellectual giants, witty and erudite and all gifted with the effortless superiority I understood to be part of the equipment of the public schoolboy. I had been secretly worried that I might find myself in some deep philosophical conversation, like one of E M Forster's youthful characters talking about the meaning of meaning. It was a relief that hardly any of that seemed to have come my way: the talk in the JCR or in other people's rooms after dinner was about the usual nothing-very-much: jokes, jazz, food, other men in college.

But then there were the buildings, the 'full sad bells' and the trees between the towers which had seemed guaranteed to send anyone who had been there – Garrett and the other masters – into a state of homesick reverie. Now at last I understood. It was the sheer antiquity of the place – the venerable stone of the college buildings which I supposed to have been taken for granted by freshmen from public schools. After New Maiden, nothing could have been more captivating than the wonderful panoramas of soaring spires, peaceful quads and dreamy cloisters, which cast a spell that has never been broken.

In Oxford then the prevailing mood, as I remember it, was a mixture of the precious and the tough, the sensitive and the coolly unimpressed, the limp-wristed and the hard-boiled. Either rôle might be adopted; sometimes both. 'Has he decided who he is yet?' the girl-friend of one of my Wadham companions once asked, of a well-known Oxford figure. 'What do you mean?' 'Well, he never seems to have made up his mind whether he's Ernest Hemingway or Oscar Wilde.'

The tradition of dandy-aesthete still lingered about the Corn and the High. In a way, it was part of the intellectual baggage I had lugged up from Raynes Park, handed on by John Garrett. His rhapsodic enthusiasm over the poetry and dramatic writing he liked was one aspect of it, and as a way into the understanding of literature, it wasn't a lot of use. Opposed to this was a certain pugnacity or contempt for the pretentious, part of which was being a jazz fan. Jazz was real life: and it fitted in with the political realities as we saw them.

I arrived at Oxford naive, gullible, easily awed, and only perfunctorily prepared. It seems strange that neither Garrett nor any other Raynes Park master gave me or my contemporaries much of a hint about the experience in store for us. I suppose Garrett himself, besides being preoccupied with his own imminent career move, was no longer particularly interested: the trick had been worked, the right levers had been pulled and, hey presto! another suburban youth was about to become an Oxford 'man' – another notch to be cut, maybe, on his book case.

Four of us, as freshmen, took the Oxford train that morning in January 1943 – two to read biochemistry, one to read law, and me. I was to read French: without consulting me, Garrett had arranged it with the Warden of Wadham, C M Bowra, in the belief (he said on my last school report) that I needed to be 'stretched'. Two of my companions, Crumley and Thompson, were bound for Balliol, and the third, Saxby, was going to Magdalen. All of us were as nervous as fledgling flyers. It was an odd time of year to be going up. Usually freshmen matriculated in the autumn, or 'Michaelmas', Term but once again the rules were being bent and we were arriving in Hilary Term, an example of Oxford nomenclature we relished because it seemed so Oxfordish: when I think of it now, the phrase takes me back to the wintry Oxford mornings of 1943, chilly walks by the Isis, a coal fire in my rooms, undergraduates with black, yellow and blue college scarves.

Of course I made a point of buying one of these as soon as possible, and, so equipped, paid the required visit to the Senior Tutor at Wadham, who took my photograph, handed me a lecture list, and told me to call on my tutors. I went to the Hall and collected the first consignment of weekly rations: one ounce of butter, two of margarine, and a pot of marmalade to last a month. There was also a small bag of sugar. These had to be carried into Hall for breakfast and carefully eked out.

So: here I was up at Oxford, aged seventeen. Too young. But within a year they would be calling me up. David had gone already. I had his rooms, and realised I was probably assumed to be much the same sort of person as he was. I had his commoner's gown, too, a scrap of black cotton, most of it having been burned when he used it to draw the fire. I put it on and looked at myself in the bedroom mirror: an Oxford undergraduate!

But when I think about the first few terms I spent at Oxford, it is with a mixture of surprise, embarrassment and self-reproach at my frivolity and idleness. A typical day would be spent lounging in the Junior Common Room until it was time to go out for coffee, then strolling around the bookshops or record shops like Taphouse's or Acott's – seldom to buy, more usually to listen in one of the booths, eyeing the sexy girl counter-assistant in a short skirt who hung about the corridor casting, as

I thought, insolent, smouldering looks at me. After lunch, perhaps some work, though if the weather were fine it would be hard to resist the temptation to go punting on the Cherwell until it was time for tea, which was shortly succeeded by dinner in Hall, then more jazz records and chat until your stomach told you to make some watery cocoa to drink with whatever food was left over from earlier on.

At least our behaviour, though shamefully marked by greed, was comparatively sober. Drinking was rare. In college I would pretend to enjoy the occasional glass of beer, or sometimes a glass of Dry Fly bought from Duke, the JCR storeman. Seldom seen without his bicycle clips, Duke was a pleasant though slightly sly man, assumed to be on the fiddle, who seemed able to get supplies of things, and sherry was one, that were hard to find. There was also a man who worked in Walter's, the tailor's shop in the Turl, a Mr Shine, who I was told could get you a bottle of gin, and I did once take advantage of this for a party, the gin being greatly diluted with orangeade. Getting drunk was highly unusual – so was fornicating. Few of us at that time had much sexual experience and could be described as rather hesitantly feeling our way when opportunities occurred, which was not often.

To have a steady girl-friend was, I believe, unusual. It had been so at Raynes Park. The boys-only milieu there left us ill-equipped for social, let alone sexual adventures with girls and I tended to regard them as regrettably unattainable. But perhaps Oxford would fix all that. Eager to discover someone sympathetic I joined the Film Society and the College play-reading group, who arranged evening dates with similar groups from women's colleges. Sometimes, we would dare to suggest adjourning afterwards to a coffee house, somewhere quiet like the Eastgate near Magdalen Bridge, for decorous conversation.

I lived in the hope that I could find a girl who would want to listen to my jazz records, but that seemed difficult. By this time I was irrecoverably jazz-struck. In addition to all the books I possessed, I had brought with me to Wadham a well-worn collection of ten-inch 78s in a couple of carrying boxes, plus a portable wind-up gramophone. Molière and Racine, de Musset and Rimbaud had to compete with Jack Teagarden, Johnny Hodges, Armstrong and Bud Freeman, and it was an unequal contest.

One of the Raynes Park freshmen, at Balliol, discovered that John Garrett was coming to Oxford – probably reconnoitring for places for the stars of Bristol Grammar, calling on heads of houses – and we decided to take him to dinner. We met at The George, a famous restaurant in the 1920s though by now past its day. Menus were printed: 'A Raynes Park Old Boys Dinner', with our names – eight of us. Garrett arrived, beaming juicily, and at the end of the meal we all exchanged signatures. Garrett wrote on my menu, 'For Paul, because I am glad he is here among this gallant and goodly company.' A good thing he knew nothing about my casual attitude towards work – and what's more, it was growing worse.

If I have any plea to enter in mitigation of my idleness, I could argue that my tutors did not fill me with any zeal for my work. My principal tutor was a venerable Frenchman named Henri Berthon, a dignified old party who lived in Norham Gardens and whose most distinguished pupil had been the then Prince of Wales, when the Prince was an undergraduate at Magdalen before the Great War. There was a signed photograph of him in a silver frame on Berthon's desk. Berthon's sole publication, as far as I know, was a book for schools called *Nine French Poets* which he would often refer to, read from, and warmly recommend to all his pupils. He gave tutorials in his densely furnished front room where there was a spluttering gas fire. Often, his mittened fingers would be painted bright purple – it was gentian violet for his eczema. He was very patient with me, even though I must have seemed quite unfitted for university studies, producing poor essays, unsupported by any very diligent reading or reflection.

In the Modern Languages faculty, only four 'sections' were available in French. I imagine they assumed a student in the School of Modern Languages would have knowledge of more than one: I only had French. But this was an example of the arbitrariness of the system: another was that the French sections seemed to have been devised without much thought to the relative scale of work involved. One section covered the plays of Molière and nothing else, but another, a notorious hurdle known as M4, entailed a vast amount of work. It required a knowledge of the major French Romantic poets (no small school), including not only the whole of Hugo's extensive output but especially the vast, unreadable, *Légende des Siècles*. Not only that, but the section also included a paper on medieval French, including the long epic poem *La Chanson de Roland*. With this exam I was to have a very bad time.

For Old French my tutor was a tall, stooping man in round professorial spectacles, called Johnston, who lived in the Iffley Road. Tutorials took place in his sitting room, around an enormous Morrison shelter: these things, sponsored by the Labour politician Herbert Morrison were intended for the inside of your house, perhaps your dining room – heavy steel structures roughly of table height, about six feet long with steel mesh around three sides. If the air-raid siren went, you were supposed to crawl in underneath, but of course that never happened. It certainly would have seemed strange to be translating *Roland*, squatting on the floor in a kind of large metal cage.

Unable to settle down to the task of learning the basic grammar of this remote tongue, I did not enjoy tutorials with Johnston, nor any part of the Old French course, which may well have been added to Modern French studies as a make-weight, in the same way that Anglo-Saxon was notoriously added to the supposedly effete English Literature course. I did my best to busk my way through, relying on the words' superficial similarity to their modern equivalents. It was a desperate approach. One way and another it is not at all surprising that I failed M4 twice, and though I eventually managed to get through, it must have resulted from a higher than usual degree of indulgence on the examiners' part.

However, if there was one thing even less enjoyable than Old French, it was the Senior Training Corps. Every able-bodied undergraduate had to belong to either the University Air Squadron, the Naval Squadron, or the Senior Training Corps – this to distinguish it from the Junior Training Corps which many undergraduates were assumed to have marched in at a public school.

I plumped for the STC, 'The Corps' for short, which being the Oxford University Senior Training Corps had a Latin motto, *Militia Nobis Studium*, punningly altered, according to a joke of the day, to *Militia Nobis Odium*. You were supposed to turn up for two parades a week, once for a whole day, once for half a day. They were spent mainly on a site which has since become St Catherine's College. The Corps were commanded by a Captain, with a Lieutenant as second-in-command, both of whom were being rested from other more arduous duties, and to assist them there was a small group of NCOs, mostly from Guards Regiments, for whom this must have been a nice cushy posting. On the whole they were pleasant to us, even though they were supposed to call us 'Sir' – an obligation they did not allow to dilute their use of picturesque, parade-ground invective. They drilled us and taught us the rudiments of the Bren gun and the Lee-Enfield rifle, how to throw a grenade without endangering the men on your own side, and how to blanco what they called your webbing – that is canvas belt, ammunition pouches and gaiters – a task to which they appeared to attach major importance. Every week we were expected to go on a ten-mile route march in full kit, alternately running and walking. The whole thing was supposed to take no more than two hours and it ended with every cadet running round an assault course somewhere along the Banbury Road: at its climax you had to spreadeagle yourself on the ground and fire five rounds at a target, despite being in the last stages of exhaustion.

Somehow I contrived to avoid taking part in this weekly event throughout my time in the Corps. Partly, it was with the help of the Warden, C M Bowra. In the normal course of college life, undergraduates had little to do with this famous Oxford personage, the celebrated wit and – by this time – elder statesman, soon to be Vice-Chancellor, who was the model for Mr Samgrass in Evelyn Waugh's *Brideshead Revisited*. There was one occasion when I was invited to lunch in the Warden's Lodge, with about half-a-dozen other undergraduates. I was so over-awed that I hardly said a word as we feasted on *filet mignon* and fresh strawberries, with a fine claret. Otherwise my only contact was the obligatory visit at the end of term, which was brief and perfunctory, and the calls I would make to enlist his help in cutting a parade. A chit from the Warden would excuse you, provided you had a convincing story, and Maurice Bowra always listened sympathetically to complaints of a cold or a 'stomach upset'. Once, I had a genuine excuse: dashing down the stairs after dinner to get to a playreading, I fell and twisted my ankle. Next morning the ankle was twice its normal size, and the college Porter, Harry, fixed me up with one real crutch and, for the opposite arm-pit, a spare broom, on which I limped ostentatiously into Bowra's ground-floor room to ask for the appropriate piece of paper. He was solicitous at once, and I went to no more parades for about four weeks, at which point a Sergeant-Instructor called at the college to find out where I was and to order my immediate attendance, threatening to march me to Corps HQ under military escort.

My bad record was no help at the fortnight's camp I had to attend, with other STC cadets, during the long vacation in summer. It was held at one of those rural sites arbitrarily annexed by the military; this one was called Churn, an abrupt and unattractive name well suited to the activities that went on there. There was a lot of drill and a lot more of tedious marching about the countryside, sometimes taking part in exercises that involved the use of live ammunition. I did badly and was identified as a recalcitrant and incompetent soldier.

My attitude to the Corps mildly astonishes me now, but then

so many of the things I did during those months in 1943 and 1944 seem to me now wholly inexplicable, as though done by someone else. Here is an example, which I have often thought about with feelings of guilty shame. It happened that at a play-reading evening, I met a girl undergraduate from St Hilda's, by the name of Gwendoline. She was from Cardiff, pretty and sympathetic, and I began to plot ways in which I might be able to put my arms round her and kiss her – this being, for the moment, the summit of my carnal ambitions: after that, we would see what developed. I was sure I was in love with her. Having invited her to tea, and been invited back, I conceived the idea of sending her some flowers. I crept out late one night and picked some from the college gardens: daffodils, narcissi and tulips, oblivious of what the gardeners might think. Then I needed a box to send them in. So, I repaired to the Porter's Lodge and asked Harry, a friendly man, if he had one. As it happened he had a shoe-box which was exactly right: he gave it to me and helped me pack the flowers in it. He did ask me where I had obtained them, and I told him. 'The gardeners are going to be cross with you, sir,' Harry said. It vaguely dawned on me that I had done something crassly irresponsible, but I sent the package via the college messenger, feeling on the whole pleased with myself.

As far as I am aware my romantic gesture had no special effect on my relationship with Gwendoline, and in any case I suffered from a chronic lack of courage in making any kind of flirtatious advances: shortly afterwards I took up with another girl, a certain Sally Plimsoll, a scholar at Lady Margaret Hall whose grandfather had been the celebrated maritime reformer and inventor of the collapsible umbrella. She copied out a medieval love poem and gave it to me but assured me it wasn't meant personally, and our relationship remained at an unsatisfactorily chaste stage. It terminated abruptly when one day, and for no reason I could understand, she slapped my face. I don't believe I had said or done anything improper. I think she just wanted the experience of slapping a man's face, and I happened to be, as it were, on hand. It seemed useless to pursue matters further.

The Wadham Amateur Dramatic Society appeared to offer the right opportunities. Its official activities were mainly limited to drawing-room performance: we had a termly fixture list with most of the women's colleges and it was a good way to meet girls, with the incidental benefit of introducing us to some theatre repertoire. Now and then, however, the WADS actually staged a play. The one I was in was Yeats' *Deirdre*, a Celtic revival piece with a Tristan-and-Isolde type plot. For this we collaborated with St Hilda's, and I played the hero, Naoise, correctly pronounced Neesha – though we didn't bother to find that out and simply pronounced it as written: Neigh-oh-ease. We did the same thing with the character of King Conchubar, which ought to be pronounced Conn-uch-ar. This rôle was taken by John Terraine, a Keble-in-Wadham man then known as a left-wing poet, now as a military historian and posthumous champion of Field Marshal Haig. We put on *Deirdre* for two performances, one in Wadham Gardens, the second in the gardens of St John's, in tandem with a production of that college's dramatic society in which John (Barry) Wain starred. I cannot remember their play. Indeed I can remember very little about our own production: my clearest memory is of Gwendoline in Yeats' chorus of musicians, uttering lines like 'Are Deirdre and her lover tired of life?' and 'The eagles have gone into their cloudy beds' – a line she gave a sweetly erotic flavour.

At the end of 1943 I was told to go to Oxford Town Hall and have a medical examination for call-up. When it was finished they informed me they had graded me B2. In brackets, they had added the word 'Eyes'. I took this to refer to the migraine attacks, which actually had ceased since I'd come up to Oxford. But the upshot was that my call-up was deferred for six months.

I left the Town Hall in a state almost of stupefaction: it was like having a death sentence postponed. I was to be allowed to remain in this enchanted environment for six months longer: more, I would be able to enjoy another Oxford spring, another

Oxford summer term – and, as my father sternly reminded me, would be able to keep the number of terms necessary for a War Degree. He hoped I would stiffen my resolution and work harder at the dreaded M4.

Alas for his hopes. On vacation in the early spring of 1944 a friend at home sold me his clarinet, a cracked instrument of antique design, which in a state of some excitement I took to my bedroom and began to blow. It didn't seem so difficult to play. So much so that within a week I was playing it in public. Peter Greaves, my friend of former years, was now playing the drums in a small band that provided music for a weekly dance at the local tennis club. Somehow I got wind of this: I went along, and joined in, playing, I have no doubt, in a raucous and uninteresting fashion, but able to convince myself that now I was of the same breed as Bix and Teschemacher.

Back in Oxford for Trinity Term, I sought the acquaintance of John Postgate, a biochemist and son of the man known as Public Stomach No 1 – Raymond Postgate, founder of the Good Food Club. John Postgate, who was at Balliol, played the trumpet and was known as one of the University's leading jazz fans. He also ran the only jazz band in the place, the OU Bandits, and was believed to be in want of a clarinettist. In no time I was taking part in jam sessions and even making recordings, in a private studio in Cornmarket Street, heavy wax-on-metal discs that all of us bore away with pride. Needless to say, they were unspeakably bad. The only member of the band with any degree of competence was the pianist, Martin Milligan, who had been stone blind from birth but was tolerant of the unconvincing noises made by the rest of us. Nevertheless, we managed to persuade the organisers of the Somerville Ball that we could supply the music for the event, and, clad in my father's dinner jacket, I sat there all evening and went through my repertoire – copied from the jazz records I had learned by ear.

Work was now well and truly eclipsed. The problem was that not only was I sitting M4 again and attending STC parades, I had to sit a fourth section if I were to get a War Degree. There being no more French sections, I decided to take one in English, and was sent to have tutorials with Nevill Coghill in Exeter, a friend of John Garrett's who had often visited Raynes Park to talk to the Sixth Form. The section was on Shakespeare – one general paper, and the other on *Antony and Cleopatra*, which by great good luck happened to have been the set play in the Higher Certificate examination I'd sat at school. By a combination of plausibility and cunning footwork I somehow passed both papers. What I remember most vividly about the examination is that the compulsory question in the general paper instructed you to make a list of the dramatis personae in any three Shakespeare plays, confining yourself to those with speaking parts. This ridiculously simple task shows how academic standards, at least in the English faculty, must have slipped for the duration. It probably explains, too, how I managed to outwit the examiners, and pass.

This long-drawn and undeserved idyll came to an end in July 1944. The exams over, I had to attend another fortnight of STC parades. The summer 'camp' was actually held in Oxford, based on the Corps HQ in Blue Boar Street, off the High, and so we lived in college and paraded every morning. It was a lot better than being billeted in bleak army huts in some Berkshire wilderness, and I decided it was time for another mighty effort. I managed to salvage my reputation, and even got promoted to Section Leader, ending up with something called a War Certificate 'B' which was supposed to be your passport to a commission. And, inexorably, my call-up papers arrived: my deferment had run out. I went to Oxford from New Maiden for one last weekend – this time with a girl companion who saw to it that I rallied to the flag with at least one major rite of initiation accomplished. There was also one last jam session, with John Postgate and a few others who were still about: at the Cornmarket Street studios we recorded a blues in C, the only key in which the pianist could play.

On the train back to London, I gazed out of the window at the spires of Oxford in the distance. As we crossed the river I remembered an afternoon a few months earlier. I hadn't taken any formal exercise at Oxford: I had tried rowing in an eight, but disliked the hectic tempo over which you had no control – thrown forward and backward on your sliding seat like some inert cloth dummy. But now and then, I would go down to the college boat house and hire a little craft they called a 'whiff, a one-man racing shell, with no covering skin. In this, I would explore the Isis and the Cherwell, making my own pace.

On the day I remembered, the air was like champagne and the river sparkled in the sun. The college barges floated sedately at their moorings waiting for Eights Week, when parents and girl-friends would crowd the upper deck to watch, and Duke would be in the little kitchen of the Wadham barge doing strawberry teas. I felt like a king in the spring sunshine. The river lapped against the bows of my little boat, and the feathering oars pattered gently on the passing tide.

I rowed up-river, then in a little while turned and began to pull downstream again, putting my back into it this time, rowing strongly and smoothly. I shot under the railway bridge and paused, resting the oars, the blades steadying the craft.

I looked up. There on the bridge, a train had stopped: like all wartime trains it was full; travellers, mostly servicemen, were packed into the corridors. Careworn faces stared down at me and on them I thought I could read a kind of wistful envy. There I was, free of all constraints, not wearing a stuffy serge uniform and not travelling back to some Army camp or Naval barracks to be shouted at by someone higher up the chain of command. I was the very embodiment of privilege. It seemed to be the high point of my youth: nothing, surely, could equal the private exultation of that moment.

Now, the case was altered. I was in the train, looking down at the waters of the Isis, the reeds at the edge, and the punts and pleasure boats and the occasional racing whiff. I looked forward to what was coming next year with no pleasure whatever.

Fifteen

HYDERABAD BARRACKS, COLCHESTER. Army place-names certainly weren't the sort that made you want to linger. This one designated a group of featureless rectangular blocks in red brick, set in parade formation within a perimeter wall: once through the entrance, manned by a permanent guard of Military Police with close-cropped hair and cheese-cutter caps, there was to be no escape, save for one or two Saturday afternoon passes, until the first six weeks' training were over. I travelled there from Liverpool Street with a copy of the latest *Horizon*, Cyril Connolly's literary monthly, prominently displayed, hoping it might attract a few like-minded fellow-travellers. It didn't. Nobody took any notice, and serve me right.

Waiting on the platform at Colchester that August morning was an NCO with three stripes and a crown. He was the Colour Sergeant. 'Call me "Colour",' he told us. He nabbed the dozen or so men who had arrived on the same train, lined us up in two ranks and marched us off in silence to the barracks, a slouching squad of mutual strangers carrying an assortment of suitcases, grips and brown-paper parcels. I was the only one in uniform – the battle-dress I had been given at Blue Boar Street – and I felt singled out, marked, as though I'd tried to get away and been brought back, just as the Corps commander at Oxford had promised I would be.

Into the barracks: names were read out and we were assigned

to various parts of this prison-like building. My uniform with its 'OUSTC' shoulder tags was handed in. In exchange I was given or, as the Army said, 'issued with' a new one plus a lot more kit, some of it with back-to-front names like Drawers, Cellular (ie underpants); Socks, Woollen; and Caps, Forage. This was how items were listed in the Quartermaster's stores' catalogue, but the nomenclature was also part of the elephantine vocabulary in common army use: lavatories were urinals ('Do Not Urinate Up This Wall' said a notice in white paint), wash-houses were ablutions and tiring menial duties fatigues. I wondered when this odd language had made its first appearance: probably around the time of the Great War. I couldn't imagine the Peninsular army using words in that pretentious way. But the conscript army of the 1940s seemed to accept it without demur, modifying it with a few obscene intensifies.

In the stores they continued to pile clothes and equipment on the counter, checking off each item: Razors, Safety, one; Trousers, denim, pairs, one; Blouses, denim, one; Vests, cellular, two; knife-fork-and-spoon, one; Housewives, one (this was the military term for a small cotton wallet of needles, thread, darning wool, etc.) . . . on and on it went, and at last a heavy canvas kit-bag to keep it all in. They also gave each of us a pay book – 'Your AB64 Part One!' somebody yelled. 'And don't fuckin' lose it!' – a small, cloth-covered notebook with an elastic band round the pages which recorded how much you were paid (twenty-six shillings a week, I seem to remember – £1.30p) and included, ominously, a 'pro forma' page on which I was told to write my will.

I lugged all this gear up to a barrack room where two youngish corporals stood talking. One was Corporal Taylor, from East London but in the Gloucester Regiment, and wearing a forage cap with two badges, one in front and one at the back, to commemorate some action against Napoleon's army when the regiment had fought back-to-back and, I gathered, been wiped out. As I went in, the present-day heir to this valiant tradition was giving voice to a torrent of obscene invective. Every other word seemed to be fuck or cunt, or variants of the same. I was impressed by the virtuoso inventiveness of his oaths but also alarmed because it seemed inevitable the other man, Corporal Fisher, would attack him and there would be a serious fight. Then I realised Corporal Taylor wasn't actually swearing at him, it was just his normal way of talking. The expletives were for emphasis, the equivalent of John Garrett's or Maurice Bowra's clipped, italicised speech. Corporal Taylor was in fact a genial, even-tempered man, sympathetic to the green and nervous recruits he was in charge of, and possessing a repertoire of Cockney jokes and stories and Army lore which he passed on to us with cheery enjoyment.

He and Corporal Fisher, another Londoner but in the East Surrey Regiment, were in immediate charge of the platoon of about twenty men. We newcomers had no regimental affiliation: we were in some reach-me-down mob called the General Service Corps. There didn't seem to be any officers about but we had a platoon sergeant; no other NCOs had anything to do with our small section of this large force of new conscripts except the PT staff – sinewy, eupeptic, elastic-looking sergeant-instructors who every day put us through a strenuous programme of body-building.

Corporal Taylor's special subject was weapon training and he approached it with due gravity. Frowning round the squad, who stood at ease in front of him, he would declare in a low, threatening tone: 'The object of all weapon trainin' is to kill the enemy.' Without pause he would ask belligerently 'What's the object of all weapon trainin'?' He pointed to one of us. 'To kill the enemy, Corporal!' Every session began with this exchange, rubbing in the fact that serious business was to be done and you might have to fire your rifle at another human being, or stick him in the stomach with the bayonet fixed under the barrel. And you might have to see his face as you were doing it.

My small personal part of World War Two was to afford no opportunities for heroism, or for licensed killing, and I was to serve my time with, as J D Salinger put it, my trigger finger itching imperceptibly, if at all. Nobody shot at me, and the only bayonet charges I took part in were against a row of sacks hanging from rough wooden scaffolds, which we were instructed by our two Cockney corporals to attack with ferocious screams, as blood-curdling as we could manage, thrusting the stiletto bayonet in to the straw as far as it would go and paralysing the imaginary enemy with fright. 'IN! OUT!' shouted Corporal Taylor. 'ON GUARD! CHARGE!'

But, truth to tell, I had seen more action in my father's dug-out at 'Wayside', or dodging the buzz-bombs on the Southern Railway, than I was to experience in the Army. This was my good luck, for the conscripts of 1944 still had a good chance of being killed in action. Even though we were winning the war in Europe, the shooting was still going on, and as for the war against the Japanese, that showed no sign of coming to an end: there was an uneasy conviction in the barracks at Colchester that it was the Far Eastern theatre of conflict, as the saying went, that we were destined for. The call-up machine, a well-oiled piece of national apparatus, was continuing to comb people out of reserved occupations and routinely hoover up every fit young man as he reached the age of eighteen. My fellow recruits at the Hyderabad Barracks all came into one of these categories, mostly the latter one. So, besides the eighteen-year-olds, there was a corpulent, rather loud man who was believed to be an actor, a grey-haired, boyish Liverpool-Irishman called MacMahon who had been a shipyard worker and a stout, humorous minor civil servant from Cardiff, called Lewis, and all of these men had somehow been prised reluctantly out of their jobs to take their places in the citizen Army. There were men from all over Britain: every variety of regional accent seemed represented. We all got on reasonably well: there were no fights, and all of us nursed a common resentment against the abrupt change in life-style the barracks represented, though no one questioned the conscription policy that had brought us all there.

One morning all of us were marched to a separate Nissen hut which was the domain of the Personnel Selection Officer, who was going to give us some intelligence and aptitude tests. There was a book of questions to go through. Then a Corporal handed me a little pile of plastic and metal objects, recognisable as the parts of a bicycle pump: I had to put it back together, and I had three minutes to get it done. Not enough! When time was up the thing I had made was an abortion. With a sigh, the Corporal wrote something defamatory on his clip-board and dismissed me to the next task. Finally each man had an interview with the Captain, who told me airily, 'We've decided you're the classical type, rather than the technical type, so we shall find something appropriate.'

Somewhere the lines of communication must have got twisted, because within a few weeks I was in the Royal Electrical and Mechanical Engineers, for training as a wireless operator and driver. Before that happened, I was bundled off to the Queen's Royal Regiment, at a place known as the Invicta Lines in Maidstone, a makeshift camp of Nissen huts and wooden buildings. Architecture apart, the daily routine was much the same as at the Hyderabad Barracks, only with longer route marches and more nerve-wracking assault courses, and even more generous helpings of bullshit – a term that could mean anything from excessive polishing and blancoing to unnecessary formalities and pointless rules. The Queen's was hot on regimental tradition: 'We are the first regiment of the line, bar none!' barked our NCO, Corporal Penn. Through some obscure regimental custom, the Queen's also practised their drill in a different way from everybody else. It was slower and more formal, heels were stamped with deadly unison after lengthy but carefully timed pauses, and guard-mounting was performed with elaborate ceremonial. For some reason I was good at this particular brand of bullshit. All those times when John Hicks and I had practised the Present Arms, the Slope and the Trail unexpectedly paid off with commendations and the odd privilege when it was my turn to mount guard.

However, someone decided that with my medical category, I wasn't really supposed to be in the infantry at all, and I was sent to a Holding Battalion in Woolwich which occupied an ancient barracks building called the Woolwich Repository, said to have been condemned around the time of the Crimea campaign. By now it was November, and extremely cold. While they decided where to send us next they invented cleaning and polishing jobs for us to do. Barrack Room Fatigue, Guardhouse Fatigue, Cookhouse Fatigue – when my turn came round for that one, it meant a morning peeling potatoes, then standing behind great steaming metal trays of food and doling out a portion to each man. My job was to serve the curry. I was surprised when they told me, but in the event this meant presiding over a dish of curry powder and asking the men as they shuffled past whether they wanted their roast meat and two veg curried or plain. If the former, I had to sprinkle a pinch of powder over the plate. *Voilà!* Curried beef.

Fatigue was certainly the word for this, so I volunteered for a group called by the Orderly Sergeant, a whimsical man, 'Count de Haan's Dance Band': it was his name for the Sanitary Squad, under the command of Lance-Corporal de Haan, another East Ender, who had lost his wife in an air-raid but wasn't popular with the men in his squad, several of whom had returned from service abroad. One or two were veterans of the Desert Campaign and had fought in Italy. De Haan had bad feet and hence was, in the military phrase, Excused Boots, meaning he was allowed to wear (another army label) Walking Shoes.

Oddly enough this was what was known as a cushy number, despite the fact that De Haan's squad had to be on parade an hour before everyone else – at 7.30 in the morning. We then proceeded to the administration building to scrub the floors, sweep the passages, polish door-knobs and clean the lavatories, or urinals. Not a very alluring set of duties but not much worse than peeling potatoes or dispensing instant curry, and the job even had its advantages. De Haan was no martinet: most of the Dance Band's time was spent in a café round the corner from the barracks and out of sight of the Orderly Sergeant, who now and then, in a perfunctory sort of way, would patrol 'the Lines', as they called the barracks area, on the look-out for scroungers. Count de Haan's squad was well placed in this respect, having the exclusive use of a small hut just outside the barrack gates, where we kept the tools of our trade – brushes, mops, brooms, polishing rags and so forth – and to which we could retire for a smoke after fifteen minutes or so of bullshitting floors, door handles and basins. De Haan, however, lived in a state of chronic anxiety over a possible unannounced visit from some anonymous superior. 'He's comin' round!' he would hiss at us as he found three or four soldiers reading the paper or playing cards in our hut. It was a useful introduction to one of the prime elements of military life, in war as – I dare say – in peace, namely skiving off or scrounging, the first essential of which, I learnt, was to keep out of sight, avoid eye contact, and be generally inconspicuous.

This interlude lasted three or four weeks, during which time, like most of the other soldiers languishing in those grim, grey barracks, I took as many opportunities as possible to get out – often back to New Maiden, an hour or so's train journey away, sometimes into London. When he wasn't in his office, my father seemed to be spending most of the time dressed in blue battle-dress, the uniform of an ARP Warden, with a whistle and a tin hat, the very image of Mr A at war, except that his social life seemed to have been screwed up a notch or two: its centre was the saloon bar of the Maiden Manor, whose regulars my mother viewed with suspicion, especially one, the wife of a war corre-spondent-photographer who was away somewhere on the West-ern Front. My mother's misgivings were to prove well-founded.

If my father weren't at the pub, you could look in at the Wardens' Post. Air raids on the 1940 pattern were a thing of the past: what Londoners now had to contend with were V2s, the rockets fired from the European mainland which landed without warning and with devastating suddenness – so making the air-raid siren an irrelevance. No wonder the atmosphere at 'Wayside' was gloomy. But I wasn't exposed to it for long, because soon my next posting came up: the Royal Electrical and

Mechanical Engineers. I was to be trained as a Driver-Operator. Believing this to be at odds with the Army's assessment of my character as 'non-technical' I asked if this could be changed: surprisingly, the request went through and it was granted. A few days later I was told to get ready to be a Clerk (Technical). It didn't sound like a very exciting job but it certainly sounded safe enough, and I was sent off to another training course, in Leicester this time – to learn typing, facts about the Army's ordnance depots, information about stores and indenting procedure: well, someone had to do it, but it was beginning to sound as if I was unlikely to make it to the Officers' Mess.

After a few weeks in Leicester, I was no longer a Private. With an infinitesimal increase in pay, I was now a Craftsman, and the next move was to a huge Army camp which had been established near the small Oxfordshire town of Bicester – it had smothered two tiny villages named Ambrosden and Arncott.

In his memoirs, the composer Sandy Wilson, who was also stationed there, relates that whenever he is in the vicinity he makes a point of motoring through the Arncott Depot just to reassure himself it isn't a dream, and that he really isn't there any longer; and it's true that for a while the place – or at least a part of it – had the reputation of being one of the most repressive camps in the British Army. My immediate destination was the 2nd Battalion at Ambrosden, where discipline was maintained by members of the Provost (pronounced Pr'vo) Corps, none of them lower than Lance-Corporal in rank, wearing red bands around their cheese-cutter caps – headgear they had steamed and worked at so that the peaks lay stiff and straight against their noses. They were under the command of a grim Regimental Sergeant-Major. I assume the Commanding Officer had grown bored and indifferent towards conditions in the camp and, perhaps out of funk, had got into the habit of leaving everything to the RSM and the other regimental NCOs. The Provost Corporals handed out 'charges' for minor breaches of discipline, for which you would be quick-marched before the company officer and given some inordinate punishment: a favourite one was to run round the parade ground in full kit – Field Service Marching Order.

The men, numbering about five hundred in the Ambrosden lines, all slept in giant Nissen huts called, for some reason, boleros, about a couple of hundred soldiers to a hut, with double bunks lined up in rows with only a few feet of space between them. These vast, hangar-like spaces were lit by naked bulbs hanging on long flexes from the ceiling and extinguished at ten p.m. sharp, and the boleros were heated, inadequately, by a small number of free-standing stoves whose pipes ascended to the curved tin roof: they burned whatever you could scrounge to put in them – usually wood gathered from round about – but there weren't enough of them and the men were wretchedly cold.

The cookhouse food was poor and the NAAFI, the soldier's haven for a smoke or for tea-and-a-wad (i.e. a bun), was small, ill-equipped and grudgingly opened only for a short time in the evenings. To get a pass to leave the camp – and go to Bicester, or even Oxford – you had to apply to a Provost Corporal whom you would find seated behind a bare desk in the guard-room. On the floor in front of the desk a thick white line had been painted: applicants for a pass, or for anything at all, had to advance to the line, come to attention with boots precisely aligned with this boundary, and with much stamping of feet and yelling of Army numbers (generally shortened to the last three digits) bawl out what they wanted, and why. If the Provost Corporal didn't feel like it, you didn't get your pass. He might even put you on a charge (a 'fizzer') if he didn't like the way you'd come to attention, hadn't toed the white line to his satisfaction, hadn't addressed him by his correct rank, if your 'turn-out' was unsatisfactory (button undone, hair too long, boots not polished) – or if he just didn't like you.

While the bully-boys in the Provost Corps spent their days sitting about in the guard-room, or perhaps sauntering about harassing people, the rest of the battalion went off to the REME workshops dotted around the Oxfordshire countryside within a radius of a mile or two. To get there we embarked on a train. The camp had its own railway, equipped with a motley collection of rolling stock, some of it bare wagons, inexplicably from France and duly painted with the famous instruction, *Hommes 40 Chevaux 8*, though some of the coaches were antiquated passenger carriages with benches, covered in torn leather or moth-eaten cloth. The morning parades were at eight o'clock: a roll-call was read out to the shivering troops, who sprang to attention as their names were called. Then it was off to the railway line, which had been laid at the edge of the battalion lines. The daily routine was brightened a little when a platoon of ATS, women of the Auxiliary Territorial Service, whose camp was nearby but out of bounds, marched past to get on their segregated part of the train. At this point, rigid discipline was strictly enforced by NCOs on both sides, male and female, with cries of 'Eyes front!' and 'No talking in the ranks!'

Standing in the swaying railway carriages as the train chugged sluggishly through the sodden meadows, I thought of Siegfried Sassoon's poem about a 1914–18 soldier who dreams nostalgically of 'going to the office in the train': here was I, in the Army but doing just that, except that the office that was my destination was in the camp sawmill. There were other workshops for tank repairs, electrical work, motor vehicles and general military ironmongery. In the sawmill the personnel were presumed to be craftsmen in wood, but nothing much was going on. A squad of men at one end was making a bedroom suite for the Commanding Officer. This wasn't considered remarkable – for the officer in charge over at the vehicle workshop a similar squad was building a car out of spare parts.

It seemed pretty remote from life in the rest of the country. Once I had to unpack a crate of supplies – nails, or screws, or some carpentry tools. I was wielding the jemmy they'd given me when a note fell out of the sawdust packing. It read, 'If you are single, drop me a line, if you are married, never mind.' There was an address and a girl's name. But I didn't write. I was more interested in reactivating my acquaintance with my St Hilda's girl friend Gwendoline, who was teaching in a girl's school in Leamington. To her I would write long attention-seeking letters complaining about the tedium and restrictiveness of army life.

My job in the sawmill was to keep track of all the jobs supposedly in progress, apply for tools, equipment or materials that weren't in the stores and keep the so-called Nominal Roll, Army-speak for a list of the men at the mill. This never took very long and I spent most of the day reading, making tea and talking to whoever happened to drop in to the office: Sergeants and Warrant Officers mostly, who had nothing much to do in the workshop, and used the office like a Common Room. They included a man I grew to like, a certain Staff-Sergeant Hartland: he was a dry, friendly person, a regular soldier, whose usual name for me, 'the fuckin' educated bastard', was amiably intended. When the mood took him, Hartland would entertain whoever had dropped in to the office with stories of the Army in Egypt, where he had served before and during the war. 'Don't talk to me about the fuckin' master race,' he would say, staring mournfully around him with bleary, pale blue eyes. 'The British was the fuckin' master race in Egypt' – an opinion he was able to support with lurid anecdotes. On other occasions he would expound his views on women: 'There's three kinds,' he told me once. 'There's those who'll do it for anybody. There's those that'll do it for their friends. And there's those that'll do it for one man. But they'll all do it.'

Hartland was in the Woodwork Shop because of his length of service rather than through any skill he may have had as a 'chippy' – i.e., joiner or carpenter. Other NCOs, who were conscripts, were genuinely entitled to be considered craftsmen, but none of them had any special respect for the work they were doing. None of it seemed urgent or even very necessary – merely something to pass the time of a battalion made up of men who were browned-off, bored and – increasingly – leaned on and abused by the barely literate yobs in the Provost Corps. Unfortunately, the NCOs at the sawmill appeared to take no interest in the conditions in the boleros. The Sergeants' Mess was well separated from the rest of the battalion lines and they lived in comparative comfort, with their own cooks, a bar, and comfortable sleeping quarters. Getting weekend passes was no problem and the Provost Corporals had no authority over them.

I fell foul of the guard-room only once, and it was with an odd result. One Sunday evening, I missed the last train back to camp and had to spend the night in the waiting room at Oxford's now vanished LMS station. Arriving back at 5.30 in the morning instead of the preceding midnight, I was instantly put on a charge for being absent without leave and had to appear before the Company Commander that same morning. Uneasy at what the punishment might be, I brooded over the best way to defend myself, and decided I would probably be better off with a written script: an absurd idea for so small an offence. However, being marched into the company office offered no reassurance. The idea was to terrify you. 'Prisoner, CHAW!! Quick march left right left right left right right wheel left right HALT!!! Hat off! 14838305 Craftsman Vaughan SAH!'

My charge was read out, and I requested permission to read my evidence. Since the officer, a Colonel, seemed too surprised to refuse, I treated him to a rather florid essay on the unreliability of the train service in war-time and some comically intended thoughts on my own absent-mindedness. The man's response was astounding. Leaning back in his chair he said: 'Where were you at school?' 'Raynes Park County School,' I told him. He smiled distantly, and said, 'Aha . . . that famous school. Case dismissed.'

'Right – TAH!! Quick march left right left right left right right wheel left right HALT!! Right, fuck off, you,' said the Provost Sergeant, who must have listened to my trial, if that's what it had been, with incredulity. I made myself scarce. Other prisoners, for no doubt equally trivial offences but with no school pedigree to advance by way of self-justification, were punished more severely. A week of 'jankers', i.e. regimental punishment, could include an hour every evening running round the parade ground, fully equipped and under the surveillance of the hated Provost Corporals.

It couldn't last. One evening, word went round that there was to be a meeting in the NAAFI to discuss grievances – an event forbidden in the Army's procedural Bible, King's Regulations; hence, it was necessary to keep it secret from the NCOs. The meeting was addressed by a craftsman-fitter who had been a chronic victim of the Provost Corporals, and a letter was drafted and sent to the War Office, bringing to their notice the repressive régime we had to put up with.

Nothing happened for a week or two. Then one morning, following some prearranged plan, the battalion resorted to mass disobedience. I wasn't on parade that morning and knew nothing about the scheme: but I learned that when ordered to turn right and march to the railway line, nobody moved. There was much shouting and swearing from the NCOs. A Lieutenant who was taking the parade panicked and actually drew his pistol, waving it belligerently and shouting about mutiny. But he fired no shots. The men stood their ground. The officer consulted the Orderly Sergeant and agreed that a deputation of soldiers would be allowed to bring their complaints before the Commanding Officer. Then, a few days later, a War Office Humber car drew up outside the guardroom, and a Staff Colonel got out, accompanied by a junior officer. They entered the guardroom, surprising the Corporal of the day, who scrambled to attention with a quivering salute. Pointing to the white line on the floor, the Colonel demanded an explanation. I am not sure what happened next: but the Commanding Officer doubtless experienced a *mauvais quart d'heure*, for he was shortly afterwards posted elsewhere, as were the Regimental Sergeant-Major and all the members of the Provost Corps, all of whom would have reverted once more to the rank of Private.

I wasn't present for any of these exciting events, and only heard about them later. For, a few days earlier, I had been moved to the 4th Battalion, up the road at the Arncott end of the depot, to work in the Orderly Room, the battalion's administrative centre.

Here, the sleeping quarters were better, and so was the food. The NAAFI was large and there was even a Garrison Theatre. I enlisted without delay in the Bicester Garrison Players, and we performed light comedies or thrillers: *The Two Mrs Carrolls*, *See Naples and Die*, *The Dover Road*, and others. Better still, there was a dance band which played at weekly 'hops' in the NAAFI and occasionally in other places – like Officers' Mess parties, when we were required to play what was called Mickey Mouse Music *pianissimo* in the background while the members and their guests dined.

When I'd been in the army for about eight months the war in Europe, in the words of a contemporary newspaper, moved with giant strides towards its end. I happened to be on leave when the celebrations took place: outside the Malden Manor pub I stood with my father and watched in a detached sort of way a huge bonfire surrounded by tipsy revellers, a conflagration that signalled among other things the end of the black-out. My father, in his blue battledress, turned to me, and as though he were a character in Noel Coward's *Cavalcade*, said, 'Well, Paul, we've come through it': all it needed was a patriotic march, *sotto voce* on the sound track . . . but I was moved by his stagey, awkward response to events. There are times when such gestures can be excused and this was certainly one of them, as the flames leaped up in the spring night, and we knew we would never again hear the air-raid sirens moaning dolefully over the suburban rooftops, or the crump of high explosive detonating in someone's back garden.

My own life, too, seemed to have moved with giant strides in the years since September 1939. Back at Bicester the Army decided everyone should be prepared for going back to what the soldiers called Civvy Street with a programme of adult education. Under the auspices of ABCA, the Army Bureau of

Current Affairs, a large-scale scheme was launched with lectures from Education Corps NCOs on Citizenship and 'BWP', or The British Way and Purpose. I was plucked from the 4th Battalion Orderly Room and despatched to a course in Bristol at which I was supposed to learn in the space of one week how to teach the troops about English Literature. Back at Arncott Depot I was promoted precipitately and without warning to Sergeant and told to organise classes for the whole battalion in French, English, Leatherwork, Motor Maintenance and anything else for which a half-qualified tutor might be available, the whole scheme to be set up within a fortnight, with all the tutors, like me, instantly promoted to Acting Sergeants. There were also a small number of semi-illiterate men who would have to be given basic instruction in reading and writing. Somehow the scheme got launched, though I cannot imagine any of my adult pupils gained anything very much from my lessons on matters like English ballads, Shakespeare's plays and how to write a job application. The lessons only happened on one day a week: Friday was the designated day, when almost every man in the battalion, with the exception of a handful who had to mount guard, was raring to go on a weekend pass. What I took to be alert attention to my French and English lessons was in reality the eagerness of men poised for a swift journey down the main line, as they sat in the education huts in their best uniforms and best brown shoes, bags packed ready at their sides.

During the rest of the week I occupied myself messing about vaguely in the Education Hut, a Nissen put down among trees a little way away from the rest of the battalion lines – putting a library together, getting things ready for Battalion Education Day and organising vocational courses in factories for men who were expecting to be demobbed: usually they were placed with firms near their homes, an enlightened scheme.

Also, there was the unit band, playing away busily most nights in the week, sometimes until two or three in the morning. The personnel changed now and then as men were posted elsewhere or demobbed, but the band maintained the character of a small jazz combo – trumpet, clarinet, saxophone, piano and rhythm section. We had no music, but played everything by ear, a repertoire of jazz standards with a few 'sweet' numbers thrown in, which improved my jazz technique but did nothing for my prowess as a soldier, supposing that were capable of improvement. I supposed I was stuck firmly in the lower ranks: but who cared – the Sergeants' Mess was a pleasant place and I was absolutely certain it was preferable to any Officers' Mess . . . cheaper, less snobbish, more tolerant and friendlier.

It was true I felt, and probably looked, ridiculously young to be a REME Sergeant, and though by this time my Oxford airs had been largely blown away, I still sounded different from the others and was occasionally mocked for my middle-class accent. Still, there were allies in the mess besides the rest of the Education Sergeants. There was Staff-Sergeant Hartland for one, plus a couple of other NCOs from the sawmill – now part of the 4th Battalion – and some who were more or less loosely connected with the unit dance band. One of them was Sergeant South, a Cockney wide boy, lean and stooping, who fancied himself as a stand-up comedian and ran an entertainment troupe in which the band figured, playing interludes between various solo acts. The show, Sergeant South's Cabaret, was performed before audiences of a fortunately lenient disposition, usually in the NAAFI but sometimes elsewhere. Once we appeared in the Randolph Hotel in Oxford, which was as near as Jimmy Sahf, as the band called him, got to the big time. Besides introducing the acts he always took a final solo spot on the programme, spinning it out interminably: his sole prop was an empty vegetable barrow and he wheeled it on dressed in cliché coster attire – cloth cap, muffler, jersey, and trousers tied with string at the knee. His material was second-hand and he would pester the other members of the troupe for contributions, jokes he would re-tell loudly and not very confidently before ending his act with 'Maybe it's Because I'm a Londoner' to an accompaniment by the band.

The other acts weren't much higher in standard. At one time

we had two tenors, who had to be placed at opposite ends of the bill because their repertoires were too similar. Neither, for example, could be dissuaded from performing *Come Back to Sorrento*, a big 'classical' favourite with the troops at that time: the better of the tenors, a certain Corporal McCann, would upstage the other singer, Sergeant Brown, by singing it in Italian, but Brown doggedly kept on singing his number. Other numbers the two rivals had in common included *Because* and *O Sole Mio*, which Brown, a Gloucestershire man, sang steadfastly in English. If they were on the programme together – and Brown didn't always turn up – there was a good chance of a clash, with one or other of them scowling in the wings while his fellow-tenor emoted through a number, accompanied by our pianist, a gaunt young Liverpudlian called Frank Robinson.

A performer whose appearances on the platform caused sinking hearts, especially among the band, was CSM Dawkes – known as Sammy – a regular Warrant Officer well into his fifties, a lewd and rather stupid man who would howl into the microphone, 'I'll be loving you, *both ways.*' This was done with a heavy leer: Dawkes was interested in buggery, indeed almost preoccupied with it, and many of his jokes turned on that subject. His singing was excruciating enough: worse was what followed, when he would wrest my clarinet from my hands (pulling rank) and play a solo, very loud, with a vulgar vibrato of the Ted Lewis pattern wide enough to make your ears ring.

Not all the acts in Jimmy South's Cabaret were musical ones. One evening a Lance-Corporal in the Royal Engineers offered his services as a conjuror: South readily took him on. The Lance-Corporal set up a small cloth-covered table in front of the band and proceeded to do his act, while the musicians watched with interest, having a clear view of how all the tricks worked. The Lance-Corporal, whose name was Schlesinger, fervently besought us not to give anything away by knowing looks or smug smiles when the trick reached its climax, and so we schooled ourselves to watch the performance poker-faced.

This encounter was the beginning of a friendship with John

Schlesinger that lasted for a while and in the course of which he many times invited me for weekends with his family, at their house in rural Berkshire. The family had come to England from Austria in the thirties: John's father was a consultant paediatrician at Great Ormond Street Children's Hospital, and his mother was a fine violinist. John had a brother and three sisters, and two of the girls played instruments, one the cello, the other the violin. I found the entire family captivating. Staying at their large house near the village of Inkpen introduced me to a level of social refinement I'd never experienced before. To me the Schlesingers seemed not only unimaginably rich, with their cook-housekeeper, their flat in Bayswater and their large, comfortable house smelling of wood-smoke and good cooking: they also seemed enviably cultivated. There were books all over the house, piles of well-thumbed music, and interesting paintings on the walls. Travelling to Inkpen by train from suburban New Maiden, I was propelled into a beautiful new world: but it made me feel clumsy and gauche – Leonard Bast to the Schlesinger family's Schlegel sisters.

I offer as further evidence of my lingering Bast-like naivety that one thing I failed to understand about John Schlesinger was that he was homosexual. A year or two went by until, reflecting on remarks he had made when we were together, I realised he might have had other motives than simple friendship, motives I neither understood nor shared. For whatever reason, our relationship was to be short-lived.

On one of those weekend visits to Inkpen John had an eight-millimetre movie camera and some cassettes of film. We concocted a film with a simple, even rudimentary plot, lasting perhaps ten minutes: it was called *Horror*. I doubt if this figures in any John Schlesinger filmography, and probably just as well. He has directed many more ambitious pictures since then – though I also doubt whether anyone could have predicted such a thing on the strength of this first rather wobbly effort. John was stage-rather than film-struck, and he and I and his brother and sisters several times put together small drawing-room entertainments for the benefit of family and neighbours, often using material shamelessly lifted from London revues like the ones at the Ambassadors Theatre (*Sweet and Low* and its successors *Sweeter and Lower* and *Sweetest and Lowest*). One of ours was called *For Export Only*: the occasion was John's embarkation leave. He had been posted to South-East Asia.

Jimmy South's Cabaret, minus the conjuring act, soldiered on. The band did the same, playing most nights of the week and sometimes during the day: loudly barracked, we played in the ATS mess hall while they ate their midday dinner, and regularly every Tuesday night at the NAAFI for the REME dance, with the same Master of Ceremonies, a genial Lancashire man called Lance-Corporal McMullen. Every week at about eight o'clock, the ATS would arrive in a three-ton truck, and McMullen, stationed by the door, would shout 'Kaifer oop!' whereupon the band would strike up with a quick-step to get things going. Punctually at eleven p.m., McMullen would announce the last waltz, and to the strains of 'Irish Eyes', 'It's Time to Say Goodnight' or 'Who's Taking you Home Tonight?', the couples would shuffle round in half-darkness under the slowly-revolving ceiling pendant. Then the drummer would let fly with a noisy volley, and the lights would go up for the final quick-step, followed by 'God Save the King'.

Army life had become comfortable enough. Technically I was still earmarked as a candidate for a commission, though this fact seemed to have been forgotten, until one day when I was ordered to appear before a Unit Selection Board, a small body of officers who were supposed to interview you and establish your 'OLQ', or Officer-Like Qualities. Somehow I managed to convey the right impression and was recommended for Wozbee, or War Office Selection Board.

However, they need not have bothered. A few days before I was due to travel to Oxshott for the WOSB – a three-day affair during which they inspected your personality from all angles – I contracted mild blood poisoning from a cut in the right wrist. Hence I arrived at Oxshott with my arm in a sling, and was not only incapable of taking part in any of the more energetic activities involved in the whole exercise, but also unable to salute. In the services that was literally a crippling disadvantage: instead of flinging my right arm up to my forage cap whenever I saw or passed an officer, I was reduced to doing the next thing on the list, namely to stare with an expression of what was meant to be mingled resolution and deference, meanwhile standing, or if appropriate, marching to attention. In exasperation the Oxshott WOSB sent me back to Bicester for another try in due course.

It was something of a relief. It was true that I was only a Local/Paid Sergeant: if ever I had the misfortune to be posted away from the Arncott Depot, then in the great snakes-and-ladders Army game I should revert to plain Craftsman. But it didn't happen: I could continue to enjoy the dance band, the easy company, the beery 'socials' and snooker games in the Sergeants' Mess, as part of a process which my father said was 'knocking the corners off'.

People weren't so bad after all. You had to beware of judging by appearances. This platitudinous truth came home to me in my dealings with one of the officers, Major Grossman. He was a 'ranker officer', in other words he'd been promoted from the lower ranks – a short, gruff, bullet-headed man aged about fifty, whom I had first come across when I had worked in the Orderly Room: then, his ill temper and bad language in front of the ATS girl clerks had, I dare say, offended me more than it did them. He was in charge of one of the big workshops and was commonly believed to be the unit's prize bastard: hot on discipline, uncommunicative, unfriendly. Sometimes they referred to him as 'the mad Major' – but then there had to be one of those in every unit.

I next encountered him at the Unit Selection Board, a committee consisting of about half a dozen officers, who sat behind a table with the Commanding Officer in the centre. It was well known that on these occasions there was always one member of the Board who wouldn't say anything: instead of pelting you with questions he merely stared at you relentlessly, the idea being to see if his steady gaze would make you uncomfortable. When I marched in, stamping about the room and saluting in the approved manner, I observed Major Grossman sitting at one end and deduced he must have been the Board member given the job of silently testing my moral courage. Well cast, I thought snobbishly: anything he said would probably be obscene or irrelevant, and they couldn't very well leave him out. In fact it didn't need Grossman's unyielding stare to put me out of countenance: I was already quaking within as the Board members questioned me and I was astounded to be told I had passed muster.

But I had misjudged Grossman. Not long afterwards, I had to go one evening to one of the tank workshops, known as D3, to collect some papers. It was about eight o'clock. In the workshop, I passed Grossman's office: the light was on, and that wasn't surprising because he was known to work late. I wasn't prepared for what happened next. After some coughing and sniffing whoever was in there began to whistle some music – and then played it on a violin. It sounded like Bach. Grossman it undoubtedly was: I could distinguish that military silhouette through the glass partition, wielding a bow stiffly and without much finesse but competently enough.

I tiptoed out on my rubber-soled shoes. Back at the Sergeants' Mess, I ran into Staff-Sergeant Hartland. 'He's fuckin' barmy,' said Hartland, not very interested, nor very surprised. Six months or so later I was in the Unit Library trying to work out how many books had been pinched. Grossman came in and told me he had come to borrow a book about birds, but he rejected the only one in the Library on the grounds that it was too elementary. Then he began to chat: mechanical engineering was his thing, he had taken diplomas and a degree by correspondence and believed in working hard to improve his knowledge. He questioned me closely about university life but wasn't too impressed with the way academic work was organised there: he thought it lacked discipline. I didn't let on that I had eaves-dropped on his violin playing, and music didn't enter our conversation.

Getting your ticket – being demobbed from the Army – was a chronic subject of conversation, with many a tall tale about how this or that soldier had 'worked his ticket', by feigning madness or illness. Demobilisation of the orthodox kind was organised on the basis of first in, first out. Every serviceman and woman had a demob number, allotted according to age and how long you had been in. Mine was absurdly high: sixty-two. If the date of my release depended on that, I was going to be in the Army until the 1950s. But there was another way out – an early demob granted to servicemen who had essential work to return to. It was argued successfully by someone that university studies came into this category. One lunch-time I was called to the telephone in the Mess. On the line was an orderly room clerk, a friend of mine called Francis Haskell, later to become Professor of the History of Art at Oxford. My B release had come through: I had less than a week to wait.

I had to ask him to repeat the words in case I had been dreaming: but it was true. Maurice Bowra had managed to get me my ticket – and had done the same for many other Wadham men. Within ten days I had been set free – complete with a demob suit and beige pork-pie hat, and a document which was my ticket. The document began, 'When you are recalled to the colours . . .' The words suggested a Recruiting Sergeant in some market square, regimental drummer at his side, proffering the King's Shilling under a flapping banner.

But it never happened, and the call never came.

Sixteen

I OFTEN LOOK back at the day I took Francis Haskell's telephone call as the most exhilaratingly happy in my life, but rivalling it for sheer exultation and optimism was the day a couple of months later when I took the train back to Oxford. The place which in the mid-forties had seemed anaemic, faltering and enervated was now, in Michaelmas Term 1947, charged with energy, an invalid made whole again by a transfusion of new blood. Already there had been symptoms of revival during the previous term. The OUDS had been given the kiss of life and put on a production of *Love's Labours Lost* in the grounds of Magdalen College: its cast included, as the pedant Holofernes, Kenneth Tynan, brilliant in the part and already identified as Oxford's star undergraduate. I had bicycled in from Bicester to see the production and its atmosphere enchanted us all: the actors sauntering off into the distance in the summer dusk, laughing at the much-mocked Holofernes' sad exit line: 'This is not generous, not gentle, not humble.'

As the new term began, Oxford became filled to bursting point with returning servicemen – older than the average pre-war undergraduate and eager for the kind of intellectual stimulation they'd been denied. Some had been in the forces since 1939; some had been prisoners of war; some had killed people, risked their own lives in battle; some had been high-ranking officers; some had sat out the war in relative comfort – either in

Britain, like me, or in obscure stations overseas. There was also an overlapping generation of school-leavers, and so there was a chaotic mixture of ages and backgrounds: ex-Brigadiers and former Naval Petty Officers dined in Hall next to nervous young men fresh from school. But older men were in the majority. Compared with Oxford in the mid-forties the whole place seemed more grown-up, full of purpose, but the seriousness was lightened by sheer relief that the war was over and we hadn't been mutilated or killed and we were in one of the most beautiful university towns in the world. You could even put up with the rationing, the chilly weather and the book shortage.

Most of us lived on Government grants: mine was £267 a year, doled out in termly instalments of £89 and just about enough to live on if you eked it out carefully and earned a bit extra by some temporary work in the vacations. Most of us had to find lodgings in the town: I found a room in St Clement's in the house of an elderly widow down on her luck, named Angela Wheeler-Booth, whose slightly dotty air was worsened, if not caused, by Parkinson's Disease. As Oxford landladies went, and for all I know still go, the kindly Mrs Wheeler-Booth, with her unpredictable cooking and weirdly swooping voice, was not very remarkable. My next landlady, plump Mrs Boswell in St John Street, an obtuse, matronly person, with mildly paranoid delusions and neurotically preoccupied with the drains, conformed more closely to type: the smell of sewage apparently pursued her by day and by night and she was forever down at the Town Hall complaining to the City Health Department. Someone, she knew, was out to get her. Down in the basement, she would adjust her steel-rimmed spectacles and peer suspiciously through her lace curtains at passers-by, some of whom enraged her – especially Kenneth Tynan, who lived a few doors along.

Tynan was famous for his outlandish wardrobe, combining such items as an orange shirt, green jacket and mauve trousers, colours which nowadays would provoke no particular surprise but in 1948 were thought crudely ostentatious, if more or less justified by the fact that his middle name was Peacock. Dandyism was back. Another undergraduate, Milo Cripps, achieved ephemeral fame through his habit of carrying at all times a golf club – upside down, like a walking stick. A third, Pierre Houédard, later an ordained priest and concrete poet, likewise affected a cane and a silk cravat: he was one of several lodgers in a house round the corner from St John Street – one of whom was the philosopher Wittgenstein – who had to be deloused and fumigated when their senile landlady died and the local authority discovered the insanitary condition of her basement living quarters.

Dandyism was back but it was somewhat hobbled by the exigencies of austerity: British citizens were being exhorted to pull in their belts, if they had any – clothing was still rationed, and in the streets of Oxford in that first chilly winter of 1947 undergraduates hurried to their lectures and tutorials in Naval duffel-coats and Army greatcoats, sometimes dyed purple, green, or navy blue.

But the Bandits were back in business, and sounded somewhat better. John Postgate was still the leader, and we secured better 'dates': a regular dance at Ruskin College, occasional college balls, and – far into the night – Ken Tynan's twenty-first birthday party, held on a boat that sailed from Charing Cross to Tilbury and back, with a passenger list of celebrities from the University and the London theatre. When the weather improved, the Bandits trekked out on Saturday nights to The Perch, a pub on the Cherwell, and played in the bar: when it closed, the band moved out to Port Meadow, unpacked their instruments and began playing again as the pub customers strolled back to town in the moonlight, sometimes stopping to dance to the jazz among the cowpats.

I got a part in an Experimental Theatre Club production of *Troilus and Cressida*, which was to be done in Worcester College Gardens. The producer cast me as Patroclus, favourite of Achilles: naive as ever, I failed at first to realise these two were meant to be lovers, but the penny having dropped, I was puzzled when someone told me I'd been recommended for the part, I thought as some kind of private revenge, by John Schlesinger: he had arrived at Balliol and was already prominent in the camp acting set who frequented the Playhouse bar at coffee time. The cast of *Troilus* also included Michael Croft as Ajax, Peter Parker as Ulysses and Russell Enoch as Troilus.

I was not a success as Patroclus, and not only because my voice was barely audible in the open air. However, this didn't stop me from trying again, this time in a Wadham College production of Shakespeare's *King John*, in which I was given the title rôle. It was performed in the Clarendon Press Institute, a down-at-heel building in Walton Street, and the producer was Tony Richardson, newly arrived from Shipley, whose appearance at that time was accurately described in his *Independent* obituary in November 1991 as 'tall and gangling, with the gait of a wading bird out of water'. I quote this now because it was written by the man who took a leading rôle in the Wadham production of over forty years earlier, Irving Wardle. Irving Wardle had already grown the beard he has had ever since and needed no property whiskers to lend him credibility in the part of the King of France. In this respect he was unlike the unlucky member of the cast who played the messenger in Act Four and came on with an ambitious set of whiskers he had fixed on with gum. Reacting to his bad news, I was required to slap his face, but slapped too hard, with the result that his beard flew into the wings. It has always astounded me that when this happened he showed no surprise, or indeed any emotion at all: a born trouper, that man. I proved my unsuitability for a stage career by laughing aloud, so noticeably altering the sound of my next line, 'O, where hath our intelligence been drunk?' The farcical character of that evening's performance (it was the final one) was underlined by the fact that while this was going on on stage, the undergraduate who played Lewis the Dauphin was throwing up unobtrusively behind the backdrop.

The undoubted hit of the production was Derek Cooper, my best friend from school, who had arrived at Wadham (Raynes

Park was well represented in Oxford's student population). He played the Bastard, Faulconbridge, an insolent, swaggering upstart like other Elizabethan stage bastards, a character Derek Cooper suffused with his own notable sense of nonchalant irony.

Tony Richardson's production gave no hint of the future in store for him: the only memorable directorial idea was that at the siege of Angiers, in Act Two, the beleaguered townspeople appeared in the gallery behind the audience, who therefore had to effect a ninety-degree turn in their seats if they wished to see the actors. What with this, and the cast making their entrances and exits through the auditorium, as well as the gloomy 'Expressionist' lighting demanded by the producer, the Wadham Amateur Dramatic Society's patrons had to work hard to keep track of the action. I kept some reviews of the production, perhaps from motives of self-punishment: none of them were very favourable, though the *Oxford Magazine* reviewer who said I had my years to contend with ('this King seemed more suited to be Faulconbridge's nephew than his uncle') remarked that Tony Richardson had 'trodden this dangerous ground with courage and enterprise'. Peter Senn, meanwhile, in the University magazine *The Isis*, recorded his surprise at being unable to locate the name of the Marx Brothers in the programme's credits.

John Garrett came up one weekend from Bristol. A small group of Raynes Parkers at Wadham invited him to sherry, then the type of invitation that supposedly combined good taste, maturity and decorum. He went round the room, distributing compliments, clearly pleased with what he had done for us. It was true they were exhilarating times, and life had a vividness and immediacy that made you realise what you had been missing. There were parties, plays, revues, even operas, summer balls, the pleasures of a small, closed and privileged community whose members knew how lucky they were, and could try whatever they wanted, however misguided and extravagant. When Princess Elizabeth visited Oxford, a specially written Masque was performed in her honour. On the anniversary of Austerlitz in December 1948 a pretended reunion of Napoleon and his marshals took place: I recall seeing the participants marching up the High in full uniform to shouts of 'Vive l'Empereur!'.

Exhilarating, but sober times. When I have been back to Oxford in recent years I have been astounded at the amount of alcohol drunk by the present student population. Astounded and, I have to admit, a little shocked: though there must have been some hard-drinking ex-service people about in the late 1940s, alcohol had nothing like the importance or prominence it has in Oxford now. There were sherry parties on Sunday mornings that would now be considered laughably tame: two or three bottles of Dry Fly or Bristol Cream would do for a guest list of fifteen or twenty. I cannot imagine what the 1990s equivalent would be. Smoking, now, that was another thing. The horrible truth about tobacco had yet to be promulgated and it was still acceptable to smoke, to pose with a cigarette held languidly between the first two fingers, or, aping Lord David Cecil, between the fourth and fifth.

An observer with a little extra acumen might have been able to pick out from Oxford's student body those who stood a good chance of becoming famous afterwards. Tynan, obviously: not only for what he did as an actor but for his speeches at the Union. He was almost the only person to achieve celebrity in both politics and University theatre. The other Union stars – Robin Day, Geoffrey Johnson-Smith, Norman St John Stevas and others, including the man who was then called the Hon Anthony Wedgwood Benn, stuck exclusively to Oxford politics. So did Shirley Williams, then known as Shirley Catlin, though her constant companion Peter Parker was famed as an all-rounder: actor, political debater, writer, even rugger player. Lurking in comparative obscurity was another politician of the future, Edward du Cann, and in an obscurity that was total, a certain Margaret Roberts, whose married name would be Thatcher.

Writers had quite a high profile: Francis King was regarded

with respect because he had actually published two novels while still, in the Oxford phrase, *in statu pupillari*. Kingsley Amis was known as a wit, raconteur, mimic and jazz fan rather than a writer: I recall an occasion during a party in St John's JCR when the Bandits were playing, and he improvised a blues lyric, which ran,

Oh, I walked down the Giler, chewing a rubber tit,
Yes, I walked down the Giler, chewing a rubber tit
It was nothing like my baby, but it was better than chewing shit.

Behind these lines, the Bandits played a low-down accompaniment. Now and again John Wain came to a Bandit session to sing, and so demonstrate his conviction that poets ought to be able to improvise to music. He had no voice and it was difficult to make out the words. I did not think it was a productive line for him to follow.

There wasn't only jazz: orchestras seemed to sprout from every corner. I joined three and during the vacations I began to take lessons in London, from an experienced old professional player by the name of George Garside, who had gone blind and had to retire from his job as principal clarinet with the London Symphony Orchestra. A bulky, slow-moving man, wise in the ways of professional music-making and orchestral lore, he had grown up in Manchester before the war of 1914–18 and remembered being taken to hear Richard Mühlfeld, the clarinet-tist for whom Brahms had written his four late, valedictory works for the instrument. And how had he sounded? 'His tone,' said George with mild contempt, 'was comic' In his flat in Twickenham he would pick up his own clarinet and, standing before me, dazzle me with the richness and power of his own sound. I began to ponder the idea of applying for a place at one of the music colleges in London after I'd taken finals. An American friend at Wadham, Bill Becker, formally known as A W J Becker III, urged me on: 'You will be that wonderful thing, the intelligent artist!' he said earnestly. But I suspected the reality might not be all that wonderful, and for all my enthusiasm I lacked the last ounce of commitment needed for a professional career in music. In any case, there were other things to think about. Derek Cooper had managed to get onto the editorial staff of *The Isis*, the oldest undergraduate magazine: Alan Brien was editor. Derek put in a word for me and for the next three terms I was *Isis* Films Editor.

The Isis became more earnest later on, in the fifties and sixties, but under its ex-serviceman editors – mine were successively Alan Brien, Derek Cooper and Robert Robinson – it was principally a platform for the usual kind of undergraduate showing-off, but it was also assumed to provide some kind of first step on the high road to eminence in journalism. Editors in Fleet Street were hopefully thought to be taking an interest in what was said in our weekly issues, their flamboyant editorials, knowing gossip, sarcastic *Profiles* (the weekly *Isis Idol*) and half-informed reviews. We had only the vaguest idea how all this might be brought to the attention of some important man behind a desk at, say, the *Daily Express*: more than likely, local stringers or agency men made it their business to send in a tip-off if anything happened that might make a paragraph or two. However, the *Isis* did seem to get read elsewhere: when Derek Cooper wrote an accurate and witty parody of Graham Greene in one issue a telegram arrived at the office in Blue Boar Street. It read: 'CONGRATULATIONS GRAHAM GREENE.'

Diligently we kept our *Isis* cuttings: there was nothing like a folder full of your own pieces, stated Alan Brien, if you wanted to impress an editor. He had already declared he was going to be a literary journalist – a critic, a literary editor, or a features man perhaps. Derek for his part let it be known that he intended to be earning a thousand a year in journalism (a respectable sum then) by the time he was thirty: if he weren't, he said, he would deem himself a failure. But this was partly whistling in the dark. In the editorial office there would be gloomy exchanges about our imminent exile from Oxford when we had gone through the dreaded ordeal of Finals and were out there on our own. 'Baby,

It's Cold Outside' was the title of an editorial that went into an *Isis* in the autumn of 1949, speculating on the scanty opportunities that might be waiting for us in the big world.

Of course, there was always the OU Appointments Committee, an organisation with an office in St Giles which was supposed to help you find your feet outside. Had they any suggestions? They certainly had. 'Commerce,' said one of the secretaries, a donnish, pipe-smoking man in his forties. 'Commerce, that's the thing. There's a place for the Arts graduate in industry – help get the country on its feet you know.' The idea was bleak. Partly in an attempt to thrust the problem out of sight I started to read for a higher degree, B Litt, with the vague idea of becoming a teacher, somewhere. I even acquired two pupils. One was a German aristocrat anxious to improve his English: he knew how he intended to achieve this and instructed me in my duties – I was to sit and listen to him reading aloud in his inches-thick accent, from Burton's *Anatomy of Melancholy*. For this I charged him ten guineas a term. My other pupil was a nervous undergraduate from Wadham who was taking a Shakespeare paper: I discovered he had been a pupil at Bristol Grammar School under Garrett and his cowed manner was attributed by the Dean of Wadham, who had assigned him to me as a pupil, directly to Garrett's influence. 'They're all the same,' he said. 'They've been Garretted.'

Now and then I met John Garrett again. There was a dinner for Old Boys of Raynes Park, held at a restaurant in Putney called Zeeta's, attended by several hundred of us, when the speeches went on until nearly midnight. Garrett turned up and we heard once again that barking, italicised laughter. Then from time to time he would visit Oxford, again with the motive, it was assumed, of helping Bristol Grammar School boys to get places. He seemed to have become grander than ever. Evidently he had struck up some kind of courtier-like relationship with Queen Mary, the widow of George V, and had persuaded her to visit his school. His pursuit of celebrities appeared to be as untiring as ever. He had also made an attempt to entrap Evelyn Waugh, and there is a curious entry in Waugh's diaries for November 1946 which records the encounter. Garrett had written to Waugh at his house, Piers Court, not all that far from Bristol, asking him to come and lecture to the Sixth Form. Waugh tried what he called his 'customary evasive tactics' and replied that he would lecture to them in his own home. 'The headmaster, an old queer called Garrett, called my bluff and they came in a charabanc about twenty strong. I had intended showing them my collection of books, urbanely. Considering afterwards what I had said, it seemed to me that I simply gave vent to peevish and otiose complaints about modern times.'

'Old queer' indeed . . . that was rich, considering Garrett, at forty-four, was only a year older than Waugh, and that they had been contemporaries at Oxford. However, one up to him for having managed to out-manoeuvre Waugh, as well as achieve his objective. As for Waugh's complaints about modern times, they would have chimed with Garrett's views by then and I imagine him nodding sagaciously, lips pursed: perhaps because of the social environment he enjoyed, he had moved in a rightward direction, disliking the Labour government and becoming more and more the image of a High Anglican Tory, mixing with important local people and automatically, by virtue of his position, on the guest list for significant civic functions.

Even so, he was not satisfied. His predecessor at Bristol Grammar School had gone on to become Headmaster at Harrow, and Garrett applied unsuccessfully for the headmastership of Stowe, and then of St Paul's. I have been told his application for the latter post was scotched by Field Marshal Lord Montgomery, who was a Governor. The job, he said, required a man who was both a scholar and a gentleman: this man was neither. It was a verdict both cruel and snobbish and one that would have bitterly wounded Garrett if it had ever been conveyed to him, as I suspect it was. At all events he remained

Headmaster of Bristol Grammar until the final scandal that finished his career.

My attempt at a B Litt course was ill-advised. Privately, I had to acknowledge that my motive was procrastinatory: anything was better than leaving the enchanted precincts of Oxford – hence I worked up some bogus enthusiasm for a research project on Restoration stage practices, and how far the closing of the theatres under the Commonwealth affected actors and their techniques when the monarchy and the English stage were back in business. This was deemed by whoever it was necessary to convince (and I forget now who that was) an acceptable subject for a thesis, and after an interview with my supervisor – a don at St Edmund's Hall who showed no interest in me or my subject – I started some desultory reading.

In fact, though, the requirements I had to fulfil in order to embark on work for a B Litt struck me as distinctly strange. You had to take a qualifying examination after your first two terms, sitting two papers, which meant attending two separate courses of lectures. I had applied late, and there was only room for me on a series of lectures on Victorian England, given by Humphrey House, then a rising star of the Oxford English faculty but destined to die young, and another series on Tudor orthography. Neither of these subjects, it is superfluous to point out, was in the remotest way connected with the Restoration stage, and my interest never rose above the perfunctory. I attended the lectures, but when at length the day of the examination on House's course dawned, and I was once more seated at a desk in the Schools building, I suddenly realised what a pointless charade I was engaged in. I read through the paper on Victorian England, more and more aware that I had nothing of interest to say about that period: I stared at the paper as though the questions were couched in Sanskrit – or just as bad, Renaissance clerical script, the fundamentals of which I had failed to master. After twenty minutes, I walked to the invigilator's desk and handed in a blank paper, left the building and in all probability went home and practised the clarinet.

I paid for this improvised decision a few weeks later when I was summoned to a viva and imperiously interrogated by Humphrey House about the reasons why I had 'walked out' of his paper. I mumbled something about being unable to write anything that would not insult the examiners' intelligence and was summarily dismissed. I failed to attend the paper on orthography and it was painfully obvious that my career in academia was at an end. Gritting my teeth, I went down from Oxford for the last time, but it was less traumatic a departure than it might have been, for I had met a girl teacher at an Oxford infants' school and fallen in love with her.

However, the way ahead began to look bleaker when I found myself back at home living with my father and his new wife – he had married his confidante from the Malden Manor pub – and started to look for a job. I went to see the editor of *Picturegoer* magazine, who was sympathetic and understanding, but had no job to offer: he sent me away wondering just what he'd meant by the advice he gave me, which was 'Don't sell yourself too cheaply.' Was he talking about money, or some intangible other quality? How could you tell?

At all events, I had been back to the Appointments Committee and agreed they could send me details of any jobs in industry that seemed suitable. Their letters began to arrive, furnishing me with enthusiastic, even glowing descriptions of companies selling cocoa, detergent, or paper products who were looking for an arts graduate to help them do it. One day one of the OUAC circulars was about a job in a pharmaceutical company called Menley and James, in Camberwell. A good deal of the space on the circular was taken up by an encomiastic description of the firm by someone named David Williams, a languidly witty St John's man whom I'd known slightly during his time at Oxford. He was now in the firm's advertising department and enthused at length about their go-ahead policy, enlightened staff relations and training-within-industry schemes. I began to think there might be something in commerce after all. Also I was rather attracted by the requirement that every candidate had to submit with his application a 500-word essay on anything at all that interested him. I suppose I may have struck a nerve with my probably rather callow 500 words on the Victorian toy theatre: at any rate they asked me to come and be interviewed. I was one of about twelve young men who attended, and had to answer a short exam paper, posing questions like, What is a Bill of Exchange? What is meant by CIF? FOB? Ex works? I hadn't the faintest idea, but all the others seemed to know, as we sat in what was apparently the board room under a photograph of the firm's founder – whose name, I noticed, was neither Menley nor James, but Ratcliffe.

When it was over, the Export Manager, to my utter astonishment, told me he believed me to be 'an M and J type' and offered me the job of Assistant Export Manager. The job would present opportunities to travel and there would be two of us: the other man, it was explained, was already well versed in export matters – he was coming from a similar job at Allen and Hanbury's, another pharmaceutical company – and the Export Manager thought the two of us would make an effective team. No doubt, he said, pursing his lips, I would like to go home and think it over.

Nobody else had shown any interest in my services. My father had taken to muttering about his son being out of work, as though it were the most shameful condition life could condemn you to, and when I signed on at the local Labour Exchange he was even more mortified, crying in anguish, 'A son of mine on the dole!'

So I took the job, and began to wrestle with problems of insurance and freight, shipping and customs procedures, currency conversions and bank guarantees. I soon realised that nothing David Williams had written was actually happening, and in any case he'd left: my suspicions should have been alerted. Later, he published several successful novels. Clearly fiction, not ethical pharmaceuticals, was his true métier.

If the Appointments Committee were to be believed, the idea of employing Arts graduates was all the rage in business, but I could not see what people like me could offer. The idea seemed to be that too many Arts graduates were being delivered out of the universities, like objects on a production line; but there were no customers to snap them up and they had no particular place to go. Well, I could vouch for that. Few of my contemporaries could have said exactly what our degrees had suited us for. Teaching? Organising the Arts in some way? There was of course the vague ambition, nursed I suspected by a large proportion of the Arts graduates in those days, to write for a living – a novel, maybe? A file of first pages, which sometimes got as far as first chapters, began to accumulate on my desk at home, and more and more the *mise-en-scène* for these efforts was a small commercial firm connected with the pharmaceutical business, and for hero, an intellectual out of his element.

Menley and James was a slightly bizarre firm. It was what was known as 'an ethical house' – that is, its products were not sold 'over the counter' in chemists' shops, but advertised to doctors and sold on prescription. The advertising was done either by direct mail or in medical journals, or through a corps of unlucky individuals known as 'detailmen', whose task it was to call on doctors at their surgeries and urge on them the benefits of this or that Menley and James 'line' – a demeaning and ignoble task which I was glad I didn't have to do.

Early on it was disclosed to me that there never had been a Menley, nor a James. The parent company was called A J White and Co. Ltd, and they were the manufacturers of an extraordinary product sold mainly for its effects on the digestive tract, called Mother Siegel's Syrup.

Mother Siegel's Syrup was still on sale when I went to work for Menley and James in 1950, but its day as a brand leader was long over. Before the Great War its sale had been backed by energetic advertising in the public prints and through leaflets and posters. The story they told was always the same. Mother Siegel, so the legend went, was wandering one day through the fields and lanes of her native Bohemia: 'driven half-mad with dyspepsia', she reached out for the berries growing by the roadside and in desperation, crammed them into her mouth. A miracle! In no time her suffering was eased, and her condition cured. Hastening home, she prepared a cordial from the fruit she had picked – and so was born Mother Siegel's Syrup.

Of course this was all boloney, and revealed as such in two campaigning publications of the British Medical Association, in which were printed detailed analyses of what really went into Mother Siegel's Syrup, along with the same information about a variety of other products with names like Antidipso (for alcoholism), Zox (for gout), Figuroids (obesity), Dethblo (ringworm) and Mul'la (piles). For a long time the formula of Mother Siegel's Syrup, one of the biggest sellers ('fastest-moving lines' in trade parlance) in this crowded market, remained a closely kept secret. But the BMA's activities eventually made it necessary for all patent remedies to have their ingredients shown on the label. The jig was up for A J White Ltd, and this was the point at which the company wisely put some of its eggs into another, more respectable basket. They bought the rights to an iodine ointment called Iodex, advertised to doctors, and invented a firm to sell it: hey presto! Menley and James.

Iodex was still a household name in the early 1950s, but it remained the only preparation the company owned. However, they had acquired the agency for a number of other ethical preparations: the biggest of these agencies was that of Smith, Kline and French, who not so many years later bought out Menley and James, keeping the name for the purpose of marketing, not an ethical product, but a remedy for the common cold advertised on television – thus the clock had come round full circle.

Meanwhile, my job was to supply about twenty or thirty assorted medicines to the firm's agents in the Middle East and Africa. This, plus the Republic of Ireland, was my personal bailiwick, and business was brisk. Every day I would spend the last half-hour or so signing dozens of customs invoices for consignments of medicines with peculiar names: Ovendosyn, Pragmatar, Eskamel, Pentnucleotide, Neuro-Phosphates and Mandelamine. There were other products which were, or became, better known: Benzedrine, Dexedrine, Drinamyl and Edrisal, some of the first of the psychotropic or mind-bending drugs and regarded as interesting novelties.

I had no idea how these things would be used or misused in the places I despatched them to. I was kept busy exchanging letters with agents in Alexandria, Nicosia, Nairobi, Beirut, Baghdad, Amman, Accra and other places but it was boring work, and the more I did it, the more boring it became. 'No experience is wasted at your age,' stated my father. No doubt he was right, but I still considered there might be some other kind of experience available, and I would counter with a saying attributed to Bernard Shaw: 'Be careful you get what you like, or you may end up liking what you get' – it was a dire warning. If I weren't careful, I would be in Menley and James for life. In the end almost five years went by before I could get a job anywhere else.

Thus far, with rough and all-unable pen, Our bending author hath pursued the story. (Garrett encouraged his pupils to be quotation sharks.) I have continued things to this point because it seemed ironic to me that, after all, my working career should have begun in the sort of nine-to-five occupation to which hundreds of thousands of suburban men are condemned to spend forty years or more. In the struggle between suburbia and the kind of freedom Raynes Park had led us to expect, suburbia had won, at least for the time being. What would John Garrett have thought? As it happened, I found out soon enough.

I had been exporting pharmaceuticals for a few months when I met Garrett again: what was I doing now, he asked me? I told him, 'I'm working in an ethical pharmaceutical house.' He pulled a face. 'It sounds like French *letters*,' he snorted, in those familiar tones, then bellowed with laughter, whether at his joke or at the hole I had dug for myself, I couldn't tell. Chagrin was my main reaction: what came back to me was the nagging thought that I deserved something more interesting than shipping and insurance, CIF, FOB and ex works.

But one thing led to another, and after a good few years as a medical journalist and broadcaster I became a presenter of an Arts programme on the radio. Now, there's a job John Garrett would have approved of. He would have been gratified to know that three Raynes Park alumni of my generation have made a living mainly as broadcasters. A fourth became a radio producer. There are a few doctors, country solicitors, teachers, accountants. Another is a Cambridge English don. Another became a successful television playwright. My brother is an historian and critic of the dance with a fair amount of published work to his credit. Quite a few of us have written books. But no one, as far as I know, has become a writer – I mean a poet or novelist, or for that matter a painter, which is what would have been expected.

I often wonder what John Garrett would have thought of the utter changes time has, in the end, made in the lives of those boys who sat at his feet in the school hall in 1935. We cannot tell. He retired in 1964 with his professional life summarily ended through scandal and illness. He had had a stroke, and had no choice but to retire. He returned to Wimbledon and set up house with a young man who had been his Head Boy: it caused outrage among those who knew him in Bristol, but Garrett and his friend were happy enough in a pleasant house in a cul-de-sac, with a fine garden and a mongrel dog for company. But then, after only a few months, a second stroke felled him. The obituary notices were short, even terse, and made little of his achievements as a schoolmaster, none at all of his charismatic personality.

So what did the Raynes Park experience add up to in the end? Not really the audacious experiment it was intended to be. What

Garrett wanted was a suburban version of a public school or the sort of conventional, long-established grammar school he was happier in. It is significant that he remained Head of Bristol Grammar School for seventeen years, though he had been Head at Raynes Park for a mere seven, only just long enough, it might cynically be said, to start the machine going and to have something creditable on his *curriculum vitae*. As he grew older, his interests shifted elsewhere – to Stratford-on-Avon, where he became a Governor of the Royal Shakespeare Theatre and organiser of an annual series of lectures on Shakespeare, published later under his editorship.

What he also liked at Raynes Park was the creation of an interesting Staff Room, peopled by teachers he wouldn't be ashamed to introduce to the poets and musicians, dons and actors he'd persuaded to visit the school. In the normal course of events, I dare say those visitors wouldn't have dreamed of venturing into such a remote, unfashionable and apparently unattractive corner of south-west London. Probably he deserves some credit for extending their horizons.

As for Raynes Park School itself, that has changed beyond recognition. If we are to believe a former English teacher on the staff, there was a time when things went badly wrong. In 1986 this teacher wrote in a national newspaper – his article given feature-page prominence – about the decade of disenchantment he claimed to have suffered at Raynes Park, which had totally extinguished his desire to work in the state secondary system. Neglect and poor discipline, it seemed, had left the school buildings in a state of virtual ruin, with leaking roofs, broken furniture, graffiti on the walls and obscene words scribbled on blackboards. There weren't enough books to go round; hooligans had set fire to the Staff Room and smeared shit on classroom walls. Staff morale was at rock bottom: if all that was true, no wonder.

Had John Garrett read this catalogue of disaster he would have been horrified, probably heart-broken. This was the place an educationalist in 1942 had hailed as one of the two best schools in England. Perhaps that ex-teacher in the *Guardian* had made things sound worse than they were. At all events, the school community now seems to have readjusted itself. Nowadays a visitor to the school who had read the *Guardian* article would be in for a pleasant surprise: all seems orderly and industrious, though Garrett would scarcely know it for the school he started. Its numbers have swelled to at least four times the size of Garrett's school population, and extra buildings have been added on or taken over from the old Central School next door. Also it is co-educational. Girls were admitted for the first time in 1990. In the nomenclature of the day, it is now Raynes Park High School. There is no Sixth Form. Pupils who want to take 'A' levels have to go to a Sixth Form College, thus leaving the school in a state of decapitation, depriving it of the intellectual élite Garrett considered essential for setting an example of scholastic attainment for the lower forms to aspire to.

It is still a place chosen by the parents of bright children, but the scramble for Oxbridge places doesn't happen any more. Claude Rogers' portrait of Garrett, which used to hang in the Headmaster's study, has been put in a cupboard, and so has his painting Boys *at Prayers*, once a milestone on Claude's way to the Euston Road ('I painted what I saw in front of me'). The school magazine, *The Spur*, is no longer published: too expensive. Prize Day has been abolished: too élitist. The boys play soccer, not rugger. The school song is no longer sung at the end of term, or at any other time, except by a dwindling number of old codgers who meet for the Old Boys' Dinner once a year. *The Poet's Tongue* is no longer used in the school. When I enquired the other day, nobody had ever heard of it.